"Littery Man"

The *Commonwealth Center Studies in American Culture*
series is published in cooperation with the
Commonwealth Center for the Study of American Culture
at the College of William and Mary,
Williamsburg, Virginia,
by Oxford University Press,
New York

Pillars of Salt, Monuments of Grace:
New England Crime Literature
and the Origins of American Popular Culture, 1674–1860
Daniel A. Cohen

"Littery Man":
Mark Twain and Modern Authorship
Richard S. Lowry

"Littery Man"

Mark Twain and
Modern Authorship

Richard S. Lowry

New York   Oxford
OXFORD UNIVERSITY PRESS
1996

Oxford University Press

Oxford   New York
Athens   Auckland   Bangkok   Bogota   Bombay
Buenos Aires   Calcutta   Cape Town   Dar es Salaam
Delhi   Florence   Hong Kong   Istanbul   Karachi
Kuala Lumpur   Madras   Madrid   Melbourne
Mexico City   Nairobi   Paris   Singapore
Taipei   Tokyo   Toronto

and associated companies in
Berlin   Ibadan

Copyright © 1996 by Richard S. Lowry

Published by Oxford University Press, Inc.
198 Madison Avenue, New York, New York 10016

Oxford is a registered trademark of Oxford University Press

Library of Congress Cataloging-in-Publication Data
Lowry, Richard S.
"Littery man" : Mark Twain and modern authorship /
Richard S. Lowry.
p.   cm.
(Commonwealth Center studies in the history of American culture)
ISBN 0-19-510212-6
1. Twain, Mark, 1835–1910—Authorship.   2. Authorship—Social
aspects—United States—History—19th century.   3. Autobiographical
fiction, American—History and criticism.   4. Authors and readers—
United States—History—19th century.   5. Fiction—Authorship—
History—19th century.   6. Self in literature.   7. Canon
(Literature) I. Title. II. Series.
ps1336.L68   1996
818'.409—dc20   95-31814

1 3 5 7 9 8 6 4 2

Printed in the United States of America
on acid-free paper

For Joyce

Acknowledgments

A s SOLITARY an activity as writing is, no one writes a book alone. After having written this one, I wonder why anyone would want to. From the time I began this project in a very different form as a dissertation, I have benefited from the generosity of a number of friends, mentors, and colleagues. R. W. B. Lewis, Alan Trachtenberg, Jean-Christophe Agnew, and Richard Brodhead not only proved to be model advisors and challenging critics, they also served, long after they had seen the last of my dissertation, as ideal readers.

A faculty fellowship from the Commonwealth Center for the Study of American Culture at the College of William and Mary came at just the right time for me to recast the dissertation into a book. Beyond that year, the center provided me and my colleagues with an intellectual environment perfectly suited to encourage interdisciplinary work. Without the center's support, and that of Director Chandos Brown in particular, this book would not have been possible. Equally important have been the students of William and Mary's American Studies Program, whose energetic engagement with the study of culture has provided me with a valuable resource for thinking through my own ideas. I am also grateful for two summer research grants from the College of William and Mary.

Scott Donaldson, Bruce McConnachie, and Richard John each read portions of the manuscript. Alexandra Michos was an exacting and adroit research assistant. Robert Gross, Christopher Wilson, Joel Pfister, and Chandos Brown each read the entire manuscript; their sympathetic and searching critiques are reflected in the book's strengths. Any weaknesses, of course, are mine.

A part of chapter 2 appeared in *The New Orleans Review* (Summer 1991); portions of chapter 3 appeared in *Rivista di Storia Contemporanea* (January 1991). I am grateful to the publishers for permission to use the material here.

I owe my deepest thanks to my wife, Joyce, to whom this book is dedicated, and to my daughters, Elizabeth and Margaret, who continue to remind me of the joy, too often forgotten in the labor, of reading and writing.

Contents

"Littery Man"

Introduction

Mark Twain's Autobiographies
of Authorship

Now then; as the most valuable capital or culture or education usable in the building of novels is personal experience I ought to be well equipped for that trade." This sentence comes near the end of a long letter Mark Twain wrote in 1891, summing up his qualifications for authorship almost as if he were writing a resumé. "I was a *soldier* two weeks once in the beginning of the war. . . . My splendid Kipling himself hasn't a more burnt-in, hard-baked, and unforgettable familiarity with . . . a raw soldier's first fortnight in the field." He was also a laborer in a quartz mill, a pocket miner, a prospector—"I know the mines and the miners interiorly as well as Bret Harte knows them exteriorly"—a reporter who "saw the inside of many things," a riverboat pilot, a journeyman printer, a public lecturer, "and so I know a great many secrets about audiences." Even his most spectacular failure, his financial backing of the Paige typesetter, a decade-long enterprise that left him bankrupt at the age of fifty-nine, serves his apprenticeship: "the history of that would make a large book in which a million men would see themselves as in a mirror; and they would testify and say, Verily, this is not imagination; this fellow has been there." And any fellow who has been there, who has seen "the inside," who has accumulated such knowledge ("all of it real, none of it artificial, for I don't know anything about books"), is qualified to be "an author for 20 years and an ass for 55."[1]

Twain insists here on what is obvious even to his most casual reader: "personal experience" supplied the raw material for the "building"—a metaphor that Twain often resorted to in describing his writing—of his narratives. Beyond that, however, he insists on highlighting that personal experience because in his mind it gives his writing a certain legitimacy, an authority over, because it grows directly out of, experience—an experience that measures favorably with that of such rival authors as Kipling and Harte. But what exactly does he do to convert this experience into something recognizable to his readers? What precisely does Twain "build"? His answer is "novels," but that only begs a number of questions: Are these novels themselves the products of "capital or culture or education"? (Can we even consider *The Innocents Abroad* [1869] or *Life on the Mississippi* [1883] novels?) Does he use his life as an investment in "trade" (to put only a slightly different inflection on Twain's use of the word), as the catalyst for literary expression, or does he use it pedagogically (for himself as a writer or for the enlightenment of the reader)? If, as he implies, the major character in these "novels" is Mark Twain, is not this character also their author? Are we to understand this hybrid figure best as a creature of the marketplace, the parlor, museum or library, or the classroom? And finally, if each of these words alone seems inadequate to Twain's purpose in characterizing the raw material of experience, if each overly restricts the connotations of "building," then what kind of activity best suggests "capital or culture or education" without being encompassed by any of them?

The immediate answer to the last question, of course, is "writing," but clearly it is the word that Twain, who prided himself on always using the right word, wants to avoid. For, like "capital or culture or education," it carried connotations too restrictive to serve his purpose. Twain more often identified himself as a "scribbler of books"; notwithstanding his use of the word in the letter, he was, after all, "not born with the novel-writing gift."[2] In other words, if he made (or wrote) novels—if, in fact, he was "an author"—he was not strictly speaking a novelist. What he did was both less and more than an art form; what he did, in fact, to borrow Huck Finn's verb for writing, was to "make" books—not only to write them but to typeset and print them, to publish them, to market them, and finally maybe even to live them. Thus, the distinction between "writing," on the one hand, and "building," "scribbling," and "making," on the other, stemmed from Twain's understanding of how profoundly social an endeavor was authorship. At the same time, his groping between "capital or culture or education" implicitly acknowledges his inability to describe with any assurance that social space writing inhabited.

In part, his indecision stems from his vocabulary: "capital or culture or education" represented some of the most important and contested terms of his era, products of a mid-Victorian reorganization of knowledge that yielded the new professional sciences of society (in particular economics, sociology, and psychology). Yet despite such lexical—or more accurately, ideological—confusion, writers like Twain regularly resorted to such terminology in response to a perceived need to define an intrinsic value for writing, in general, and for literature, in particular. The sources of this need were manifold. On the one hand, an expanding market for reading—formed by magazines, newspapers, and a slowly rationalizing book trade—made it possible (if still difficult) for writers to make a living, even a career, as authors. "[S]tory-telling is now a fairly recognized trade," admitted Twain's close friend William Dean Howells, the era's "Man of Letters as a Man of Business," as the title of Howells's seminal essay put it, "and the story-teller has a money-standing in the economic world." On the other hand, these new prospects brought danger. As Howells warned the prospective novelist, "literature has no objective value really, but only a subjective value"; to write solely in pursuit of "objective," or economic, gain was to reduce culture to mere capital.[3]

Implicit in this caution was a social ideal, an Arnoldian sense that Howells shared with many of his peers in the arts, that the practice and products of culture stood between civilization and anarchy in a society too caught up in the fever of technological and financial progress. Matthew Arnold saw culture as England's only protection against becoming too American; in America, writers tended to define culture specifically against what was seen as a nationwide obsession with material wealth and practicality.[4] Such culture would, in effect, save the country from itself by embodying or disseminating (the distinction was never clear) forms of value other than the "objective" or economic. As such, the ideal of culture was tied intimately to education; it represented, for instance, to Thomas Wentworth Higginson "the training and finishing of the whole man." Literature and the arts fostered "a learning which makes no money, but helps make men"; it raised minds, which "as yet lie chiefly in our machine-shops," to higher things.[5]

But as Howells, Higginson, and, above all, Twain were well aware, clear distinctions between "capital" on the one hand and "culture or education" on the other were difficult, if not impossible, to maintain. Writers, especially those ambitious to produce a literature that assumed a cultural responsibility, were among those who most persistently professed the discourse of culture and education even as they were most aware of the limits and contradictions inherent in this rhetoric. The magazines for which they wrote, the publishers who sold their books, the universities, art museums, lecture halls, and libraries that fostered and perpetuated culture: all were, if not businesses themselves, products, even signs, of the power of capital. If as authors they sought to build a transcendent culture that would educate readers into citizens of humanity, as professional writers they made their living selling their goods in a market rigorously subject to the laws of capital.

Most important, the contradictions between rhetoric and experience left writers who took seriously the idea of culture unsure of just what it was they did. As Howells put it, "In the social world, as well as in the business world, the artist is anomalous, in the actual conditions, and he is perhaps a little ridiculous."[6] No one voiced these contradictions more eloquently than Howells, but no one made the anomalies, indeed the ridiculousness, of the author so much the center of his fiction as did Twain. Even as he came to form his career within the rhetoric of culture, he pursued his vocation with what he called "a mercenary eye"; even as his pursuit of capital led him to deride the pedagogical pretensions of high culture, he insisted on a fundamental "truth-value" in all his writing.[7] So immersed was he in the culture of capital that Philip Fisher has argued that his name "should be seen not so much as a pen name but as a trademark (as it always appears on the copyright page of his works), a brand name for the various enterprises of lecturing, door-to-door subscription sales of novels or travel books, printing investments, and public appearances, all headquartered in that gaudy Hartford mansion that would, like his name itself, come to be seen as part of his identity."[8] Yet even as he built this name on the strength of his carefully fashioned public image as a humorist, a "jack-leg novelist," and an "American vandal," Twain was equally capable of seeking and relishing the recognition of such high cultural figures as Oliver Wendell Holmes and Charles Eliot Norton and of treasuring the honorary degrees he received from Yale and Oxford.

In what follows, I argue that the contradictions and uncertainties implicit in "capital or culture or education" not only lie at the heart of how Twain pursued his career, they also framed how what he aptly called the Gilded Age defined the social role of authorship. To continue Twain's metaphor with the words he used to introduce *The Adventures of Tom Sawyer* (1876), the conjunction and, at times, the collision of what these terms represented for his era not only made possible his career, but also shaped "the order of architecture" in his texts—defining the design and formal labor with which he constructed his narratives—and his understanding of what an author did, how he related to his audience and his society in general.

Critics have long been aware of Twain's uneasy relationship with culture and capital. Van Wyck Brooks argued that Twain's involvement in the market—as a writer and publisher, as a speculator, as an inventor—was an important part of the "ordeals" that prevented the writer from realizing the full powers of his creative genius.[9] In the last few decades, however, critics have followed the lead of scholars like William Charvat, Lewis Simpson, and Raymond Williams to step beyond modernist concepts of an autonomous literature to recapture both the historicity of "the literary" as a category in nineteenth-century America and the importance of the market in constructing that category.[10] Explicitly or otherwise, Amy Kaplan, Richard Brodhead, Daniel Borus, Christopher Wilson, and Michael Denning have sought to position the making of the literary in a historical period that was undergoing two closely related yet contradictory movements in the field of culture.[11] The first was a growing interpenetration of writing and marketing so profound as to change the very nature of the literary itself. Borus characterizes this point most clearly when he argues that the "central historical determinant of the realist writing process was the consolidation of the literary marketplace as the locus of literary production, exchange, and circulation."[12] It now is difficult to imagine accounting for the literary output of writers as diverse as Louisa May Alcott, Charles Chesnutt, Horatio Alger, and Henry James without a sense of how a newly recognizable mass market for culture affected not only their relations with editors, publishers, audience, and other writers, but also how they conceived of the writing they did (and did not) produce. Studies in the history of reading have noted a complementary shift in how this writing was received. As audiences for the written word expanded from the coteries of the early century to at least potential national markets, as editors and publishers forthrightly sought writing that was more "timely" than "timeless," readers began to consume writing more extensively than intensively.[13]

Yet even as writers grew more firmly incorporated into this national market for reading, there also emerged an autonomous sphere of "highbrow" culture of which literature was an important component. In part this autonomy was the product of conscious labor on the part of writers like Howells, who adopted a stance toward both his product and his audience that resembled that of the newly emerging professions of law, science, and medicine. The literary novelist (Howells labeled such a writer a "realist," but his label was more prescriptive than descriptive) emerged in this paradigm as an expert in a field of knowledge described loosely as "real life," which he or she mapped with assiduous care both to material and to ideological detail. Lawrence Levine and Michael Denning have detailed the emerging hierarchies of culture—defined as much by their, at times, explicit conditions of use as by their content—while Alan Trachtenberg has emphasized the pedagogical, or, in a term that draws on Raymond Williams's work, the *incorporating* work of such hierarchies in organizing the production, dissemination, and use of culture in a society undergoing vast changes.[14]

None of these critics, however, position Twain with any degree of assurance in the dynamics they describe. Denning most compactly exemplifies this difficulty when he characterizes Twain as a "classic American writer" who nonetheless came "closest to the dime novel in practice, influence, and audience."[15] Brodhead suggests that it is possible to include Twain in the self-consciously highbrow school of Nathaniel Hawthorne, while Borus and Amy Kaplan place Twain in what the latter calls the "mass-mediated realism" exemplified most by Howells.[16] In all these discussions his inclusion is decidedly conditional; in none of them is he a major figure of study, this despite almost universal agreement that he was a major contributor to the late nineteenth-century field of culture. It is almost as if contemporary scholars of literary culture have as much trouble positioning Twain in the cultural dynamics of his time as he did. Given his importance, as well as his subsequent status as one of the founders of a particularly American kind of writing (one could almost speak of a "school of Twain" including Chesnutt, William Faulkner, Ernest Hemingway, Ralph Ellison, Toni Morrison, and Norman Mailer—not to mention H. L. Mencken, Ring Lardner, and even Stephen King), this unease over Twain suggests problems in our understanding of how the literary field, in particular, and the cultural field, in general, function.

Indeed, Pierre Bourdieu's work suggests that "capital or culture or education" did not so much represent the material "determinates" of writing (to inflect Borus's term with perhaps more than he intended) as they constructed what Bourdieu has called "the space of possibles" of cultural production. A relatively autonomous sphere that is nonetheless subject to a dominant hegemony, literature functions as a discursive "field" structured as much by a symbolic economy as by the market per se. Thus, what writers do—indeed, why writers do what they do at all—is shaped both by the actual conditions that make writing possible and that establish its social value, and by writers' perceptions of those possibilities, based on their capacity to risk what capital they

have for symbolic or economic profit.[17] Nor does the process end there. For not only
are writers made out of the tensions between position and perception, they themselves negotiate those tensions in such a way as to transform the social conditions of
writing.

Thus, it seems more profitable—to adopt a trope of capital to the analysis of culture—to understand the professional paradigm advocated and even pursued by writers like Howells and Frank Norris, and elaborated by contemporary critics, as a stra-
tegic rhetoric aimed at validating and reconfiguring a form of labor that nonetheless
eluded the discourses produced to define it. As Bourdieu argues, despite attempts to
link the making of culture with the "making" of law, medicine, and science, a large
gap separates the first from the others. The boundaries of the cultural field are much
more permeable than those of other fields; there are no established career tracks, no
partnerships or degrees that confirm one's professional success. So open is the field,
so vulnerable is prestige and status to "symbolic challenge" (one need only think of
Howells's precipitous fall from grace in the early decades of the twentieth century),
that "it is the arena *par excellence* of struggles over job definition."[18]

Thus, what Brooks has characterized as Mark Twain's "ordeal" refers as much to
a critical difficulty as it does to the historical challenges of writing. But there is no
question in either the broader scholarship and in Twain criticism at least since
Howells's *My Mark Twain* appeared in 1910, that Twain wrestled with the contradictions of authorship embodied in his hesitation between "capital or culture or education" in a way that sets him apart from his contemporaries. Self-educated yet widely
read, a man for whom "the language of money" was as integral as his famous drawl,
who attended as many minstrel shows as operas, Twain engaged these contradictions
with unique energy. The solution for critics of Twain at least since Brooks has been
to resolve such contradictions by literally dividing him in two. Justin Kaplan's 1962
biography solidified this split by interpreting its subject through a series of dualities—
a self-taught man of the West and the South living in the cultural centers of the
Northeast and Europe, a popular humorist moving in the highest literary circles, a
frustrated financial speculator who wrote novels—that culminated in the trope that
titled the book, *Mr. Clemens and Mark Twain*.[19] "Mark Twain" emerges in Kaplan's
hands as a Spencer Brydon–like alter ego to Samuel Clemens, an expression and
projection of his inner turmoil. More recently, Susan Gillman has endeavored to
historicize these dualities by exploring the ways in which Twain himself employed
tropes of doubleness, linking what she describes as a psychology of imposture with
his era's confused constructions of identity. Thus, Twain responded to the contradictory social grounds for writing by developing an idea of his labor in the tensions
between conscious authorial control and unconscious and uncontrollable creativity, a
duality that he finally internalized.[20] Yet even after emphasizing the constructedness
of Twain's "unconscious," she in the end retains the category for her own analysis:
the Mark Twain we have come to know is the product of Samuel Clemens's dark
struggles with control.

Both of these studies have the virtue of reminding us that Mark Twain was a social fiction "authored" by a particular man. But they also obscure the extent to which, as I shall detail in chapter 1, *all* writers' names took on a fictional status, that, in effect, all writers lived "double" lives. Like Mark Twain, they were public figures, inhabiting not only the texts that bore their names on the title page, but also the entire cultural system—the newspapers and magazines, the book reviews and advertising, the public performances and readings—through which their texts circulated. If "Mark Twain" was initiated by Samuel Clemens, the moniker soon took on, and retained, like all products in a market economy, a life of its own. As the title to Howells's eulogy suggests, and as the more recent title of Louis Budd's *Our Mark Twain* reiterates, once created, "Mark Twain" followed what seemed to be its own rules of character, taking on a personality shaped by its position in culture and its relationship to different audiences.

Twain put the case in similar terms about his more strictly fictional characters. "I never deliberately sat down and 'created' a character in my life. I begin to write incidents out of real life. One of the persons I write about begins to talk this way or another, and pretty soon I find that these creatures of the imagination have developed into characters, and have for me a distinct personality."[21] If characters like Tom Sawyer and Huck Finn begin in "real life," as Twain suggests, there is only limited utility in reading them as biographically determined; if Mark Twain began as Samuel Clemens, he too became a semiautonomous figure who began to *write* "this way or another." Thus, if there is an unconscious to Mark Twain, I find it more productive to construe it as a *social* unconscious that made possible a specific form of writing. Doing so reminds us, as does Twain's search for the right word in the letter quoted at the opening of this chapter, of how collective a process writing is; it reminds us that writers do not write *for* a market, but *in* a market, one that functions as much socially and culturally as it does economically and one that wields an influence far beyond the realm of writing. When Edith Wharton fantasized about seeing her book displayed in a bookstore window, she not only imagined the author she would become, she projected the woman she already was.[22] As a writer, Mark Twain was all Samuel Clemens ever was; to separate the two is like separating the writer from the speculator, the family man from the public raconteur.

Thus, to return to the opening letter, if Twain's life "equipped" him for his trade, how he and his era defined "capital or culture or education" taught him how to value and finally use that equipment. The "Mark Twain" that his audience knew and who survives today exists in the writing itself, figured in the tensions between narrator and character, audience and form, as both a comic signature of the author and a sign of the culture that produced him. I take this process of figuration as both the site and the product of Mark Twain; the result, I will argue, runs through his work as a loosely segmented autobiographical narrative of an authorial self that emerges from and inhabits the economic, cultural, and educational discourses of his society. Thus, at stake in this book is not strictly a narrative of Twain's career as a writer, nor an analysis of

Twain's public persona, although both dimensions as described by Henry Nash Smith, Everett Emerson, Louis Budd, and others, play an important role in my argument.[23] Nor am I interested in offering comprehensive readings of all of Twain's "major" texts; in fact, my study ends with *Adventures of Huckleberry Finn* (1885). Rather, my purpose is to reconstruct how the tensions and continuities of capital, culture, and education animated his autobiography of authorship as it unfolded in the tropes, voices, structures, themes, and practices that created "Mark Twain" as what Michel Foucault identifies as an "author-complex."[24] The very constructedness of this subject, in turn, both allows a better positioning of Twain in his history and provokes a specific insight into the emergence and reproduction of that peculiarly historical category we have come to call the literary.

This said, however, I do center each chapter on specific texts, embedding my readings in a range of relevant discourses: travel writing, literary criticism, boys' fiction and domestic advice literature, autobiography, and writings on education. These texts, in turn, are taken as important manifestations of cultural practices—tourism, bookselling, childrearing, literacy education, and, most important, the writing and reading of fiction. The purpose of this expansiveness is to probe what is commonly taken as the border between discourse and "material experience," in order to develop an argument that reaches in two directions. On the one hand, no discursive practice can be understood without a sense of its materiality. On the other hand, no material practice can be adequately discussed without looking at how it was "textualized": how it produced and emerged out of its own specific discourses, how those discourses circulated through society, how they represented and finally authorized that practice. If, as Miles Orvell has argued, the era's sense of reality was made unstable by the proliferation of, and its fascination with, artifice, the interplay between the authentic and the inauthentic, the discursive and the material, was central to its self-understanding.[25]

Thus, I approach Mark Twain and the writing he and his peers produced as what Joan Scott has characterized as "a linguistic event," even as I insist, in her words again, "on the productive quality of discourse."[26] Each of the chapters centers on specific texts in the conviction that much of the literary history relevant to any writer resides in the figural movement of the texts themselves: with each word Twain labored over, with each trope, he literally and literarily made history. My object is not to narrate the history he made, but to explore how he made that history. And to address this issue we must follow Twain's lead, who believed that no language was original.[27] Thus, to choose a brief example from one of the texts I shall later discuss at length, there are a number of relevant explanations for Twain's writing of *Tom Sawyer*: an ongoing fascination with boyhood provoked both by his culture's "discovery" of childhood and his own sense of historical disjunction, the emerging market for boys' fiction, changing patterns of masculinity, perhaps even the death of his infant (and only) son, Langdon, in 1871. All of these contexts are important, and I shall address the most relevant ones in turn, yet none of them account for the particularly disruptive presence of Injun Joe. What does begin to account for it is, bluntly, the novel itself: a rhetorical logic that produces both "innocent" boyhood and vengeful manhood as the necessary constituents of an adult male narrative voice.

This logic I, in turn, see as a key element of the most compelling drama in Twain's autobiography of authorship: his searching exploration for the grounds of what I shall call cultural authority. What is it, Twain asks time and again, that legitimates his authorship? What is it that gives him not only the authority to write, but the legitimacy to be read? These are not merely thematic questions, though they do structure his narratives of boys, "innocents," and "cubs" undergoing comic educations in (the often absurd) lessons of capital and culture. More profoundly, these questions turn attention to the self-parodying voice of *The Innocents Abroad* and *Tom Sawyer*, the final chapters of *Huckleberry Finn* that Hemingway dismissed as "just cheating," indeed the unfinished quality of virtually all his "novels," all of which attest to an author struggling in the act of writing to test and explore what it means to "make" public fictions. Finally, these questions allow us to read Twain's writing as participating in a tension-fraught, even contradictory, dialogue with his readers, other writers, the public in general, and with himself over the place of fiction in social life.

What makes Twain's writing both particularly useful and particularly difficult for pursuing such an inquiry is its wide variability in genre, intent, and quality. Yet the most consistent thread running through it, and what most fundamentally distinguishes him from his contemporaries, is the degree to which he employed narrative to sustain his humor rather than, as did for instance Howells and Harriet Beecher Stowe, employing humor to develop narrative. As James Cox has eloquently argued, Twain wrote—and hence must be read—first and foremost as a humorist.[28] Twain's humor accounts for what can be called the sustained "authorial intention" of virtually all of his work; it both shapes the formal logic of each text and positions that text in a combative relationship to other texts and discourses of the time. In this sense his work is profoundly rhetorical: its pleasure derives from how Twain writes his readers into the text, offering us a place to stand, a perspective from which to best enjoy and even participate in its humorous performance. This position, however, is a slippery one, a comic trap laid by a wily narrative voice—half author and half character—that encourages us to indulge readerly expectations for unity and closure, only to pull out the rug from under our feet and then, as it were, slip it back under us again, fulfilling our expectations in unanticipated ways.

Such humor of course derives from the standard repertoire of literary burlesque, which, as Franklin Rogers has argued, Twain discovered early in his career while a member of Bret Harte's and Charles Stoddard's self-styled "Literary Bohemia" in San Francisco.[29] More recently, Shelley Fisher Fishkin has located the origins of Twain's characteristic humor in the voices of slaves and other African-Americans he knew.[30] Both formulations go far toward accounting for the strange blend of conservatism and subversiveness that characterizes Twain's work, but Rogers in particular accounts for its specifically literary quality. As he describes it, burlesque served as a form of literary slapstick, a pie-in-the-face humor that thrived by ridiculing and travestying specific texts by such popular writers as Charles Dickens and James Fenimore Cooper. This hit-and-run comedy played a dual role in shaping Twain's apprenticeship as a writer. It taught him the fine points of violent juxtaposition, hyperbole, defacement, and mimicry—tactics he employed for rhetorical effect throughout the rest of his career. But it also served as an important form of mimesis: by mimicking and travestying other authors, genres, and texts, the burlesque artist came to master his own literary craft.[31]

Twain's embrace of burlesque thus yielded a fiction which is, in Cox's term, "parasitic": "its reality depends upon a double vision, half of which imitates the parent form, the other half which mocks it."[32] Cox's use of the word "parent" here of course suggests what Harold Bloom would term an anxiety of influence inhabiting Twain's work: even as each of Twain's texts seems to "adopt" its own textual "parent," the comic disfigurement of its travesty exposes as "conventional" what is assumed to be an autonomous, individual "expression" of unique power.[33] Ultimately, however, Twain's work is best understood not as burlesque, but as parody: his mature humor takes as its target not specific texts, but certain forms of discourse that claimed authority to represent and finally, in his mind, to legislate particular versions of reality. To be sure, he never forsook burlesque altogether, and he felt strong rivalry with authors like Stowe and Harte, but as a parodist he developed a much more complex practice of authorship than burlesque would allow. For the parodic text, in effect, shares, no matter how uneasily, its authority with other, often "authorless" forms of discourse. As Cox puts it, the Twainian text works to "impersonate a cliché"—not just to quote it, but to reconstruct it, re-present it, and finally employ it in representation.[34] The result is fiction that plays with and ultimately challenges the reader's trust both in the integrity of the narrative form, and, what is more important, in the languages that make that form seem "real" or "true." Insofar as Twain's texts affiliate with other texts and languages, they position the reader and writer in a skeptical relationship with more general languages of authority. His narratives not only represent other ideologies, they are, in a limited but very real sense, self-consciously crafted sites of contradiction: his parody targets not only languages "outside" the text, but its own language as well. They question, even as they "build," his authority as an author.

Twain's texts thus work, as David Sewell and Forrest Robinson have made explicit, in ways that anticipate Mikhail Bakhtin's theoretical explorations of parody as both a profoundly constructive and deconstructive use of language.[35] Twain's irreverent humor, his suspicion of the sham and hypocrisy of any authoritative language, suggest his unequivocal opposition not only to the nineteenth-century rhetoric of high culture, but also to those emerging professional discourses of the social sciences, the law, and medicine, which were also predicated on effecting the kind of linguistic and social unification described by Bakhtin. Smith, in particular, has described this oppositional stance by characterizing both Twain's style and his subject matter as generated by the collision of two languages. One, composed in the elegant rhythms of "conventional language," carries the weight of "official culture"; the other, full of the common phrasings of the "vernacular," is born of "everyday experience, the vulgar world of the natural man."[36] Thus, in Smith's argument, Twain's fiction subverts conventional genteelism with a colloquial common sense, exposing "the distorting effect of conventional notions of propriety on the individual's responses to experience."[37]

As does Bakhtin, in his analysis of the novel, Smith misses the extent to which Twain, in particular, and the literary, in general, participated in, as much as it contested, "official culture." To a large extent, this stems from Smith's equation of the genteel and the vernacular as they are found in Twain's writing with specific social classes: genteel people used genteel language; common folk spoke in the vernacular. Thus, in Smith's formulation, Twain's fiction upheld the rights of "common man."[38] In fact, however, the "vernacular perspective" was a point of view constructed *within* literate culture to represent those on the linguistic margins. No matter how accurately dialect may have been transcribed into narrative—and Twain took great pride in his ear for speech—it was nonetheless, as it appeared in the novel, as "conventional" as other languages.

Twain understood this; he was as apt to parody the vernacular as he was to parody the language of "culture." In Twain's hands, *no* language was outside the purviews of parody; any language—be it fictional or nonfictional, "conventional" or "vernacular"—served him as vehicle for composition. So omnivorous is his humor that even his own work provided him with a target for parody, as is suggested by Huck Finn's dismissal of "Mr. Mark Twain," the author of *Tom Sawyer*, as a liar. As Bakhtin puts it in a more general context, Twain "participates" in his fiction as a ventriloquist; he writes "with *almost no direct language of his own*."[39] The result is not a cultural critique as it is normally understood—Twain's texts do not work to establish any space outside the culture it travesties. Rather, they enact a parodic performance of authorship, a performance whose success depends paradoxically on establishing the very authority such performance calls into question.

It is precisely this performative nature of Twain's "parasitic" discourse that makes his work so useful for reconstructing the cultural theater that not only set the stage for his literary antics, but also made necessary the strategies of authorship he employed. To read Twain is to be repeatedly brought up against fundamental questions about how fiction worked: how it was made, how it asked itself to be read, how it perpetuated and altered the assumptions and values with which readers and writers built their worlds. This textual work "documents" not just the individual life of the author, but also the society that made possible the conception, writing, publishing, dissemination, and reading of fiction.[40] And here Twain's humor is of special value. For humor, as he was well aware, is extremely timely; a joke grows quickly old when it has to be explained. But if time works against the humorist, humor works for the cultural historian. In reconstructing the "joke" of Twain's work, not solely to recapture its comedy but to understand how and why it worked for author and readers, I hope to make visible what Williams has called "the structures of feeling" of Gilded Age America.[41] It is a limited history to be sure, yet its very focus replicates in part that of Twain and his peers, who ascribed a social power to printed language and hence produced a world shaped by that assumption.

At the historical core of my exploration of Twain's writing, then, lie three major cultural transformations falling roughly under the three rubrics that index Twain's hesitant attempt to describe his writing: capital, culture, and education. I emphasize each of these separately in chapters 2, 3, and 4, respectively, though my argument is attentive to how closely the meaning of each depends on our understanding of the others. Chapter 1 sets the stage by framing Twain's well-known problems with finishing narratives as the practical manifestation of his larger concerns about his own authority. It then turns to what has emerged as a kind of locus classicus of Twain scholarship: his Whittier Birthday Speech. There Twain most explicitly positioned himself in relation to the emerging literary hierarchies of his time. My interest, however, lies not in "explaining" Twain's ambivalences in any biographical way, but in exploring how he and his peers produced a new set of writerly possibilities out of the tensions between cultural, economic, and educational capital. Thus, I argue that central to the dinner, and ultimately to Twain's practice as a writer, was the question, What is an author?—a question that Twain, in particular, used to establish the field of possibilities that would fuel his best work.

Chapter 2 returns to the beginnings of Twain's career as a national author, reading *The Innocents Abroad* (1869) and *Roughing It* (1872) as texts that resolve the contradictions between the discourses of high culture and popular entertainment with a comic embrace of a commodity aesthetic. Looking closely at the narrative personas of the tourist and the prospector, I explore how Twain suggests a self whose very desire is structured by fantasies of commodity speculation and whose cultural authority is certified by his ability magically to transform language into currency. Chapter 3 focuses on how *The Adventures of Tom Sawyer* (1876), Twain's first independently authored book of fiction, brings into collision this commodity aesthetic with a narrative voice built in response to one of the earliest languages of the expert—a language found particularly in the narrative voices of boys' fiction and in childrearing advice. I also situate this discourse on boyhood in emerging forms of middle-class manhood in order to explore how the intervention of print culture into the domestic space informed how Twain and his era understood the uses of fictional forms of entertainment. I then read "the problem of Injun Joe" as a sign of Twain's own ambivalence about his role as domestic entertainer.

Adventures of Huckleberry Finn serves both as the point of departure for the fourth chapter and as the conclusion of my study. Beginning with its characterization of an illiterate boy writing his own "autobiography," to use Twain's working title for his novel, I argue that the narrative enacts a parody of Benjamin Franklin's *Autobiography* and constitutes Twain's most profound entry in his own autobiography of authorship. Drawing on the rhetoric linking literacy and character building initiated by Franklin and reproduced and refined by nineteenth-century pedagogues, Twain crafted a text that linked literacy and the literary in order to question the very grounds of authority on which the text, and Twain's status as a "littery man," was premised. The result is a text that explores what Twain saw as a pattern of violence and humiliation underlying his era's endorsement of what it called "the power of writing."

Thus, the letter that opens this introduction occupies a curious place in his oeuvre. Written in 1891, after the resource of "personal experience" had all but been exhausted (virtually every incident he catalogs had been written about), Twain's letter represents the words of a man whose career, at least as the letter describes it, was closed— this despite nearly two more decades of writing ahead of him. Whatever he would write after that would, as Susan Gillman has eloquently detailed, explore new forms of authority. Yet whatever direction those explorations would take, they would negotiate the terrain of "capital or culture or education" that Mark Twain traversed during the first two decades of his career; they would build an authorship that expanded, contradicted, but never repudiated the one constructed by the authorial autobiography that shaped his early work.

ONE

❧

"Littery Man"

The Rhetoric of Authorship

I. "The Sole Form"

For a writer as prolific as Mark Twain—he produced nearly 18,000 pages of material during his career—writing was never easy. His nine-year struggle with *Adventures of Huckleberry Finn* (1885) is simply the best-known example of his compositional trials. Nearly every book he undertook, and virtually all of his fictional efforts, followed a pattern of rush and stall, furious productivity and frustration. At times he underwent an almost intoxicating "fierce irruption" of ideas; in letters and in the margins of his manuscripts he would compute how many words he wrote each hour.[1] At other times, Twain endured equally "fierce" struggles with direction that often as not resulted in his putting away manuscripts for months and even years at a time. This on-again-off-again writing was in part the result of his compulsive involvement in an often bewildering labyrinth of business and socializing, public speaking, party politics, and travel. So hectic were his various commitments during the period of his greatest productivity—from 1870 to 1895—that he only found time to write during the summers, when he would remove himself from the social whirl of life in Hartford, Connecticut, to the relative quiet of a small study set apart from his sister-in-law's farmhouse in Elmira, New York. Yet even as he managed there to produce *Roughing It* (1872), *The Adventures of Tom Sawyer* (1876), *Adventures of Huckleberry Finn*, and *A Connecticut Yankee in King Arthur's Court* (1889), he would often find himself "idle," waiting for "a 'call' to go to work" before he could dive into his writing.[2]

Another, more fundamental, reason for Twain's struggles stems from his writerly strategies. Justin Kaplan has characterized Twain as a largely "intuitive" writer, more focused on line-by-line composition than larger matters of form. As Kaplan notes, this "characteristic method of improvising from chapter to chapter, of letting the story shape itself, had its pitfalls. One day's failure of invention coupled with the absence of an over-all plan could mean that his books came to a dead stop."[3] Twain described such halts as "very simple—my tank had run dry; it was empty; the stock of materials

16

in it was exhausted."[4] In book after book, Twain would reach a point of decision, a point where he had exhausted the original impetus for beginning the story, and put the manuscript away, either to be picked up later, discarded, or cannibalized for another project.

Twain described his writing frustrations to his close friend William Dean Howells in a letter discussing his travails over "Which Was the Dream?" (a piece he never finished). He begins by recounting the struggle he had experienced twenty years earlier with the manuscript "Simon Wheeler," which in his estimate had reached 40,000 words before Twain had lost control of the plot. "I didn't finish the story," he writes, "though I re-began it in several new ways, & spent altogether 70,000 words on it, then gave it up & threw it aside." He then generalizes his experience in a way that casts light on his overall strategy of writing:

> Speaking of that ill luck of starting a piece of literary work wrong—& again—
> & again; always aware that there *is* a way, if you could only think it out, which
> would make the thing slide effortless from the pen—the one right way, the
> sole form for *you*, the other forms being for men whose *line* those forms are,
> or who are capabler than yourself: I've had no end of experience in that (&
> maybe I am the only one—let us hope so.) Last summer I started 16 things
> wrong—3 books & 13 mag. articles—& could make only 2 little wee things,
> 1500 words altogether, succeed;—only that out of piles & stacks of diligently-
> wrought MS., the labor of 6 weeks' unremitting effort. I could make *all* of
> those things go if I would take the trouble to re-begin each one half a dozen
> times on a new plan.[5]

If these are the comments of an improvisational writer, they also reflect his sense of the sheer labor entailed in finding the "right way, the sole form." In fact, so intimately linked were form and effort that, as his letter implies, he judged the success of his work in terms that were forthrightly practical: the "right" form can be recognized only when it yields "effortless" writing. As he put it in 1906: "As long as a book would write itself I was a faithful and interested amanuensis and my industry did not flag, but the minute that the book tried to shift to *my* head the labor of contriving its situations, . . . I put it away and dropped it out of my mind."[6]

Yet for all of the talk about active labor, both passages suggest a writer waiting for something to happen, or rather, as Susan Gillman has described it, waiting for his unconscious to take control. This suspension, she argues, between active writer and passive amanuensis characterizes the psychic splits of "a writer permanently confused over what category his work belonged to," the genteel world of the literary or that of vernacular humor.[7] Was Twain the master of his own literary craft, the man whose sense of control over his material led him to insist that "the difference between the right word and the wrong word is the difference between the lightning bug and the lightning"? Or was he the slave to a literary marketplace that demanded that he "paint himself stripèd & stand on his head every fifteen minutes"?[8] Twain never resolved this struggle for control; throughout his career he wrestled with what Gillman calls the "paradoxical double desire" of domination and submission, a doubling she sees as having "striking affinities to the contradictory divisions many have perceived in the Mark Twain–Samuel Clemens relationship."[9]

Gillman's analysis usefully points to how intimately Twain's sense of authorial identity was related to the practical problems of writing, particularly as that identity was shaped by his sense of audience. After all, the search for "the sole form" serves to differentiate his writing from those of other "men whose *line* those forms are." However, as Twain's use of the word "line" suggests (as "a line of business" and as a signature), the identity he has in mind is less psychological than it is authorial, less shaped by internal struggles of a split personality than by the social contradictions of a fractured labor. In short, the "labor of contriving" links the creation of an authorial identity with the practical matter of getting the job done, all of which Twain represents as a problem of form. Thus, any attempt to reconstruct Twain's authorship must begin with defining the labor that went into solving the problem of form.

Twain's equation of successful "literary work" and effortlessness may well have had its origins in his stagecraft as a popular lecturer. For it was in front of the countless audiences on the lecture circuit and in the banquet hall that he perfected what can be called an art of effortlessness designed to charm his listeners. And, fittingly, his most compelling discussion of his art in any form comes in an essay on the stagecraft of popular lecturing, "How to Tell a Story" (1897). There he develops what he sees as a crucial distinction between the "comic story" and the "humorous story" that reflects directly on his writing struggles. The former is essentially nothing but a joke told badly: whatever attraction it may have lies so thoroughly in what Twain calls its "*matter*" that anyone, even a machine, can tell it. The latter is "a work of art—high and delicate art," precisely because it "depends for its effect upon the *manner* of the telling."[10]

He makes his point by contrasting two versions of the same joke. The comic version unfolds in a perfunctory manner, with the teller belaboring the punchline. The humorous version is, in fact, a description of its telling by James Whitcomb Riley. What recommends Riley's performance to Twain is how, by adopting "the character of a dull-witted old farmer who has just heard it for the first time, thinks it is unspeakably funny, and is trying to repeat it to a neighbor," he works to "spin out to a great length" a supposedly simple story, allowing it to "wander around as much as it pleases, and arrive nowhere in particular." What emerges is what Twain called elsewhere "a running narrative," an open-ended story fashioned "according to the temper of the audience."[11] In other words, the art of humor manifests itself in a performative fashioning of "the sole form" Twain searched for as a writer, a narrative unique to the occasion, shaped deliberately if not effortlessly by the mutual engagement of artist and listeners in a ritual dialogue. The teller "quakes in a jelly-like way with interior chuckles" while the audience laughs and starts "until they are exhausted, and the tears are running down their faces."

As tempting as it may be to see Twain's formulation of the art of humor as celebrating a tall-tale tradition of oral storytelling, it nevertheless remains the product
of a professional performance. Despite all of the give-and-take between audience and
performer, a clear line between active control and passive enjoyment, initiation and
response, divides them. These dynamics emerge most clearly at the end of the essay,
where Twain illustrates the fine art of the pause ("it is a dainty thing, and delicate,
and also uncertain and treacherous") by scripting in dialect, complete with stage directions, "a negro ghost story," "The Golden Arm." Presented as it is at the end of
the essay, the tale exemplifies the art Twain has learned from "the most expert story-
tellers," professional humorists like Riley, Artemus Ward, Bill Nye, and Dan Setchell,
all of whom he names in his essay. But there is one figure whom he does not name,
and from whom he learned both the style and substance of "The Golden Arm": "Uncle
Dan'l," a slave on his uncle's farm, where Twain as a boy spent his summers. "I know
the look of Uncle Dan'l's kitchen," writes Twain in his autobiography. "I can see the
white and black children grouped on the hearth, . . . and I can hear Uncle Dan'l telling the immortal tales which Uncle Remus Harris was to gather into books and charm
the world with, by and by; and I can feel again the creepy joy which quivered through
me when the time for the ghost story of the 'Golden Arm' was reached."[12]

As Twain tells it, the story hour emblemizes his uneasy nostalgia for a past of
innocent boyhood lived in the shadow of slavery. "All the Negroes were friends of
ours," writes Twain, "and with those of our own age we were in effect comrades." "In
effect," because "color and condition interposed a subtle line which both parties were
conscious of and which rendered complete fusion impossible."[13] It is only as an audience "grouped" under the spell of Uncle Dan'l that this line disappears until the
children must go to bed. The same dynamics apply to the more professional setting
for the tale described in his essay, though the line drawn is not one of race. For the
purpose of the story is to draw "the farthest-gone auditor—a girl, preferably," into
the story's suspense, and then, with the right use of the pause and the tale's ending
"snapper," elicit "a dear little yelp" that will make her "spring right out of her shoes."
As he lays it out, the story's magic emerges in the performer's skill at provoking his
lone female auditor into violating decorum.

I will return to both the gendered and racial issues in Twain's vision of authorship; for now I want to emphasize how the art of humor served to empower a
performative self by cleansing the environment of social tensions and bringing audience and teller face-to-face. And it was precisely this space that disintegrated when
Twain turned to writing. For if a story well told—"understand, I mean by word of
mouth, not print"—could bring art to life, its transcription could well entomb it. As
Twain put the issue in a letter to Edward Bok:

The moment "talk" is put into print you recognize that it is not what it was
when you heard it. . . . [T]he varying modulations of the voice, the laugh, the
smile, the informing inflections, everything that gave that body warmth . . .

and commended it to your affections—or, at least, to your tolerance—is gone
and nothing is left but a pallid, stiff and repulsive cadaver.[14]

Twain made more explicit the latent sexuality of his image in another letter recalling,
with an enthusiasm he reserved only for oral performances, some speeches "which
carried away all my wits & made me drunk with enthusiasm": "Lord, there's nothing
like the human organ to make words live & throb, & lift the hearer to the full attitudes of their meaning." In the newspaper the next morning, however, the identical
speeches "don't seem the same—their still sentences seem rather the prone dead forms
of a host whom I had lately seen moving to the assault."[15]

If the voice was vital, potent, if its control an art, print threatened to kill, to cas-
trate. Important here is how the sexualized language underscored Twain's sense of
the absolute differences in the mediums. Print froze the warmth of performance; it
flattened the humorous into the comic, because it severed the intimacy of performer
and audience, destroying what Walter Ong has called the "circumambient actuality"
that so sparks oral performance.[16] If, as Howells insisted in "The Man of Letters as
a Man of Business"—his own searching inquiry into the social grounds of authorship—"The only thing that gives [a] writer positive value is his acceptance with the
reader," how is a writer alone with the words on the page, or face-to-face only with
publishers and editors, to gauge his reader?[17] For Twain, the question was never clearly
answered. "My audience is dumb," he wrote to the English critic Andrew Lang in
1889. "[I]t has no voice in print, and so I cannot know whether I have won its approbation or only got its censure."[18]

In 1874, Howells, who was then editing Twain's "Old Times on the Mississippi"
for the *Atlantic Monthly*, seemed to sense his author's anxiety over medium and audience when he advised his friend on the article's tone. "Don't write *at* any supposed
Atlantic audience," he urged, "but yarn it off as if into my sympathetic ear. Don't be
afraid of rests or pieces of dead color. I fancied a sort of hurried and anxious air in the
first [installment]."[19] In providing his contributor with an ear for his yarn, an audience for his performance, Howells rightly understood that for Twain the dynamics
of speech communication—the face-to-face intimacy, the sense of power—represented not an alternative medium of expression to writing, but an imaginary screen
on which he could project an ideal writing. Conversely, if as a writer Twain performed
for a mute audience, his problematic search for the "right form" actually represented
an effort to create the right performative context. The struggle to write was a struggle,
in Ong's terms, to "fictionalize in his imagination an audience" that would endorse
his performance.[20] When this frame was firmly in place, he was capable of writing at
a prodigious rate; when it slipped, he was left adrift.

In fact, Twain's career can in many ways be understood as a restless effort to find,
or imagine, an audience. On the one hand, he was capable of claiming the genteel
readers of the *Atlantic* as his true audience. Twain replied to Howells's advice on "Old
Times" with characteristic gusto: "It isn't the Atlantic audience that distresses me;

for *it* is the only audience that I sit down before in perfect serenity." It was not an audience that would demand he "paint himself stripèd."[21] On the other, he rejected just this audience for its cultural opposite, insisting as he did to Henry Huttleston Rogers, the Standard Oil baron who guided Twain through his bankruptcy, that his readers were "factory hands and the farmers. . . . *They* never go to a bookstore; they have to be hunted down by the canvasser. When a subscription book of mine sells 60,000, I always think I know whither 50,000 of them went. They went to people who don't visit bookstores."[22] Yet even as he pursued a mass audience, by the turn of the century he grew so uneasy that he expressed his intentions "to stop writing for print as soon as I could afford it," a promise that he made good in part by restricting the publication of his sprawling autobiography, a work that he in fact dictated rather than wrote.[23]

In many ways, Twain's often contradictory efforts to identify his audience reflected broad changes in the economic and institutional conditions of publishing that transformed relatively homogeneous (and restricted) readerships into markets.[24] Since the 1850s, authors such as Susan Warner, Fanny Fern, and Harriet Beecher Stowe (Twain's Hartford neighbor, whose *Uncle Tom's Cabin* [1852] would always serve him as a benchmark for his own success), as well as publishers like the New York *Ledger*'s Robert Bonner, had discovered and finally cultivated an economically viable reading market. By the end of Twain's career, a subsequent generation of editors and writers succeeded in establishing a relatively organized market for reading that linked different modes of writing with differing segments of the public. The result was a market shaped more or less as a hierarchical pyramid, with an elite form of literature occupying both the top of the structure and the smallest proportion of the market, and the penny press and dime novels serving as the base. In between lay a vast array of fiction, journalism, essays, textbooks, advice books, general interest magazines, and trade journals.

Writing during a period when cultural hierarchies were relatively fluid, Twain moved remarkably well up and down this pyramid, making shrewd use of its cultural codes and economic differentiations in a way that few writers—especially few male writers—could. His work appeared in the most elite magazines; an edition of his collected works was published in a handsomely bound set by Harper Brothers, one of the most committed (and successful) marketers of literature. At the same time, he continued, as an author, publisher, journalist, and finally as a celebrity, to exploit the burgeoning capabilities of mass publishing that so threatened the more conservative members of the genteel elite.[25] In a literary world of increasingly diverse readerships, Twain was exceptional—the popular "Lincoln of our literature," as Howells aptly named him.[26]

Despite this versatility, or maybe because of it, Twain relied heavily on his sense of a split market to define his audience and his broader intentions. In his well-known letter to Andrew Lang quoted earlier, Twain defended *A Connecticut Yankee* against its negative notices in England by arguing that it was the victim of critical standards based on artificially narrow assumptions concerning the value of high art. "The critic assumes, every time, that if a book doesn't meet the cultivated-class standard, it isn't valuable." Such a "law" risks condemning all but the finest works of art as useless; in the pursuit of revering culture, it obviates "all the steps which lead up to culture and make culture possible." It is thus a criticism in danger of catering only to "the thin top crust of humanity—the cultivated," while ignoring the interests of "the mighty mass of the uncultivated who are underneath." The kind of art that Twain practices, however, stands categorically outside of such standards because it caters "for the Belly and Members" and not the head of the social body:

> I have never tried in even one single instance, to help cultivate the cultivated classes. I was not equipped for it, either by native gifts or training. And I never had any ambition in that direction, but always hunted for bigger game—the masses. I have seldom deliberately tried to instruct them, but have done my best to entertain them. To simply amuse them would have satisfied my dearest ambition at any time; for they could get instruction elsewhere, and I had two chances to help to the teacher's one: for amusement is a good preparation for study and good healer of fatigue after it.[27]

Twain's letter makes clear that he thought of audience not only as a matter of identifying *who* read his books, but also of articulating *how* those people read: the "masses" were to be entertained and amused, the "classes," cultivated. Thus to imagine any given audience entailed imagining both a particular kind of writing and a particular mode of authorship. Just how complex this ensemble of writerly and readerly assumptions, expectations, and roles was for Twain is suggested by how, despite his avowed pursuit of the masses, he still retains a trace of the "cultivated" standard ("amusement is a good preparation for study") in justifying his choice of audience. More pointedly, the letter suggests that the public art of humor that Twain celebrates in his essay on storytelling may not be so much a performative act as it is a formative one: humor achieves its highest success only when a performance creates out of the audience's pleasure the truly humorous artist. James Whitcomb Riley's mastery is measured by the efficacy of his authorial persona: "The simplicity and innocence and sincerity and unconsciousness of the old farmer are perfectly simulated, and the result is a performance which is thoroughly charming and delicious."

Without an immediate audience, without a circumambient frame supplied so neatly by the lecture performance (a frame to be sure within which Twain constantly chafed), authorship—the written art of performative humor—became that much more difficult to create. Yet it was precisely this self-creation that Twain pursued relentlessly. It was, after all, the presence of the speaker, "everything that gave that body warmth" and identity to an audience, which in print threatened to become "a pallid, stiff and repulsive cadaver." That which Twain wants to "slide effortless from the pen" is not so much, to change his original emphasis, "the sole form *for* you" as it is "the sole form *of* you." Form here constitutes identity; when it is "right" it inhabits, gives warmth to, writing.

Twain's compositional strategy intimates how essential, how vital to his work as a writer, was this often frustrating drama of self-creation, or self-authorization. At stake for Twain with each text he began was the invention of a rhetoric that would create a reader who, in the absence of an immediate audience, could authorize the continuation of his voice. R. Jackson Wilson has clarified this dilemma by arguing that nineteenth-century authors laid claim "to a kind of authority that [gave] their work something of the character of a performative utterance" akin to that of ministers and judges. Just as the latter's language held the power to pronounce and define such states as criminality and marriage, so too did authors seek to endow their own "utterances"—poetry, fiction, and belles lettres—with a similar social authority. The words of ministers and judges, however, became law, as it were, because they were backed by institutional support. Writers, on the other hand, had few such extra-linguistic resources. Instead, the validity of their performance and the legitimacy of their authority depended on how well they figured an authorial presence worthy of their readers' attention. In short, they had to ask "the reader for the authority to employ such devices, to speak in such voices, to adopt this or that persona, to display—or conceal—a particular kind of narrative presence."[28]

This figured author was as much the product of writing as the producer of writing: the evident skill of a form of writing, the extent to which it met, without completely reproducing, the expectations of readers, gave the author a provisional authority to claim public attention. In turn, the more often this "style" appeared under the author's name—with room, of course, for variation, "artistic maturity," "stylistic innovation," and so forth—the more secure that authority. Thus, books by the most successful authors were identified strictly by a name: one was as likely to read "Stowe," as *Poganuc People* (1878), "James," as *The Bostonians* (1886).[29]

For Howells, so permeable were the distinctions between author and authored, so essential the process of self-construction, that he argued that "every novel if it is honest will be the autobiography of the author and biography of the reader."[30] But it was Twain, struggling as he did to form an authorship with his writing, who more than any of his contemporaries used autobiography to build the mutually dependent identities of author and reader. In preface after preface, he stressed to his readers that they were about to read "personal narrative," based on "personal familiarity" and "experiences of my own": "I am sure I have written at least honestly."[31] His travel books centered Mark Twain as the main character, whose doings were at least as foregrounded as where he visited, while texts like *Roughing It* (1872) and "Old Times on the Mississippi" (1874) stood virtually as a form of autobiography. So pervasive was this tendency that the introduction to his pieces in his own *Mark Twain's Library of Humor* (1888) notes that his books "continue the story of his own life, with more or less fullness and exactness."[32] The importance of the "autobiographic element" to his actual readers is suggested by the critic who went so far as to argue that "the interest of his books varies directly in proportion to the presence of this personal element."[33] Another noted the tendency of Twain's admirers "to regard themselves as his personal friends" by referring to him by his first name, a distinction he shared with the likes of Andy Jackson, Abe Lincoln, and Teddy Roosevelt.[34]

This mass appeal of course had more to do with the "personal narrative" he offered the public than with his jealously guarded "private history."[35] Indeed, the protection he gave his personal life to a great extent stemmed from his regarding it as a form of literary property: to allow someone else to "steal" his biography was to put at risk what became his final projects—his own autobiography and the authorized biography by Albert Bigelow Paine.[36] In any case, whatever motivated Twain's hold on privacy, the public figure that came to be Mark Twain was more than a pen name to "mask" Samuel Clemens. Rather, it was the name of an autobiographical persona "self-made" by the act of fictional narration. Mark Twain is, in all senses of the term, the subject of his writing: a figure whose personal experience supplies the material, the voice, the stylistic contours of what he called "the building of novels" and other narratives; the often hazy, but always present, historical reference point for the innocent abroad, Tom Sawyer, the cub pilot on the Mississippi; and the author figure who, as the "maker" of books supposedly exists prior to, but ultimately inhabits, is in a sense subjected to, the language of the texts. Finally, Mark Twain is a persona engendered by his narratives to occupy the position of "author," a role that Mark Twain himself understood as formed in a social arena. His supreme fiction, his most explicitly artful humorous performance, was Mark Twain, the fiction that authorized his fiction.

II. LITERARY REVERENCE: THE WHITTIER BIRTHDAY BANQUET

If in "How to Tell a Story" Twain imagined an ideal performance, then certainly he realized his nightmare with his ill-fated speech delivered at the banquet, attended by fifty of the most important figures of New England letters, honoring the seventieth birthday of John Greenleaf Whittier in 1877. Planned as a broad burlesque of three other eminent poets in attendance—Ralph Waldo Emerson, Henry Wadsworth Longfellow, and Oliver Wendell Holmes—a tale meant to enliven a long evening of eating, drinking, and platitudinous speechmaking, became, under the pressure of Twain's anxiety over his own authority, a source of "pain and shame . . . so intense" that nearly thirty years later its author still felt at times like "an imbecile."[37] Both the undeniable intensity of Twain's memory of the speech and the way in which it compellingly crystallizes the humorist's ambivalent relationship with the Boston world of genteel letters has rightly made this banquet a kind of primal scene of Twain criticism. For in burlesquing the other writers, Twain's vernacular story not only seemingly travestied an occasion meant to self-consciously celebrate the institution of literary authorship, it also challenged him to confront his own authority as a writer. As Gillman has put it, Twain spoke at the dinner "suspended between two roles: the California humorist mocking the institution of the Men of Letters while being accepted as a member of that institution."[38]

The neatness of these dualities, however, are challenged by the fact that, in 1877, there was no single "institution" of letters. Rather, Twain delivered his talk to an audience of writers as suspended between roles as he was. An event that may, at first glance, seem to have been a relatively straightforward affirmation of a canonical tradition was, in fact, a conflicted moment in a complex reordering of the institutions of authorship, one that would both alter the economic and cultural bases on which writers could build their careers and would revise the values and uses that their work represented to society at large. Thus, at stake in the burlesque, for both Twain *and* his audience, was the right to define what he calls in his tale "a littery man." On a more immediate level, the speech reveals in a remarkably concentrated manner how Twain's search for "the sole form" generated his strategies for plotting his autobiography of authorship not on the private geography of identity but on the shifting public terrain of his society's construction of the literary. If Twain wrote in a way that figured an authorship of writer and audience, he did so in this speech at a moment when his strategy entailed a cultural struggle as much as it did a formal one.

Drawing on the familiar vernacular convention of framing one story with another, Twain begins his speech by offering it as a "reminiscence" of traveling the gold country of the Sierras as a young writer. While there, he stops "at a miner's lonely log cabin," seeking hospitality and eager to test "the virtue of my *nom de plume*."[39] Rather than receiving the greeting he hopes for, he meets a miner who glumly lets him in and serves him a meal in virtual silence. Twain, piqued by his host's "jaded, melancholy" demeanor, attempts to get the miner to explain his enigmatic behavior, which he does only after much persuasion and three whiskeys. Twain, the miner tells him, is "the fourth littery man" to visit him in the past twenty-four hours: the others were "Mr. Longfellow, Mr. Emerson and Mr. Oliver Wendell Holmes. Consound the lot!" Emerson is described as "a seedy little bit of a chap," Holmes "was as fat as a balloon . . . and had double chins all the way down to his stomach," and Longfellow was "built like a prizefighter" and looked "as if he had a wig made of hair brushes." All three had been drinking; they were stopping at the cabin to rest on their way to Yosemite. The miner continues by describing how he had offered the customary hospitality of food and rest only to have his guests insult him with condescending recitations of their poetry, consume his whiskey, and cheat at a game of cards. The evening had almost ended in a drunken brawl with knives and guns until Holmes threatened to smother his comrades under his folds of fat. After inflicting further indignities on their host, the three ruffians left in the morning, with Longfellow taking the miner's boots as his just due as a great man.

Whatever the reaction by the three poets to such a burlesque—Longfellow and Holmes were apparently politely amused; Emerson too befuddled to react—Twain's irreverent caricature left him swinging between humiliation and defensiveness. After ten days of misery, he remained so convinced that he had deeply insulted his listeners that he wrote humble letters of apology to all three of his "victims." Five years later, he reacted to the news of Longfellow's death by admitting that he still felt like "an unforgiven criminal" because of his remarks.[40] Yet alongside this at times almost abject remorse ran an equally persistent conviction that, as he put it in a letter just months after delivering the speech, while it "was in ill taste . . . that is the worst that can be said of it. . . . nobody has ever convinced me that that speech was not a good one."[41] Decades later, in his autobiographical account, he still found the speech "as good as good can be. It is smart; it is saturated with humor."[42] Then he reversed himself yet again two weeks after dictating those lines, calling the speech "gross, coarse . . . offensive and detestable. How do I account for this change of view? I don't know."[43]

Twain, of course, suffered his share of poor performances during his career as a public speaker, but his persistent return to the incident suggests that the talk represented for him more than a literary indiscretion. In his autobiographical account, in particular, it stands out as a failure of craft and conception so complete that it shakes his confidence. As he describes it, the problem lay in his relationship with his audience, composed not just of Whittier and his peers, but including as well some of the most eminent men of New England culture—Thomas Wentworth Higginson, Charles Eliot Norton, the publishers Henry Houghton and James Fields, the naturalist John Fiske, and fifty other writers, editors, and educators. Twain tells of beginning his tale with a "genial and happy and self-satisfied ease," as "[t]hose majestic guests, that row of venerable and still active volcanoes, listened, as did everybody else in the house, with attentive interest." However, instead of playing to that attention, Twain loses all contact:

> Now then the house's *attention* continued, but the expression of interest in the faces turned to a sort of black frost. I wondered what the trouble was. I didn't know. I went on, but with difficulty—I struggled along, . . . always hoping—but with a gradually perishing hope—that somebody would laugh, or that somebody would at least smile, but nobody did. I didn't know enough to give it up and sit down, I was too new to public speaking, and so I went on with this awful performance.

The masterful awareness that characterizes the humorous artist is here displaced by the groping self-consciousness of the comic who tries to incite laughter by laughing at his own jokes. Such ineptitude is fatal: "When I sat down it was with a heart which had long ceased to beat. I shall never be as dead again as I was then."[44]

According to Twain's account, his failure is contagious. The next speaker, the novelist William Bishop, rises, "facing those awful deities—facing those other people, those strangers," only to "hesitate, and break, and lose his grip, and totter, and wobble, and at last [to slump] down in a limp and mushy pile." Like Twain's, Bishop's speech is fatal. As Howells puts the case in mildly chastising his friend: "The world can never look upon Bishop as being a live person. He is a corpse." So, too, is the audience: the program, scheduled to run much longer, ends abruptly, everyone too "dazed, . . . stupefied, paralyzed . . . to do anything, or even try."[45]

Twain was not alone in characterizing his failure as complete. Howells—who as editor of the *Atlantic Monthly* and master of ceremonies had nervously introduced his friend as a humorist "whose fun is never at the cost of anything honestly high or good"—recalled Twain's "amazing mistake, . . . bewildering blunder, . . . cruel catastrophe," as ending with the speaker "standing solitary amid his appalled and appalling listeners, with his joke dead on his hands."[46] But both accounts, and Twain's in particular, certainly exaggerate the dire impact of his talk, and by most reports actually contradict what happened. To be sure, not everyone was comfortable with Twain's burlesque (some of the out-of-town papers questioned its propriety), but on the whole it seems the speech was delivered with aplomb and received with laughter and applause. The program continued well into the early morning before breaking up, while local newspaper reports the following day contain no hint of a scandal or problem.[47]

Then why does Twain, whose memory was always more creative than accurate ("When I was younger," he wrote later, "I could remember anything, whether it happened or not"), cast as an utter failure what was at worst a qualified success?[48] The answer lies in how completely Twain's autobiographical account displaces the actual events with a fantasy of infectious failure that itself inversely mirrors the performance in "How to Tell a Story." His narrative links performative breakdown, brought about by his naïve misreading of the audience, with a breakdown in authority. "What could have been the matter with that house?" he asks in his autobiography. "Did I lose courage when I saw those great men up there whom I was going to describe in such a strange fashion? If that happened, if I showed doubt, that can account for it, for you can't be successfully funny if you show that you are afraid of it."[49] For Twain, the speech failed because it did not do what any good performance must do: figure an authorial identity capable of grasping the authority to face an audience "with a speech to utter."

By his account, then, the speech represents an extraordinary stage failure because it took place in front of an extraordinary audience; Twain "fails" not only as a speaker, but as a writer in front of his peers. Alongside this nightmare, however, runs a curiously apocalyptic fantasy in which Twain's death figures as but the first in a chain of dysfunctions that ultimately lead to the audience's death as well. The humorist humiliated forebodes, in his account, not just his own demise, but the death of all authorship as represented by his audience. It is precisely out of this general debacle that Twain's authority reemerges, in his autobiographical account, as triumphant—powerful enough to silence his peers.

Twain's contradictory versions of the reception of his performance do more than merely reflect his ambivalence about his speech; they perpetuate the subtle tension of identity and antagonism with his audience that generated his tale in the first place. They refigure the ambiguities that Twain inscribes in his talk when he casts himself both as the innocent bearer of someone else's puzzling tale—after all, he merely tells his audience what the miner told him—and, of course, the author of the tale he tells.

Finally, the imagery of death, castration, and impotence in Twain's autobiographical account (Bishop wobbles "in a limp and mushy pile," the audience sits "paralyzed") recalls his anxieties of print and suggests that the significance of his "mistake" lay, for him, not so much in misjudging his audience as in staging his performative demise in a way that implicated his peers in his own struggles of authorial self-fashioning. That it did implicate others is suggested by Howells's overreaction. It is suggested, as well, by the questions about the propriety of his speech that appeared in out-of-town newspapers for several weeks, questions that echoed Twain's own vacillations.[50] Finally, it is suggested by the ways in which the banquet became part of the "usable past" of subsequent critics, marking a distinctive break between an older world of genteel New England letters and a more national, and ultimately more modern, literary practice anticipated by Twain.[51]

Writing to a close friend just two months after the banquet, Twain expressed regret over insulting the poets, but nonetheless insisted that his speech was a good one. His barbs, he argued, were not personal; he as easily could have "substituted the names of Shakespeare, Beaumont, & Ben Jonson" for those of the three New Englanders, an assertion that at least reveals how highly Twain thought of his victims.[52] It also suggests that his target was quite literally their names, the virtue of *their* noms de plume, which like those of Beaumont, Jonson, and, above all, Shakespeare, had come to signify at least as much as their writing, Literature itself. Indeed, the Shakespeare whom Twain had in mind was not the playwright whose work during the century had been adopted and even bowdlerized by a tradition of popular performance, a writer whom Twain himself had repeatedly burlesqued early in his career, even making him a member of Queen Elizabeth's earthy court in the ribald farce, *1601* (1876).[53] Rather, it was the playwright whose profile since mid-century had hardened into a sacred icon of high culture, whose every word was the utterance of genius, whose language was so elevated that, even as it was scrupulously preserved, it was certified as hopelessly obscure to all but the most educated. This was the Shakespeare who frustrated Twain's attempted burlesque of *Hamlet* by precluding any change in the text of the play, "for the sacrilegious scribbler who ventured to put words into Shakspeare's [*sic*] mouth would probably be hanged."[54] It was the Shakespeare collected in an eleven-volume set, complete with study guides, notes, and introduction, which Twain endorsed as "invaluable; they translate Shakespeare to me and bring him within the limits of my understanding."[55]

Twain was not the only one to invoke this Shakespeare when referring to the New England poets: the Boston *Daily Advertiser* compared the scene of Whittier and the fifty men gathered to pay him tribute to an imaginary portrait of "Shakespeare and his friends." "The trio," went on the report, "—Whittier, Emerson, Longfellow— gave a reverend, almost holy, air to the place, and their gray hairs and expressive, joyful faces formed a beautiful group."[56] This language, in turn, reflected the rhetoric of many of those who spoke at the banquet, honoring as it did more the men than their work. Josiah Gilbert Holland, the conservative editor of *Scribner's*, captured the language best when he sent his regrets in a letter (read aloud during the ceremonies) that traced the public influence of "these beloved and venerated poets" to their "simply . . . being lovely and venerable." Did his "fellow citizens" know, he asked, how the poets "help to save the American nation from the total wreck and destruction of the sentiment of reverence?"[57]

It was just this burden of reverence that Twain profaned—he later wondered "how I ever could have been inspired to do so unholy a thing"[58]—when he caricatured the poets. In the words of one critical review of the speech, to bring "these poets and philosophers, whose lives have been passed amid books, in college cloisters, and in refined society, into intimate relations with whisky, cards, bowie-knives and larceny" was to take the names of literature in vain, to deflate the ideal image of authorship with the gritty physicality of a fat Holmes, a seedy Emerson, and a bristled Longfellow.[59] The thrust of Twain's speech, then, was aimed not at the men in attendance, as he makes clear in his letter, but at their *names*. It was a distinction that Holmes, for one, recognized quite well when he responded to Twain's apology by assuring him that "It never occurred to me . . . to feel wounded by your playful use of my name."[60]

In graciously pardoning Twain, Holmes seems to acknowledge a distinction between self and name. But then, if this name does not refer to Holmes personally, to whom, or what, does it refer? Could it be that he makes the same distinction between public author and private self that Twain made? Holmes himself complicates these questions by implying in his tribute to Whittier at the banquet that, in fact, a real human being gazed at the reader through his poetry. Quoting himself, he said, "'the style is the man,' and the nib of one's pen / Makes the same mark at twenty, and three-score and ten." Thus, he praised the "sweet singer's" writing for revealing to the careful reader the very man as he is: "How we all know each other! no use in disguise; / Through the holes in the mask comes the flash of the eyes."[61] On one level, Holmes implies that the Whittier he admires is the poet created in the writing—an artificial if persuasive character—yet, with the same gesture, he then equates this figure with the man sitting near him. Does the reader glimpse the person or the name, an essential humanity or a constructed self?

This confusion of authenticity and artifice is also reflected in Howells's characterization, made decades later, of the poets as "men of extraordinary dignity, of the thing called *presence*, for want of some clearer word, so that no one could well approach them in a personally light or trifling spirit."[62] At once present and distant, they occupy some difficult-to-determine sphere of notoriety or fame. And thus, Twain's barbs, as Howells saw them, both struck home and missed at the same time: "To be sure, [the poets] were not themselves mocked; the joke was, of course, beside them; nevertheless, their personality was trifled with."[63] "Personality," "presence": like Holmes, and like Holland, who saw the poets at once as good men and good icons,

Howells insists on an essential selfhood in characterizing the authority of the poets, even as he acknowledges something artificial that hovers about or "beside" them.

The tremors of confusion registered by the banquet speakers over the status of a name, a pen name, have less to do with any explicit crisis of identity than they do with an essential anxiety over the cultural authority of the literary. In praising Whittier for what is, in effect, his sincerity, Holmes (and his praise is characteristic of much of the dinner's rhetoric) implies that his fellow poet's authority lies in how directly his writing reflects what is essentially an exemplary character. As such, the rhetoric of reverence locates the burden of authority not in the performative text, but in the men themselves, who, like Shakespeare, are presumably worthy guardians of stable values.[64] To paraphrase Holland, Whittier's writing is venerated because he is venerable. Twain's burlesque, however, provoked Holmes and Howells, especially, into confronting, if for only a moment, the possibility of a disjunction between revered name, writing, and writer. When, in Twain's tale, Longfellow makes off with the miner's boots, the poet turns to his abused host and says, quoting his "A Psalm of Life":

> Lives of great men all remind us
> We can make our lives sublime;
> And departing, leave behind us
> Footprints on the sands of Time.

Even as the words perfectly express the assumptions underwriting the banquet's reverential tone, the incongruity of such language coming from the mouth of an ill-bred ruffian raises some provocative questions. Who is it that authorizes these words; who is it that gives them their meaning? Are these the words of a "Longfellow" whose very vision makes him one of the great men he writes about? Or are they those of the ruffian, sublime in his impertinence? To insist on the author's claim to meaning denies literary language any special status; to cede these words to the ruffian breaks the links of sincerity that presumably give literature value.

The banquet's rhetoric of reverence sought to establish a unitary value for literature by repressing the potentially disturbing disjunctions that Twain's burlesque teased to consciousness. But what makes his tale so vital is that, even as the evening's celebratory language sought to elevate authorial authority, the banquet itself actually had much to do with unsettling it. For Whittier's birthday was not the only reason for the banquet; the participants also met to commemorate the twentieth anniversary of the founding of the *Atlantic Monthly*. Indeed, virtually everyone in attendance, from Whittier to "younger" writers like Charles Dudley Warner (Twain's Hartford neighbor who coauthored *The Gilded Age* [1873]), the poet Edmund Clarence Stedman, the novelist William Bishop, and Twain himself had contributed to, edited, or in some way supported the magazine. Thus, Henry Houghton, who only four years ago had bought the magazine for $20,000 from James Osgood (who also attended), was using the occasion to give his periodical the same public "presence," the same cultural authority, as the men he celebrated. He wanted to endow the *Atlantic* as the institutional voice of elite American letters—to establish its language as the country's preeminent literary language and its writers as the embodiments of an identifiable tradition of canonical literature. To do so, he needed to carve out a niche for the magazine in what was emerging as an increasingly rationalized literary marketplace.

He had already used the magazine's eminent prestige to elevate Whittier and his peers to the summit of culture. At the banquet, he could then use their reputation to winch the magazine still higher. In his speech, Houghton welcomed Whittier and his famous peers as the magazine's "founders and constant contributors, . . . who still give it the influence of their great names and well-earned reputation, as well as the matured product of a genius enriched by a lifetime of labor." In his remarks, Howells even more bluntly acknowledged the banquet's purpose. The *Atlantic*, he urged, "has represented, and may be almost said to have embodied, American letters. With scarcely an exception every name known in our literature has won fame from its pages, or has added lustre to them."[65]

It was just this fame that Houghton and his stable of writers and editors worked assiduously to cultivate. The most prominent sign of such effort was the extensive coverage given to the banquet not only by newspapers in Boston, but across the country. Not only did Sylvester Baxter of the Boston *Herald* and Delano Goddard of the *Daily Advertiser* attend as invited guests, speeches and toasts were copied for the papers ahead of time in order to make the morning editions. Nor did Houghton's publicity stop there. He also marked the dinner by publishing, as a companion to those of William Cullen Bryant and Longfellow, "A fine life-size portrait" of Whittier, "this beloved and honored poet."[66] During the dinner, seating charts were signed by each of those present and subsequently auctioned for as much as $65 apiece at the South Church Bazaar. ("These autographs will, of course, be very valuable," noted the *Advertiser*, "both for their several worth and as memorabilia of the occasion.")[67]

For Houghton, reverence thus served as the language of cultural publicity, the means whereby literature could enter the marketplace without being of the marketplace. More important, it joined most of those attending the dinner in a remarkably unified sense of value and purpose. For while Howells could distinguish "very well the difference between an author whom the Atlantic has floated and an author who has floated the Atlantic,"[68] the guest list made no such distinctions of fame, including equally those who worked assiduously to create a canon and those who were targeted for canonization. Both Francis Underwood—one of the originators of the *Atlantic*—and Thomas Wentworth Higginson wrote biographies of Whittier. Horace Scudder, one of Houghton's most important editors, organized an American Men of Letters Series edited by Charles Dudley Warner, for which Holmes wrote a biography of Emerson, and Higginson of Longfellow.[69] While Higginson, Holmes, Howells, Richard Henry Stoddard, Warner, Whittier, and Twain were featured in the "Authors at Home" series published in the *Critic* during the 1880s, among the writers contributing to the series were Bishop and George Lathrop. Scudder, himself, championed the same coterie of New England writers in his Riverside Literature Series for schools.[70] These more deliberate efforts were the products of, and in turn reinforced, the more informal networks and relations that animated what Richard Brodhead has called "paraliterary institutions"—men's clubs, Harvard College, *The North American Review*, James T. Fields's Old Corner Bookstore—all of which served not only to regulate the cultural commerce of Boston but also to identify it with a class of religiously liberal, culturally secure, and economically stable social peers.[71] Attending the banquet were members of the Saturday Club, which included all four of the honored writers—all of whom had helped to found the Atlantic Club, out of which had emerged the *Atlantic* itself—the Papyrus Club, the Radical Club, and a number of other equally exclusive clubs that met regularly for less formal, but equally sumptuous, meals.[72]

The rhetoric of reverence thus served to consolidate aesthetic taste, cultural value, and social identity into a figured author who "embodied" the literary for a reading market. It celebrated Whittier, Holmes, Emerson, and Longfellow by ratifying a literary system of distinction, a system that distinguished as literature a particular kind of writing produced by a particular kind of author who wrote for, and in turn was read by, a fundamentally homogeneous audience supplied by periodicals like the *Atlantic*.[73]

In one sense, Houghton's efforts were not especially innovative, marking as they did but one more stage in the late nineteenth century's merging of poetics and economics. Robert Bonner, the enterprising publisher of the New York *Ledger*, had made his reputation by relentlessly broadcasting the reputations of his writers, such as E.D.E.N. Southworth and Fanny Fern (Longfellow would also publish with Bonner).[74] As early as 1843, Horace Greeley could write to the reclusive Henry David Thoreau: "[T]hough you may write with an angel's pen yet your work will have no mercantile value unless you are known as an author."[75] Even Hawthorne, one of the most retiring and exclusive authors of the century, was urged in 1845 by his publisher to pose for a daguerreotype: "By manufacturing you thus into a Personage, I want to raise your mark higher."[76] By the 1870s, not only was a name essential for economic success, a work had virtually no *literary* value unless it was known by its author. Thus, Horace Scudder would differentiate "nursery classics" from "major classics" by stressing the former's lack of "individual authorship," implying that the maturing reading process could be gauged by a child's interest in the author of the work: "Only when its interest has begun to take note of some personal relation of author to work does the child need to pass from the realm of the great unknown stories to that of the known."[77]

Yet even as literature and authorship were being bound more tightly together, authorship itself, even that rooted in the genteel canon, was increasingly subject to "manufacture" by institutions dominated by the exigencies of a mass market for reading. Within twenty years, writers like Higginson and Holmes, not to mention Howells and Twain, became "personages" of a kind only imagined by most of those at the dinner, celebrities known as well as Andrew Carnegie and Thomas Edison.[78] The dinner thus began a transformation of the literary from a genteel tradition into a genteel endeavor; it did so by celebrating a canon of the past in the media of the future, by commemorating fame even as it manufactured celebrity, by insisting on literary distinction in the leveling language of the mass media.[79]

Twain's tale thus represents more than a personal ambivalence on his part, and its reception represents more than an instance of the intolerance of cultural Boston. Rather, in its humorous challenges to its audience, it inscribes many of the anxieties about the changing authority of the literary that the dinner sought to allay. Thus, the "mistake" of Twain's burlesque lay not in his insensitivity to his audience, but in his reflecting perhaps too accurately for some a shared sense of transformation. If, for many of those at Whittier's banquet, the "value" of the nom de plume, and with it the value of literature, was shifting uneasily between authenticity and imposture, Twain's irreverence did nothing to settle them. Nonetheless, it is not quite accurate to see his humor as strictly subversive. For if his talk partakes of sacrilege, it also secularizes; if it defiles, if it deconstructs, it also reconstructs the authority of authorship. Far from establishing a stance wholly outside the institutions of literature that underwrote the banquet, Twain's story entangles its writer in a complex play of travesty and accommodation; challenging the values of literature and the cult of the author, it reproduces the authority of the literary and so makes a place for Twain in the cultural world he depicts. In short, it allows him to make a name for himself.

Twain's best-known burlesque of Shakespeare comes, of course, in Huck Finn's garbled transcription of the Duke's equally suspect recitation of Hamlet's soliloquy. "To be, or not to be; that is the bare bodkin / That makes calamity of so long life," intones the sham actor as his awed amanuensis sets down the words.[80] The entire passage hovers on the verge of sense, perfectly mimicking the Shakespearean voice, drawing faithfully on his words even as it disfigures his language. The result is a passage that images the literary as, in the words of the book salesman in Twain's parody of *Hamlet*, "the grandest kind of book-talk. . . . Why, it ain't *human* talk; nobody that ever lived, ever talked the way they do."[81] Similarly, in Twain's burlesque of the poets, when Oliver Wendell Holmes inspects the miner's cabin, he too speaks inhumanly while quoting his poem "The Chambered Nautilus":

> Through the deep caves of thought
> I hear a voice that sings:
> Build thee more stately mansions
> O my Soul!

The miner can only reply, "'I can't afford it, Mr. Holmes.'" Emerson continues the comic duel of the human and the inhuman when he comments on the fare of bacon and beans by quoting from his own "Mithridates": "From air and ocean bring me foods, / From all zones and latitudes," which draws the bewildered answer, "this ain't no hotel." This carnival of quotation culminates in the drunken card game, when the lines from Emerson's "Brahma"—"They know not well the subtle ways / I keep, and pass, and turn again"—are transformed into: "They know not well the subtle ways / I keep. I pass, and deal *again!*"

In both texts Twain presents literary language as an image of itself: rather than speaking literarily, the poets and the Duke speak a language that signifies the literary. His texts thus create a vast gulf between the common sense of everyday speech (Huck, the miner) and the abstract and finally nonsensical rhetoric of literature. In effect, he inverts the vernacular paradigm, in which literary texts commonly highlight the rich strangeness of colloquial speech. Instead, it is poetry that intrudes as fragments of an inscrutable and ultimately irrelevant world, even as it demands action and incites replies. In his banquet speech, the play of nonsensical authority—the ability of the ruffians to *make* sense, to enforce their will even as they make no *sense*—reaches a crisis after the card game degenerates into a boasting match over whose work is "bulliest." Emerson grows restless for more company and asks, pointing to his host, "Is yonder squalid peasant all / That this proud nursery could breed?" No comic misinterpretation is needed to decipher the language's chauvinism: the context of mayhem and abuse converts Emerson's poetic musings into an epithet. Its aggression is underscored by the fact that it is uttered as the poet is "a-whetting his bowie [knife] on his boot." With that, the miner's comic resistance to the impertinences of his guests collapses. For the rest of the evening he serves as their fool, singing for their entertainment until he drops from exhaustion, only to awaken to see Longfellow appropriate his boots.

It is not, however, the miner who alone must respond to this gulf in meaning: Twain's use of literary quotations also demands that he and his listeners negotiate the divide. In quoting poets who not only were present as cohonorees, but who spoke at the banquet in the very language he parodies, he punctures the self-satisfaction inherent in the occasion, in effect visiting on his listeners the linguistic violence he fantasized about in his autobiography. Yet it is also the quotations that best secure the codes of taste and distinction the banquet celebrates. For, as in the case of the Shakespeare passage in *Huckleberry Finn*, the success of Twain's burlesque depends on his audience's knowing the writing at least well enough to recognize its travesty. Thus, if as quotations the poets' language burlesques and affronts, as *citations* of original texts, they affirm in their unreality and pretension those values that enforce the idealist nature of poetic language.[82]

If Twain's art here is no mere art of subversion, neither is it one of secret accommodation: the confrontation between the literary and the nonliterary is left bristling with all the cultural arrogance of Emerson's bowie-whetting. Rather, the burlesque represents Twain's attempt to test in front of his literary peers, as he does in the tale, "the virtue of my *nom de plume*," to figure himself in the cultural landscape he represents. As a Western humorist and former gold and silver miner, as an "innocent" traveling the sacred roads of European culture, Twain is most quickly figured as the miner.

On the other hand, by 1877, his identity was already established—in part, by the very writing that had brought him to the attention of the *Atlantic*. As an author speaking at the banquet, recalling the early days of his fame, Twain claims at least a qualified bond with his audience and the poets he lampoons. Nor is this situational posturing resolved by how he casts himself as narrator. In opening the talk as a "reminiscence," Twain takes the stance of a reporter: neither the tale, he implies, nor the caricatures, are strictly his. In closing, however, he admits that "In my enthusiasm I may have exaggerated the details a little." With this he dissolves the frame of objectivity and confesses—to whatever indeterminate degree—to its authorship. No longer does he stand as an auditor as bewildered as his audience over an inverted comedy of manners; he is its creator. Like the visitors in his story, Twain the speaker has abused the hospitality of his hosts by travestying the occasion and parodying their shared values; in the words of one newspaper account, he "lays hands on Emerson and Longfellow in that rough way."[83] Emerson as a ruffian is an inverted image of Twain as an author.

He links himself and Emerson more closely and disturbingly than that. For when the miner concludes his tale, the narrator rises to defend the reputation of the "real" poets by insisting, in language that echoes Holmes's praise of Whittier, that "*these* were not the gracious singers to whom we and the world pay loving reverence and homage; these were imposters." But then it is the miner's turn to grow skeptical as he asks, "Ah—imposters, were they?—are *you?*" The narrator has no answer. The question not only silences him, it devalues his pen name: "since then I haven't traveled on my *nom de plume* enough to hurt." But the question is a crucial one, for not only does it thrust the burden of proof on the narrator, and, by implication, on Twain himself, it links his own imposture at the banquet with the reverent posturing of the canonized poets. Who, he seems to ask, in this world of reverend names and manufactured personages, is *not* guilty of imposture? What is the "virtue" or the "value," what is the authority, of not just a nom de plume but of literature?

Like his peers, Twain could not answer these questions directly. He seemed genuinely troubled by them just after the banquet, ready, in fact, to silence himself, to realize the literary death he would fantasize about nearly thirty years later. He confessed to Howells that he felt "my misfortune has injured me all over the country; therefore it will be best that I retire from before the public at present. It will hurt the Atlantic for me to appear in its pages."[84] Howells quickly disabused his friend of his wishes, but there can be no doubt that the tensions between Twain and his audience—and the world of Boston letters that audience represented—played a large part in his own conceptions of his authorship. Certainly, elements of the speech directly reflect his ambivalence over his growing affiliation with the organs of high culture. But to figure Twain solely as a crasher at the gates of Culture, an outsider who envied as much as he distrusted genteel Boston, a Western humorist confronting the Eastern canon (to reiterate a few of the standard critical formulations), both obscures the shape of Twain's authorial career and overly simplifies the complex and changing world he had entered as an author.[85] As one of the speakers at the banquet, Twain

had every reason to see his audience as full of friends and peers. He was invited to
speak—this was in fact the second such program in which he had participated—not
just because of his well-deserved reputation as a banquet speaker, but because he was
one of the *Atlantic*'s most valued contributors. As early as 1868, he had been identified as a writer to pursue, but it was only when Houghton became publisher that
Howells, who was then editor, was urged to solicit manuscripts from his close friend.[86]
By the time of the dinner, Twain had published a number of pieces, including "A
True Story" (1874), the serialized "Old Times on the Mississippi," and "Some Random Notes of an Idle Excursion" (1877–78), the last of which would conclude with
the January issue. He had also been approached directly by Houghton to serve as the
lead author in a "Library of American Fiction" comprised of "the foremost American novelists."[87]

If Houghton understood the advantages of tying Twain's name to his magazine
and his publishing house (he never managed the latter), Twain had a clear sense of
the significance of publishing in the *Atlantic*, a magazine that he would later characterize in his autobiography as "a place which would make any novel respectable and
any author noteworthy."[88] However, Twain did not need the kind of respect and name
recognition the *Atlantic* could offer him; he submitted work more on the appeals of
Howells than out of any commitment to the magazine. He refused Houghton's offer
to serialize *Tom Sawyer* before book publication because it would leave him vulnerable to newspaper reprinting, and hence dilute his market. There just was not enough
money in the proposition. As he put it to Howells: "I would dearly like to see it in the
Atlantic, but I doubt if it would pay the publishers to buy the privilege, or me to sell
it."[89] He also turned down Houghton's American Fiction project on the same grounds.
("I like the whole plan except the money side of it.")[90] Instead, he published with
Elisha Bliss's American Publishing Company in Hartford, which marketed its books
directly by "subscription" or installment, with armies of agents traveling door-to-door.
Not only were middle men like distributors and booksellers eliminated, such books
more easily reached a much larger market than did trade books sold in bookstores.
The result for publisher and writer alike was highly profitable.

Twain's explicit pursuit of "the money side" of authorship of course separated him
from many of the concerns of his peers (it is difficult to imagine his agreeing with
Howells's conviction that "there is something profane, something impious, in taking
money" for art).[91] But this distance is best measured as a difference in emphasis.
Houghton himself insisted at the banquet on the need for combining "the best business talent with the loftiest efforts of authorship."[92] Nor did Twain stand outside of
the dinner's canon-making project. With the exception of Howells, Twain would
benefit more than any other participant at the dinner from the efforts of Houghton,
Fields, Holmes, Longfellow, and their peers to establish a market capable of sustain-
ing canonized literature. Despite that, at the age of forty-two, he was considered a
"junior" member of the party and despite the condescendence he often endured for
being "merely" a humorist, Twain was well on his way to becoming an American

Rabelais or Cervantes, if not a Shakespeare. By 1877, Twain had established his reputation as a writer and was in the midst of the most productive and creative period of
his career. Just eight years later *he* would be honored with a banquet celebrating his
fiftieth birthday, complete with a poem written for the occasion by Holmes; his seventieth would celebrate "the uncrowned king of American letters" as 170 literary guests
"showed by word and manner and act that they looked upon the chief guest as the
master."[93]

Far from standing outside his era's literary establishment, Twain engaged with
the central cultural issues of his era. His very popularity lead him by 1877 to confront
the issues of fame and celebrity, audience and medium, canonized literature and the
marketplace, more directly than virtually any other writer at the dinner, and, by the
end of his life, any other writer of his era. It is from this stance that the miner's question is so important. For at the center of Twain's parody lay not just a question about
his own identity, but a challenge to the presumed authenticity of literary authorship
in general. If the value of Twain's nom de plume depended on the authenticity of the
"gracious singers," then their names, of course, depended on his. And his was, of
course, in the terms of reverence, a fraud, a name manufactured in the marketplace
of culture. But if his literary value was based on an imposture, it was capable, as he
was coming to realize by 1877, of carrying an imposing authority.

In Twain's tale, the cultural authority of the literary collides with everyday speech,
reverence meets manufacture, in order to test and finally produce an authoritative "sole
form"—one that simultaneously maps a terrain of cultural differences and a voice
appropriate to that geography. The result is neither an affirmation of reverent distinction nor an oppositional critique of it, but rather a narrative of posture and imposture generated by parody and held together by humor. What emerges is not so
much an expression of cultural conflict as a tale that lays claims to being the site of
that struggle; it is quite literally a contra-diction—a narrative speaking against itself.
Twain's formal strategies, his art of humor, far from resolving the collisions of cultural languages, actually work to sustain them.

III. LOCAL DIFFERENCES

In emphasizing the performative dynamic of Twain's speech, a dynamic that is fully
intelligible only when read both as part of the evening's celebration of names and
Twain's subsequent revision of the evening's events, I want to suggest the intimate
link between Twain's formal struggles with writing and what we can understand as
the evening's cultural politics. In the end, the speech's irresolution (what *is* "the virtue" of his pen name?) represents both an example of a whole career of unresolved
writings and a particularly pointed challenge to the banquet's aspirations—which, of
course, the humorist shared. The autobiographical account attests to the persistence—
indeed, to the importance to Twain's style—of this mingling between the mechanics
of writing and the situational posturing of public authorship. For, in the autobiogra-

phy, not only does he revise what happened following his speech, he also edits the speech itself, most strikingly by changing "*nom de plume*" to "*nom de guerre*."[94] The new wording of course fits well with his fictionalized account of the burlesque's devastating effect on the evening's celebration. It also captures aptly the arrogance, even the aggression, beneath the rhetoric of reverence—much as Emerson's bowie knife did. Most important, it suggests that if Twain's pen name, like that of Whittier, Emerson, Holmes, and their colleagues, was a name of war, it was also a name *at* war with itself and those of other writers.

The figurative conversion of pen into sword also suggests that, decades later, Twain may have seen his "war" on names extending beyond the field of, to borrow Bourdieu's term quoted earlier, "job definition." Although not explicitly mentioned in his account, there were those who had expanded the theater of conflict in a direction unforeseen by the literary men participating in the evening's celebration. The day following the dinner, the Women's Christian Temperance Union published a formal complaint about the six rounds of wine served. More pointedly, there appeared in the Boston *Daily Advertiser* a letter signed "A Few Among Many" protesting the exclusion of women from the guest list. (Women were allowed in only after the men had finished their meals, having waited in the lobby to hear the speeches.) In voicing an unease over the exclusionary realities of the evening's ritual of consensus similar to that implicit in Twain's burlesque, and brought more into focus by his adoption of "nom de guerre," the letter helps to clarify both the possibilities and limitations of Twain's cultural politics. Ultimately, it suggests that Twain's struggles with writing and his ambivalence over the significance of his authorship, far from inhibiting his development as a writer, provided the energy animating his fundamentally social engagement with issues of capital, culture, and education.

"Some of us feel as though our own mothers had received a slight," opened the letter. If in "the republic of Letters, if nowhere else, woman is a citizen," then why were "the brilliant women" of the *Atlantic*—writers like Harriet Beecher Stowe ("one of the chief contributors of the Atlantic"), Elizabeth Stuart Phelps, Louisa May Alcott, Rebecca Harding Davis, and Lucy Larcom—"conspicuous only for their absence"? These contributors "had *earned* a seat at Whittier's own right hand"; why were they denied a seat at the table honoring a man "accustomed to see women honored equally with men in his Quaker home and church"? Indeed, not only were these women not invited, they were not even so much as mentioned: "from generous publisher and genial editor to grotesque humorist, all combined 'to let expressive silence muse their praise.'"[95]

The letter struck a telling blow to the dinner's canonizing aspirations. Higginson, long an outspoken supporter of women's rights, suffered a particular arrow of outrage ("And Colonel Higginson was there, and he forgot us, too!")[96] and responded a week and a half later with a public apology. The New York *Evening Post* picked up the story by reminding its readers that "the Atlantic Monthly's staff of writers is much more largely masculine than is that of any other magazine in the country. It is, in a

certain sense, our masculine magazine, and has always been so."[97] Houghton presumably saw his mistake and worked to expand his canon by inviting women to a
breakfast held for Oliver Wendell Holmes two years later, where he offered a lame
excuse for their earlier absence (the *Atlantic*, in its youth, was "too bashful" to invite
the ladies).[98] In 1882, the magazine was careful to celebrate Stowe's seventieth birthday. Nor did the "grotesque humorist" escape the taint of exclusion. Nearly thirty
years later, Twain's own seventieth birthday celebration was praised for "the strength
of the feminine contingent. There were fully as many women there as men, and they
were not present as mere appendages of their husbands, but as individuals representing the art of imaginative writing no less than the men."[99]

The letter of protest shifts what Houghton tried to put off as merely a social gaffe
to an issue of literary "citizenship" in a "republic of letters." In part, the exclusion
may have been determined by the very confusions over the nature of publicity that
Twain exposed in his talk. As an outgrowth of earlier, exclusively male, banquets held
more informally, and with little or no public notice, the Whittier celebrants may not
have realized the full scope of their aspirations. (Any violation of taste on Twain's
part may have stemmed from his anticipating something more like the ribaldry of
the private, all-male banquet for the *Atlantic* he had attended three years earlier, where
he had delivered a toast to "The President of the United States and the Female Contributors of the *Atlantic*.")[100] But it is precisely this almost universal blindness that
the letter of protest makes so eloquent. Why were women not invited, queries the
writer. "Was it because 'women are angels'" and thus too delicate for a banquet awash
in wine? "Was it because Eve, being 'first in transgression' . . . her sons determined
she should never more sit down beside them at the convivial board? Or was it that
prestige of sex is not yet offset by the chivalry of justice even among the liberals?"[101]
Indeed, the writer suggests that the whole enterprise of canonization is misconstrued;
Whittier should not be celebrated as a "gracious singer," as a literary descendant of
an enshrined Shakespeare, but as the "Dear Bard of Freedom" notable, as was
Higginson, for his liberal politics.

In this way then, the letter makes explicit what Twain may have belatedly realized in revising "nom de plume" as "nom de guerre": there are larger issues than professional gamesmanship at stake in any war of names on the cultural battlefield. (It
may be no coincidence that Twain made the revision six months after his own seventieth birthday celebration, in response to the query of a female correspondent.) By
and large, Twain's tale blindly accepts the implicit assumption that this was a man's
dinner and that the problems of authorship and literary canonization were exclusively
male problems. Yet there are suggestions that his burlesque at least complements, if
it does not advance, a cultural politics of gender. In their bullying swagger, boasts of
preeminence, and intimations of violence, the three rogues suggest a mythic masculinity derived from the riverboat boasting of Mike Fink, Davy Crockett, and Sut
Lovingood.[102] The miner, on the other hand, in his insistence on domestic decorum,
in his anxiety over expressing anger or outrage, bears a trace of feminization. Most

important, it is he who insists on questioning the value of names. The miner, too, had earned the right to sit at the head table, by virtue of being a host, but was excluded on essentially arbitrary grounds.

In its broader outlines, then, Twain's parody anticipates, or at least leaves open the possibility for, the critique by the feminist correspondent. Both understand authorship as a contest of pretension taking place within literary institutions and the reading marketplace. An author's status, his or her place in the canon of fine writing, is determined not by innate character, but by a demonstration of consensus authorizing certain uses (and users) of language while precluding, or at least ignoring, others. But there all similarities end. By interpreting the evening's bonhomie cheer as a rite of gender exclusion, by criticizing the elevation of representative men with the language of representational democracy, the letter's author moves quickly beyond issues of professionalization to tie authorship with "citizenship," recasting the evening's cultural politics as a symbolic enactment of social politics. The dinner, the letter points out, was not merely an exercise in constructing literary hierarchies: by identifying men as potential insiders and women as de facto outsiders, it reproduced ideological categories of gender. Twain's parody, on the other hand, from its very inception, resists any such reading of its content. (One need only contemplate the effect of the tale on its audience if Twain had chosen as the poets' host a New England housewife, an African-American, or an immigrant, to recognize the care he used in selecting a miner.) Working clearly within the confines of the masculinized literature established by the dinner, it parodies the language of reverence in order to certify Twain's own authorship.

To emphasize the limited focus of Twain's speech here is at once to acknowledge the evasive quality of his humor and to point to how it thrives on the very cultural insecurities the celebrants sought to allay and even hide. In a larger domain, it is to insist that Twain's performative engagement with the discourses and institutions of literary professionalism lay at the root of, in Jane Tompkins's phrase, the "cultural work" carried on by his writing.[103] In other words, Twain's insistence on what can be broadly defined as the rhetorical aspect of his writing suggests that to read in his texts what Walter Benjamin calls "the *attitude* of a work to the relations of production of its time" without attention to "its *position* in them" is to risk missing how intertwined the two textual dimensions were.[104] The analysis of one depends on the interpretation of the other. In questioning the link between an author's public identity and the avowed right to write, in rewriting "nom de plume" as "nom de guerre," in identifying an essential arrogance—even aggression—implicit in literary reverence, Twain linked social power with cultural elegance in a way that not only yielded burlesque, but exemplified the most searching dimensions of his important work. Implicit in the uncertainties of literary professionalism as he saw them lay larger questions. If reverent homage casts authors as representative men, what are they representative of? And why does that give them the power to represent others? In short, to lay claim to the right to write is to project and act on an implicit theory of social order.

The possibilities for social critique inherent in Twain's struggles with authorship—particularly how they placed in tense juxtaposition cultural authority and social power—emerge more clearly in another dinner speech he delivered four years after his self-styled debacle at the *Atlantic* dinner. Once again Twain was invited to speak at an occasion designed to affirm ritually the historical continuity and cultural authority of a particular community; in this case the dinner, held by the New England Society of Philadelphia, celebrated 250 years of Puritan heritage. In contrast to the Whittier dinner, Twain had little invested in identifying with his audience. Nevertheless, his acceptance of the invitation and the way in which he presented himself to the group make clear how his self-presentation was critical to how he fashioned his public identity as an author. By constructing a character in opposition to the collective identity of the audience, Twain pointedly challenged the New England Society even as he claimed an element of it as his own.

His talk begins with a "protest" that immediately questions the grounds for the dinner: "I have kept still for years, but really I think there is no sufficient justification for this sort of thing. What do you want to celebrate those people for?—those ancestors of yours, of 1620—the *Mayflower* tribe, I mean."[105] After defusing his challenge with some straightforward absurdity—"Why shouldn't they come ashore? . . . a horse would have known enough to land"—he moves to a more disturbing point. The Pilgrims, he argues, were a "hard lot": "They took good care of themselves, but they abolished everybody else's ancestors," including, he adds, his own. He then proceeds to offer a baleful history of his persecuted lineage. In doing so, he clearly positions himself not as a distinguished member of the group, but as an outsider.

His "first American ancestor," he declares, was an Indian: "Your ancestors skinned him alive," and thus "I am an orphan." Later ancestors include the Quakers, Roger Williams, and the Salem witches ("Your people made it tropical for them")—all victims of religious persecution. As he sums up: "Your ancestors—yes, they were a hard lot; but, nevertheless, they gave us religious liberty to worship as they required us to worship, and political liberty to vote as the church required." Twain's chronicle of the Puritan past then expands beyond religion to include racial intolerance: his listeners' forebears were responsible for opening the slave trade, thus introducing yet another of Twain's ancestors. And finally, after "I had acquired a lot of my kin—by purchase and swapping around . . . with the inborn perversity of your lineage, you got up a war and took them all away from me."

In revising a tradition of Puritan virtue as a history of oppression and exclusion, Twain amplifies the social conflict implicit in his Whittier Birthday Speech. Emerson's bowie knife, no longer the ambiguous costume accessory to a caricature, reappears as the stake, the chains of slaves, and the rifle. At the same time, Twain ostensibly abandons the compromised and contradictory position of imposter he assumed earlier; instead, his claim to ancestry clearly positions him as an outsider. "[A]gain am I bereft, again am I forlorn," he cries in mock dejection: his listeners may be able to chart their lineage directly to the Mayflower, but "no drop of my blood flows in the veins of any living being who is marketable." Instead, he himself is a "border ruffian from the state of Missouri," neither pure westerner nor pure "Connecticut Yankee." He is a cross-bred "orphan" of a heterogeneous culture, a creature of "mixed breed, an infinitely shaded and exquisite mongrel. I'm not one of your sham meerschaums you can color in a week. No, my complexion is the patient art of eight generations."

From his stance as an outsider, Twain urges himself on his audience as a prophet from the wilderness, their "only true friend" able to see clearly enough their degradation: "Disband these societies, hotbeds of vice, of moral decay—perpetuators of ancestral superstition." But, as his speech reaches its hyperbolic apogee, his voice becomes as "cross-bred" as its ostensible speaker:

> Oh my friends, hear me and reform! I seek your good, not mine. You have heard the speeches. Disband these New England societies—nurseries of a system of steadily augmenting laudation and hosannahing, which, if persisted in uncurbed, may some day in the remote future beguile you into prevaricating and bragging. Oh, stop, stop while you are still temperate in your appreciation of your ancestors!

The ambivalent reference of the word "speeches" sets the tenor of the passage: does it refer to the mongrelized voices of past victims of intolerance newly introduced by Twain's "genealogy," or does it refer to the banquet speeches celebrating the official tradition of the Mayflower descendants? This doubled voice continues as the figurative outsider indicts his audience for its historical intolerance in a language mimicking that of temperance and revival meetings, the nineteenth-century residue of Puritan morality. "[C]ease from varnishing the rusty reputations of your long-vanished ancestors—the super-high-moral old ironclads of Cape Cod . . . go home, and try to learn to behave!" By substituting the relatively mild and "remote" condition of "prevaricating and bragging" for the conventional threats of imminent misery and perdition, by accusing his audience of intemperate "laudation and hosannahing" rather than the sins of alcohol and vice, and, finally, by capping his parodic jeremiad with the comic deflation of urging his listeners to "behave," Twain legitimates the very self-satisfaction he challenges. In assuming the comic guise of a preacher he reestablishes a bond between himself and his listeners based on their mutual sharing of the joke.

It is a mistake, however, to understand his humor as diffusing his critical challenge to his audience. For in Twain's hands, critique is the material of humor as much as humor is the vehicle for critique. The inflated language of reverence, of "laudation and hosannahing," by virtue of its aspirations to authority, supplies the pretext for Twain to establish his authority not over the language so much as in it. The result is parody, a "mongrel" speech of contradiction that challenges both speaker and audience to once again confront the miner's question: "Ah—imposters, were they—are *you*?" In Twain's hands, any language of reverence and authority becomes an imposture, a partial truth masquerading as a complete truth. Thus, in both dinner speeches, the imposture of comic subversion was itself the product of the posturing rhetoric of cultural authority made material by the banquets themselves. To parody that language represents for Twain both an opportunity to expose its hidden partialities and to master it, to render problematic the authority of others who use that language and to claim his own authority over it. The challenges and evasions that characterize both of Twain's speeches—indeed, virtually all of his texts whether delivered orally or written—are best viewed as rhetorical tactics in a local politics of authorship.

Thus, within each text, and over his career as a whole, Twain's authorial self-construction represents what Fredric Jameson, drawing on Kenneth Burke, has characterized as a "symbolic act." Insofar as each text engages with historically shaped contradictions—in the cases under discussion here, the split between insiders and outsiders—it embodies "a genuine *act*, albeit on the symbolic level"; but the effectiveness of that act in social terms, its ability to directly change society, remains entangled in "the ambiguous status of art and culture."[106] It is in its complex confrontation with this ambiguity, and in its searching and conflicted exploration of culture's status, that the local, cultural, and, eventually, the social politics of Twain's writing most powerfully emerges.

❦

TWO

Consuming Desire

The Innocents Abroad and *Roughing It*

I. Speculating in the Market

In describing Twain's debacle at the Whittier Birthday banquet, Howells recalled how "the subtle fiend of advertising, who has now [1910] grown so unblushing bold, lurked under the covers," causing him, as a "young editor," "fine anguishes of misgiving as to the taste and the principle of" consorting with it.[1] Howells's reservations here characterize his lifelong unease over what he saw as a tightening bond between business and letters. The market for reading, which of course the *Atlantic* played such an important role in shaping, threatened to impose on writing an economic value that would overwhelm its social value. Economics, he wrote elsewhere, would pollute the "literary atmosphere," plunging literature into "a vast mart, [where] literature is one of the things marketed here; but our good society cares no more for it than for some other products bought and sold here; it does not care nearly so much for books as for horses or for stocks."[2]

The same lament was voiced by a range of critics protesting that "literature and art [were being] treated like common merchandise."[3] For Howells, however, the issue wasn't one of simply quarantining writing from the marketplace: as a professional author, he saw too clearly that success in the arts depended on the emerging national market for reading. Negotiating his contracts shrewdly, placing his work in the most prestigious and lucrative outlets—he left Boston and Henry Houghton for the "vast mart" of New York on the strength of a salary of $10,000 a year from Harper's— Howells made his work precisely the kind of product that "good society" cared for. He built his career as, in the title words of his most important essay, "The Man of Letters as a Man of Business." As the essay made clear, he consciously worked "to establish the author's status in the business world," to compare practitioners of "the hungriest of the professions" with "bank presidents, and railroad officials, and rich tradesmen, and other flowers of our plutocracy." No matter the writer's "low rank among practical people": "story-telling is now a fairly recognized trade, and the story-teller has a money-standing in the economic world."[4]

At stake in Howells's market anxiety was his effort to endow novel writing with a certain kind of authority in and over culture. Sensing the erosion of older institutions of acculturation such as the family and the church, Howells sought to install the novel, in Richard Brodhead's words, as "the cultural force most powerfully authorized to form and maintain, in individual minds, a collective definition of the permitted and the proscribed, the normal and the aberrant, the serious and the unserious."[5] The Howellsian novelist aspired to produce and, finally, to legislate a field of knowledge that would resemble in its status and its rigor those presided over by professionals in medicine, law, and the social sciences. Like them, the novelist was to undergo a thorough apprenticeship in the study of reality. Unlike them, however, the novelist's expertise could not be grounded in specifically defined areas and methods of research nor could it be legitimated by a university degree. Instead, the novelist's expertise would be grounded in the domain of knowledge that lay in the everyday life of common experience; the proof of apprenticeship would lie in the veracity of representation.

Therein lay both the promise and the threat of the market. On the one hand, the distribution networks of publishing promised the writer an unprecedented access to a national audience. Reaching into the private minds of readers alone with a novel, the writer, as imagined by Howells and his genteel peers, could potentially realize a powerful influence over the collective mind of America. On the other hand, the market was equally capable of, indeed very successful at, disseminating a potentially pernicious fiction of fantasy, novels that "hurt because they are not true . . . because they are idle lies about human nature and the social fabric."[6] Such writing, recognizable by its emotional excess and melodramatic indulgence, threatened the reader by offering literature as nothing more than "the emptiest dissipation, hardly more related to thought or the wholesome exercise of the mental faculties than opium-eating; in either case the brain is drugged, and left weaker and crazier for the debauch."[7] The marketability of this fiction threatened the writer in two ways. First, as Howells was well aware, writing for entertainment sold in vast quantities; the potential for financial success could seduce the hungry writer into writing for the demands of the market. As another critic put the case, the popular novelist, "in haste to get his wares on the market, . . . is inspired by the idols of the market-place rather than by the spirit within him. If one of his books makes a hit, he copies and copies it until his manner becomes mannerism, his characters dolls or caricatures, his scenery like that of the old-fashioned drop-curtain."[8]

The second threat was, for Howells, more subtle and more immediate. For the seductive power of mass-marketed fantasy threatened to contaminate even the serious writer, the one who aspired to professional authority, by encouraging him to ply the same fictional tools as the dime novelist. Thus, behind Howells's repeated confessions of "the guilty conscience of the novelist in me,"[9] behind his distrust of Houghton's "subtle fiend of advertising," lay a sense that the very mass market that underwrote the novelist's authority threatened to reduce writing to entertainment, fiction to fantasy, reading to mere consumption. Writing for the market, rather than in the market, was for Howells a form of literary and economic speculation. Serious novelists, he argued, entered the market as artisanal laborers willing to sell a finished product; "[i]t ought to be our glory that we produce something, that we bring into the world something that was not choately there before; that at least we fashion or shape something anew."[10] His ideal was a moral capitalism, a market in which the social responsibility of the realist was perfectly complemented by pecuniary return. Indeed, for Howells, literature was recognizable by its resistance to speculation, by the author's refusing the temptations of writing directly for the market, and by the author's refusal to indulge in the sentiment of romantic entertainment.

Amy Kaplan characterizes Howells's realism in just these terms when she argues that his aesthetic project served to resolve the threat of the market with his aspirations for professional authorship. As author and critic, Howells called for both a turn to subject matter grounded in a quotidian life not dominated by the excesses of love and for an equally important "revaluation of the activity of reading and writing." Realism, for Howells, embraced a morality of production grounded in "a system of value which privileges industriousness and self-discipline as the basis of communal life. As a cultural force, realism turns reading into work, an act which unites its practitioners . . . through the mutual recognition of a common identity rooted in the productive sphere." In this way, Howellsian realism emerges as "a strategy for defining the social position of the author. To call oneself a realist means to make a claim not only for the cognitive value of fiction but for one's own cultural authority both to possess and to dispense access to the real."[11]

As close friend, editor, literary confidante, even, at times, as mentor, Howells wielded a profound influence on Twain's career as a writer. He facilitated Twain's appearance in the *Atlantic*, edited many of his friend's manuscripts, and was virtually the only author from whom Twain would take any advice. As a critic, he never ceased to champion the humorist's work as important literature, from his first review of *The Innocents Abroad* (1869) in the *Atlantic* to his memoir of their friendship, *My Mark Twain* (1910). Indeed, what is most remarkable about his critical assessments of the humorist is the degree to which he made Twain *his*, a realist who, despite—indeed, perhaps because of—his mass appeal, wielded a moral authority over the democratic masses who nourished his vision.[12] In an essential way, however, Howells's nomination of Twain to the school of realists misses the extent to which the two writers diverged. If Howells sought to displace mass fantasy with realism, to counter speculation with production, Twain, in his writing and as a professional author, reveled in his power to exchange fantasy for value and fully embraced the role of speculator.

There can be no doubt about the enthusiasm with which Twain pursued the business of authorship. Writing for him entailed much the same kind of speculative "invention" as went into "Mark Twain's Self-Pasting Scrapbook," his "Improvement in Adjustable and Detachable Straps for Garments," and of course the Paige typesetter.[13] Copyrighted instead of patented, his books were nonetheless expected to realize for him the same profits as his financial schemes and his investments in everything from patent medicines to railroad stock. To read Twain's correspondence with his publishers, to follow the tortuous urgency of his own publishing business, to trace his endless lawsuits over copyright and plagiarism, is to encounter a writer intent on cornering markets and accumulating profits not by labor, but by magic, particularly that magic of converting words into money. Income from writing, he wrote to Charles Webster, the nephew he put in charge of his publishing house, "like stock speculations, is money got for nothing, so to speak."[14]

For Twain, writing was a business; as he put it in his autobiography, his "experiences as an author" began not with pen in hand, but when he negotiated his first book contract with Charles Webb.[15] It was not that the market "influenced" his prose in any determinate way, but rather that for Twain "speculation" was not a pun: so closely linked were money and writing that it is impossible to refer to one without the other. The same determination to get rich that led him to the silver fields of Nevada led him to write his account of his experiences there in *Roughing It* (1872). It also led him to go prospecting by proxy by sending one James Henry Riley to South Africa in pursuit both of diamonds and of material that Twain himself would later massage into yet another book for the subscription market.[16] If his success as an author brought him fame, it also generated profits to be invested in grandiose projects like the Paige typesetter or the Kaolotype printing process, which would allow him to corner the market on all published material. What more natural a fantasy for a man who at times saw himself as an author capable of generating money with words?

Taken together, Howells and Twain seemed to follow widely diverging, but ultimately complementary, paths in the economic landscape of fiction writing. In part, their divergence may have been a matter of personal style: one a magazine editor, the other a publisher; one drawn to the security of a regular salary, the other willing to risk his talent in the marketplace, building a fortune book by book. (Twain's happiest moment as a publisher came when he presented President Ulysses S. Grant's widow with a check for $250,000 from the profits of her husband's memoirs.) But what most differentiates them is how, in this shared but heterogeneous market economy, they figured their authority. In embracing a variation of the professional paradigm, Howells sought to establish a relationship of qualified autonomy with the economic requirements of authorship. As his invocation of the ideal of artisanal craftsmanship suggests ("it ought to be our glory that we produce something"), he envisioned writers first preparing their text and then offering it to the market. He also took seriously his self-assumed responsibility as a broker of culture: working as author, editor, and critic, he was a professional tastemaker, selecting, at times interpreting, for his audience not just the modern world, but its representations as well. In other words, Howells— perhaps because he so firmly grounded his sense of literary purpose in a self-conscious literary tradition—was able to imagine productive spaces outside the market. Later in his life, he would envision the Boston he had discovered as a hopeful young poet as such a space; that poet's direct descendant would reside metaphorically within the "Editor's Study" (the name of the regular column Howells contributed to *Harper's Monthly*)—a room symbolically removed from the street, protecting the writer from the harsher winds of commerce. Howells worked to create such spaces by those activities that substantiated and finally institutionalized a writer's career: book reviews, newspaper notices, clubs, literary dinners, reading tours, magazines, and certain "serious" publishers.

Twain, of course, participated in all of these activities. Unlike Howells, however, he did so with little sense of their defining even a semiautonomous space of culture. He wrote virtually no criticism; he saw book reviewing as a form of publicity useful (or harmful) to the sales of his books (and he was enraged by what he saw as personal attacks). Though he read more widely in the Western canon than he acknowledged publicly, he borrowed very little directly from the belles lettres tradition. The market for him was ubiquitous. It did more than establish external values for writing; it penetrated the very language of the literary itself, shaping its purposes and defining its uses.[17] The "sole form," after all, distinguished one writer's "line" of goods, of business, from another. Even Huck Finn, the "juvenile pariah" who flees St. Petersburg as much to escape his share of the loot he and Tom find in McDougall's cave as to escape the "sivilizing" of Miss Watson, "don't take no stock" in biblical stories of Moses. Like Huck, Twain was "mixed up in the business" from the beginning; unlike him, however, he embraced it with remarkable energy. If he shaped his career figuratively on the lecture platform, practically it unfolded in the emerging forms of mass culture: advertising, the newspaper syndicate, the news magazine, the celebrity interview, and the subscription book.

It was by virtue of this last cultural medium that Twain was able fully to realize his speculative energies, both as a writer and a publisher. More important, it was the mass market for subscription books that seemed to promise a chance for maintaining the performative context for authorship that Twain feared print in general sundered. The attraction to Twain of subscription selling was obvious: profit. Instead of relying on the business acumen and favor of the bookseller and distributor to sell a book to the public, subscription publishers eliminated the middlemen and carried their volumes, often one at a time, directly to customers' doorsteps. In a sense, this process was one of the oldest methods of merchandising: peddlers like the famous Parson Weems had included books among their wares since the early part of the century. Twain's earliest publisher, Elisha Bliss of the American Publishing Company, followed more directly in the footsteps of the Hartford, Connecticut, publishing firm Oliver D. Cooke & Son, which in 1822 had sold the *Family Encyclopedia* door to door. This method proved so successful that by the Civil War there were as many as twenty subscription publishers in Hartford.[18] Between 1861 and 1868, Hartford publishers used 10,000 door-to-door agents, sold nearly 1.5 million books, and grossed 5 million dollars in sales.[19] During the decades between the war and the end of the century, subscription publishing grew until it accounted for two-thirds of all books sold in America.[20]

Bliss and his colleagues were able to reach this volume by efficiently organizing their production and distribution apparatus. Books were sold by geographically organized bodies of agents, many of whom were women or freshly discharged Civil War veterans who, working on commission, canvased vast territories of the country. Each customer was offered for examination a prospectus, bound as a replica of the book and containing twenty or thirty pages of excerpts and illustrations. After agents had accumulated enough sales, they ordered the volumes from the publisher, who only then printed and bound the book in massive runs. They were then rushed by rail to the waiting agents, who distributed them and collected payment.

Executed successfully, a subscription book campaign could quickly realize huge profits. The lure of this kind of profit led Twain to forego what was becoming a lucrative career as a popular lecturer and journalist and sign with Bliss to publish what would become *The Innocents Abroad*. In fact, the attraction lay not just in how much money he could make, but also in how he could make that money. As a reporter, Twain wrote either for a salary, or, when a traveling correspondent, for a fee. As an author, he could become a literary entrepreneur. Turning down an offer of $10,000 for rights to his book, he instead chose to realize a 5 percent royalty on each volume sold—he sought literally to bank on his success.[21]

The decision was the right one: within sixteen months Bliss sold nearly 85,000 volumes of Twain's first book, yielding its author over $16,000 in royalties.[22] Twain was elated, comparing his success, with characteristic hyperbole, to that of his Hartford neighbor, Harriet Beecher Stowe, whose *Uncle Tom's Cabin* (1852) had sold 300,000 copies in its first year. Twain was so impressed by the sales success of *The Innocents Abroad* that he wrote Bliss:

> I never wander into any corner of the country but I find that an agent has been there before me, and many of that community have read the book. . . . What with advertising, establishing agencies &c., you have got an enormous lot of machinery under way and hard at work in a wonderfully short space of time. It is easy to see, when one travels around, that one must be endowed with a deal of genuine generalship in order to maneuvre a publication whose line of battle stretches from end to end of a great continent, and whose foragers and skirmishers invest every hamlet and besiege every village hidden away in all the vast space between.[23]

Over the years, his fascination with the sales machinery, and a growing sense that Bliss cut the profits pie a little too liberally for himself, led Twain to involve himself more and more in the American Publishing Company—as its most important author, he eventually served on its board of directors. By 1880, sure that he had been swindled out of thousands of dollars, Twain finally began publishing his own books; by 1883, he established his own firm, Charles L. Webster and Company—named for the nephew who served as Twain's puppet—to publish his work. By 1886, the company carried an ambitious list of subscription titles, including reminiscences by Union

Army heroes like William Tecumseh Sherman, Philip Henry Sheridan, George Brinton McClellan, and Ulysses S. Grant, Henry Ward Beecher's *Autobiography*, and a collection of travel and history books.

As onerous as the business of publishing sometimes proved to be for Twain—he often complained of its taking him away from his writing—his immersion in the book trade complemented, and in turn shaped, his writerly concern for audience. It allowed him to cast the necessarily fictionalized reader as an individual customer, the author as a salesman, and the text as both the object of and the contract stating the terms for cultural and economic consumption. From the moment he accepted Bliss's offer to publish *The Innocents Abroad*, Twain shared his pen with the invisible hand of the market.

Twain's first book represents his most explicit effort at exploring the economics of cultural consumption. It was, after all, a travel book of Europe and the Holy Land, a rigorous albeit humorous tour of many of Western Civilization's most sacred cultural monuments. Hence, it fit perfectly with Bliss's list: he had built his company by marketing, often with very little attention to accuracy, books of history, travel, natural history, etiquette, even some mild pornography. (With the exception of reprinted or pirated issues of European classics, Bliss and his colleagues virtually never took a risk with novels. *The Gilded Age* [1873] was the first new work of fiction published by subscription.) Twain had initially made the trip as a traveling correspondent for the New York *Herald* and *Tribune* and for the *Alta California* in San Francisco, which had earlier sponsored his trip to the Sandwich Islands; his dispatches, with their irreverent humor, had been reprinted across the country and made him a celebrity. The book, however, required more substance. The average reader expected just such information. "The winning card is to nail a man's interest with *Chapter I*," Twain advised a prospective author in 1875, "& not let up on him till you get him to the word 'finis.' That can't be done with detached sketches. . . . Bring along *lots* of *dry statistics*—its the very best sauce a humorous book can have. Ingeniously used, they just make a reader smack his chops with gratitude."[24]

Twain may not have offered his readers dry statistics, but in rewriting his newspaper material he did fill his book with the kind of conventional history and description—much of it, in fact, lifted almost verbatim from other guide books—that his readers had come to expect from subscription books.[25] In fashioning a book that, in the words of Bliss's advertisement, would "interest all classes and ages," he also eliminated much of the rougher humor and the references to the Pacific coast that characterized his *Alta California* material.[26] In addition, he discovered that his articles only amounted to 250 of the 600 pages required to make the standard subscription volume (material substance justified in part the often steep prices charged for such books). Twain's revisions thus represent more than just a writer working to improve his manuscript; they also signify a writer who saw his relationship to his audience in essentially economic terms. At the same time, however, the medium of his rhetoric invoked high culture: his humor, and the information it dispensed, concerned some of the most revered cultural icons of the period.

Thus, *The Innocents Abroad* offered Twain an ideal stage for his debut as a literary personage, a platform on which to enact an authorship scripted by the resources of high culture and the habits of consumption and one lighted by the garish energy of Gilded Age speculation. The result is a text that plays with the tensions between authenticity and imitation, object and image, to rewrite aesthetic experience—exemplified in particular by the viewing of art—as a consuming experience. Beyond this, however, it also figures writing as the activity that most effectively traverses the line between culture and the marketplace, producing what can be called an authentic inauthenticity.

II. Siteless Sights: *The Innocents Abroad*

One of the best-known moments in *The Innocents Abroad* comes when Twain visits what he calls "the most celebrated painting in the world—'The Last Supper,' by Leonardo Da Vinci."[27] Barely a quarter of the way into the narrative, which has thus far galloped almost frantically through hotels, cathedrals, and museums, the episode represents just one more stop on a hectic itinerary. In Milan alone, itself sandwiched between a few days each in Genoa and Venice, the travelers already have visited the Duomo and its "7,148 marble statues" (129), the Ambrosian Library—where they see, along with an autographed letter of Lucrezia Borgia, some drawings by Michelangelo and Leonardo ("They spell it Vinci and pronounce it Vinchy; foreigners always spell better than they pronounce" [132])—and a public bath, before they find their way to "an ancient tumble-down ruin of a church." There, in this anonymous place, they pause to see for themselves the "wonderful painting, once so beautiful, always so worshiped by masters in art, and forever to be famous in song and story" (136).

The episode opens as a rehearsal of what by 1869 had become a familiar ritual of viewing art, described time and again in travel literature. Primed to a high pitch of expectation by guide books, art reproductions, lectures—the whole range of nineteenth-century cultivated education—travelers approached European art much as Harriet Beecher Stowe did, who, as she mounted the steps of the Louvre, felt a "flutter of excitement and expectation."[28] For her brother Henry Ward Beecher, the flutter became a crescendo on his visit to the painting collection at the Palace de Luxembourg in Paris. If not typical in its intensity, his account nonetheless exemplifies the disorienting shock many felt when encountering authentic art. He felt himself undergo an "instant conversion, if the expression be not irreverent": "[t]o find myself absolutely intoxicated—to find my system so much affected that I could not control my nerves—to find myself trembling and laughing and weeping, and almost hysterical, and that in spite of my shame and resolute endeavor to behave better,—such a power of these galleries over me I had not expected."[29] Even the more urbane art critic James Jackson Jarves, who lived much of his life amid the European art he loved and collected, recalled wandering the Louvre feeling "oppressed, confused, uncertain, and feverish," struggling "in a convulsive effort to maintain mental equilibrium."[30]

In part, these accounts record honestly overwhelming experiences of confronting, after years of having access only to reproductions, the authentic works themselves.[31] "I have seen good copies all over the world," confessed one traveler, "but they
lose their charm after seeing so much of heavenly beauty and earthly sweetness as
this glorious work of Raphael exhibits."[32] Another attested to "the new sense which
is developed by the sight of a masterpiece. It is as if we had always lived in a world
where our eyes, though open, saw but a blank, and were then brought into another,
where they were saluted by . . . grace and beauty."[33] These were Americans finding
for themselves, by following a program of leisured (if not leisurely) self-cultivation
first codified in the eighteenth-century Grand Tour, what many intellectuals felt their
country lacked: a rich tradition of culture made sturdy by a backbone of canonical
masterpieces and ancient monuments.[34] It was this expectation of enlightenment that
had persuaded Harvard earlier in the century to send abroad such prospective faculty
members as George Ticknor, Edward Everett, George Bancroft, and Henry
Wadsworth Longfellow to prepare for their roles as educators.[35] Their experiences,
in turn, helped inspire Americans to import as much of Europe as they could for their
own edification. Boston's Anthology Society Reading Room—later to become the
Athenaeum—was founded on the strength of books that travelers brought back from
Europe.[36] Later in the century, Jarves, inspired by his experience at the Louvre, as-
sembled an impressive collection of Renaissance Italian art, which Yale acquired in
1868 for its own museum.[37] Similarly, New York's Metropolitan Museum of Art and
Boston's Museum of Fine Arts both opened their doors in 1870 stocked with the
products of their patrons' European buying tours.

Thus, when Bayard Taylor, the most popular travel writer in America after mid-
century, confessed, "I cannot disconnect my early longings for a knowledge of the
Old World from a still earlier passion for Art and Literature," he merely made explicit what many travel accounts took for granted: Europe was for nineteenth-century
Americans a vast museum, a collector's cabinet that made solid what had only been
dreamed of.[38] To visit Notre Dame and Shakespeare's home, Florence and Athens,
was to make literal the literary, to make authentic the imaginary, to divest allusion of
illusion: "The Capitol, the Forum, St. Peter's, the Coliseum—what few hours' ramble
ever took in places so hallowed by poetry, history and art?"[39] Thus, it was the viewing
of art—consolidated in impressive collections in Paris, Florence, and, above all, in
Rome—that in many travelers' accounts most concisely symbolized the experience
of visiting Europe.[40]

In visiting the Leonardo, then, Twain walks a path already well trod by Americans eager for authentic art and culture. In fact, he represents "The Last Supper" as
the essence of Art, "celebrated" not just by travelers and critics but by other "masters
in art"; it is, in short, the masterpiece of masterpieces, created by the original and
originating Master. Twain's language deftly echoes a tradition of almost giddy homage to the painting both by critics and travel writers; an earlier traveler had described
"This celebrated painting, a copy of which, in one form or another, everybody has

seen, [and which] has been pronounced one of the finest in the world."[41] In their use of the word "celebrated," both writers, in turn, echo one of the most powerful pronouncements of the painting's value, by Johann Wolfgang von Goethe, whose essay on Leonardo's "Celebrated Picture of The Lord's Supper," published in English in 1821, cited it as "The picture . . . known to all that have ever heard the name of art pronounced."[42] According to Mrs. [Anna] Jameson, whose *Sacred and Legendary Art* (1848) went through numerous editions, Leonardo, "the greatest thinker as well as the greatest painter of his age," had with this painting brought forth "a creation so consummate, that since that time it has been at once the wonder and the despair of those who have followed in the same path."[43] Leonardo was more than a great artist, he embodied Art; he was, according to Charles Eliot Norton, a "great genius, one whose power all the world recognizes and honors, . . . [one who] stands apart from his time, unapproached, alone."[44]

Twain's visit to the painting, then, is framed by a set of expectations linking the genre he writes in—European travel literature—with a discourse of art appreciation that demands a response to the painting. If he had avoided such a confrontation earlier at the Louvre with a casual reference to "its miles of paintings by the old masters" (100), here he faces the demands of convention. He reacts, but in a way that deliberately travesties the reactions of others. The painting he describes is "battered and scarred in every direction, and stained and discolored by time. . . . The colors are dimmed with age; the countenances are scaled and marred, and nearly all expression is gone from them; the hair is a dead blur upon the wall, and there is no life in the eyes" (137). Despite the image's inscrutability, Twain finds himself alone in his disappointment. Around him artists assiduously copy it onto canvases, while tourists stand "entranced before it with bated breath and parted lips," uttering "catchy ejaculations of rapture." Gauging their reactions against his own, he wonders: "How can they see what is not visible? . . . You would think that those men had an astonishing talent for seeing things . . . which had faded out of the picture and gone, a hundred years before they were born." Indeed *his* eyes lead him to notice "how superior the copies were to the original, that is, to my inexperienced eye" (138).

The moment captures in miniature the irreverent texture of the text as a whole. Twain visits "The Last Supper" as what, he calls elsewhere, an "American Vandal": "the roving, independent, free-and-easy character of that class of traveling Americans who are *not* elaborately educated, cultivated, and refined, and gilded and filigreed with the ineffable graces of the first society." Unburdened by education (if "one has no opportunity in America to acquire a critical judgment in art," [170] then he will parade, rather than hide, his "uncouth sentiments" [171]), the Vandal gazes at Art "with a critical eye and says it's a perfect old nightmare of a picture and he wouldn't give forty dollars for a million like it."[45]

Twain's innocent may represent a stereotypical American abroad—one English reviewer characterized him as "a very offensive specimen of the vulgarest kind of Yankee"[46]—but he is also a close relative of the Vandal, whose uncultivated or "inexperienced eye" underwrites a clear-eyed skepticism, always quick to expose the empire's new clothes, to dismiss as shams the fruits of civilization offered to him by breathless guides and sanctimonious guidebooks. If Europe is a museum, he suggests, it resembles more one curated by P. T. Barnum than Charles Willson Peale: a house of humbug filled with disfigured paintings by "Old Masters" and buckets of nails from the True Cross. It is this humbug, distilled in the catch-phrased awe of visitors to "The Last Supper" and perpetuated by other travel writers, that Twain will expose. "This book," he posits in his preface, "has a purpose, which is, to suggest to the reader how *he* would be likely to see Europe and the East if he looked at them with his own eyes instead of the eyes of those who traveled in those countries before him. I make small pretense of showing anyone how he *ought* to look at objects of interest beyond the sea—other books do that, and therefore, even if I were competent to do it, there is no need."

While this bravado led Bret Harte, for one, to praise Twain as a "hilarious image-breaker," Twain's contentious stance is not as straightforward as his preface suggests.[47] In fact, his disappointment about the Leonardo was, by 1869, in many ways no less a cliché than the rapture of those who stood around him. "I sat before it for some time," noted one traveler, "and looked at it, and read all the guide-books said about it, but was not able to work myself up to the point of extravagant admiration expressed by some travellers in its contemplation."[48] Bayard Taylor admitted to a similar reaction in viewing the comparably admired Venus de Medici: "It may be considered heresy, but I confess I did not go into raptures, nor at first perceive any traces of superhuman beauty."[49] Even Harriet Beecher Stowe's flutter of excitement on approaching the Louvre subsided once she entered it and experienced "nothing of that overwhelming, subduing nature which I had conceived."[50]

The persistence of such reactions, coming as they often do hand in hand with expressions of giddy elation, suggests that disappointment itself was as integral a component of the reaction to authentic culture as was rapture. Twain writes not so much as an image breaker as an image exploiter, reproducing even as he travesties the conventions of travel writing (the claim of seeing truthfully stood as one of the most clichéd apologies in the genre). Indeed, his purpose is not so much to denigrate art—he admits to being "satisfied that the Last Supper was a very miracle of art once" (138)—but to explore his, and by implication his readers', relationship with that art. The narrator's disappointment in "The Last Supper" stems from the fact that the painting—far from being *too* cultural for his vulgar taste—is not authentic enough; as merely a scarred piece of history, it cannot deliver the pure experience that the conventions of rapture, constructed in countless travel accounts and reproduced in the expectations voiced in Twain's text, lead him to anticipate. In his disillusionment, the narrator is as much a victim of reverent expectations as are his fellow travelers in their illusion. He, too, visits the painting to experience in the original what he had known only in reproduction and in prose. Once there, his "impartial" description of the disfigured picture, by virtue of how thoroughly it negates the rapturous comments of others, perfectly expresses his disappointed expectations. Indeed, so caught up is he in his search for aesthetic experience that he endorses the copies as "superior" precisely because they, at least, help him recall what he came to see.

Thus, the irony in his carefully worded praise for the painting: "The Last Supper" is "the picture from which all engravings and all copies have been made for three centuries" (137). This seemingly naive statement points to the final significance of Twain's staging his confrontation with Art with the Leonardo rather than in, for instance, the Louvre. As informed commentators were well aware, because "The Last Supper" had suffered such damage from flooding and heavy-handed restoration—not to mention the deterioration that resulted from Leonardo's choice of media—the "original" masterpiece had long since, in Goethe's words, "almost ceased to exist, in its own substance."[51] To later connoisseurs, the picture was no more than the "wreck of a glorious presence"; less educated travelers could "distinguish little beside the composition and the general sentiment of the picture."[52] By the nineteenth century, the real picture had been for centuries known best only through copies; its fame and its "beauty" lay solely in its "aura" of authenticity, paradoxically attested to by the ubiquity, if not always the skill, of its reproductions.[53] Thus, in turning his "impartial" but "inexperienced" eye from the original to its copies, Twain suggests that the rhetoric of reverence finds as its true object nothing more than the mental image such language has shaped beforehand. In short, his double take represents the peculiarly modern experience of culture in an age of comic reproduction.

Art is not the only sight on Twain's itinerary to disappear behind the flood of images and expectations framing it. At virtually no point does his tour elicit an experience "authentic" enough to exceed his expectations. The issue is comically foreclosed at one of his earliest stops on his tour, in the city of Tangier, "the spot we have been longing for all the time. . . . We wanted something thoroughly and uncompromisingly foreign—foreign from top to bottom—foreign from centre to circumference—foreign inside and outside and all around. . . . And lo! in Tangier we have found it" (57–58). As the apotheosis of the authentically foreign, the city's architecture, its inhabitants' exotic dress and customs, and its history reaching to the time of ancient Thebes, all lead Twain to invest Tangier with an uncanny "foreignness":

> Here is not the slightest thing that ever we have seen save in pictures—and we always mistrusted the pictures before . . . they seemed too weird and fanciful for reality. But behold, they were not wild enough . . . they have not told half the story. Tangier is a foreign land if ever there was one; and the true spirit of it can never be found in any book save The Arabian Nights.   (58)

Just as in front of "The Last Supper," Twain's attention oscillates between the object (the city, the foreign) and its image, as he weighs the reality of one against the expectations generated by the other. At first, it seems that Tangier does indeed exceed its images, which tell only "half the story." In citing *The Arabian Nights*, however, Twain finally locates the authentically foreign in a "reality" measured not by its difference from images, but rather by its resemblance to what travelers know beforehand. Tangier, as he sums up, is nothing less than "an oriental picture," an image of the foreign best embodied in a book of fantasy.

In interpreting the "foreign" or the "authentic" by its image, as he does both in Tangier and while visiting "The Last Supper," Twain casts what he sees in essentially aesthetic terms. Indeed, under Twain's "ignorant" eye, all of Europe emerges as a form of art. Whether he visits the Vatican, the dungeons of the Castle D'If, the markets of Constantinople, or Notre Dame ("We recognized the brown old Gothic pile in a moment; it was like the pictures" [95]), his vision tears each site from any historical or social context—any foreign or authentic reality—and transforms it into a "sight" framed by preexisting images that link it to other "site/sights."[54] The Leonardo, Notre Dame, Rome, Tangier: no matter the scale, everything in Europe is there to be visited, recognized, and categorized with other images. The result is an experience that is remarkably uniform, even at times boring. "What is there in Rome for me to see that others have not seen before me?" he asks in mock desolation. "What is there for me to touch that others have not touched? What is there for me to feel, to learn, to hear, to know, that shall thrill me before it pass to others? What can I discover?—Nothing. Nothing whatsoever. One charm of travel dies here" (190–91). Like the "twelve hundred pictures by Palma the Younger . . . and fifteen hundred by Tintoretto," much of Europe leaves Twain "weary with looking" and incapable of interest, much less enthusiasm (169–70).

Twain's prefatorial claims notwithstanding, what differentiates him from previous travel writers is not a particularly scrupulous veracity—the standard avowal of virtually every writer—but the fact that he travels Europe as a tourist rather than as a cultural pilgrim. In his irreverent haste, he anticipates what Henry James would later characterize as the "passionless pilgrims" who evinced "a disposition, which had perhaps even most a comic side, to treat 'Europe,' collectively, as a vast painted and gilded holiday toy, serving its purpose on the spot and for the time, but to be relinquished, sacrificed, broken and cast away, at the dawn of any other convenience."[55] The commentaries that Twain offers, the history that he supplies, the comic comparisons he constructs, all serve to fragment "Europe" into a touristic collection of interchangeable sights; these sights are then shuffled and reintegrated in a narrative organized as much by the contingencies and coincidences of Twain's tour and by his personal predilections as it is by the countries he visits.

Although James characterized the modern tourist as "passionless," Twain's pilgrim emerges as a creature of enthusiastic anticipation, riding waves of expectation and consumption or expectation and disappointment. Far from rejecting aesthetic experience, he revels in it; from the opening pages, he immerses himself wholeheartedly in the leveling vision of tourism, trusting in the very equivalence of one sight to another to sustain his passion. The excursion, he is sure even before he sees the itinerary, will be "a picnic on a giant scale," a "royal holiday" during which passengers would "scamper about the decks by day, filling the ship with shouts and laughter" (17). Nor does the dry language of the prospectus advertising the trip's itinerary—"The undersigned will make an excursion as above during the coming season" (18)—dampen his enthusiasm. Its catalog of sights gives shape to the innocent's revel by invoking a litany of magical names: Lyons, Genoa, Correggio, Corsica, Napoleon, Joppa, Jerusalem, Caesar—places and names connected only by the timetable of travel. Twain opens the list of marvels by asking, "who could read the programme of the excursion without longing to make one of the party?" (18) and closes by answering emphatically, "Human nature could not withstand these bewildering temptations" (22).

The Innocents Abroad opens with the tourist already preformed, keyed to a pitch of comic hyperbole by the anticipation of travel itself. This culturally produced lust for travel, more than the desire to visit any particular place, fuels the pilgrims' trip. Despite their repeated disappointments—indeed, despite their growing skepticism as to whether these promises can be fulfilled—Twain and his companions time and again eagerly strain for the first glimpses of Gibraltar, France, Milan, and Jerusalem, their appetite whetted by pictures, guidebooks, religious and historical associations. Once having arrived, no matter how completely each place may satisfy or disappoint their expectations, the pilgrims quickly succumb to an unslakable thirst for travel that pulls them to the next sight.

In this sense, *The Innocents Abroad* unfolds as a sustained exegesis of the opening prospectus, which Twain, in a parody of Puritan sermon forms, prints in full as "a text for this book." For, if Europe promises a certain kind of "experience," this experience is valid only insofar as it recreates and fulfills the promises of the prospectus. Europe emerges as a metonymic series of buildings, paintings, streets, and vistas; like the words in the prospectus, it is linked as a system of equivalent signs. Indeed, Twain ends his text by evaluating the success of the excursion in precisely these terms: "I have no fault to find with the manner in which our excursion was conducted. Its programme was faithfully carried out. . . . our holiday flight has not been in vain— for above the confusion of vague recollections, certain of its best prized pictures lift themselves and will still continue perfect in tint and outline after their surroundings shall have faded away" (474–75). The "pictures" he has in mind are not those by the "Old Masters" but the very sites, impressed now as images, vaguely hinted at in the prospectus: "We cannot forget Florence—Naples—nor the foretaste of heaven that is in the delicious atmosphere of Greece—and surely not Athens. . . . We shall remember . . . Baalbek—the Pyramids of Egypt" (475). Twain thus ends his book where it began, with another catalog of sights, one that registers his experience only by the few modifiers with which he now surrounds each "sacred" word.

As Twain conceives it, tourism, then, is not strictly a form of enlightened travel, but a comically philistine cycle of anticipation and consumption—a process that entails reading about each site, evaluating the actual place in light of its prior image, and comparing it to other sites and experiences. Geographic places and material objects are torn from their social context and transformed into images of themselves, tourist "sights" framed by the touristic imagination. Sights, for Twain, are commodities, their

cultural value established not by any "aura" of authenticity but by guides and guidebooks, by the planned activity of tourism and its relentless itinerary, and, most of all,
by the act of consumption itself.

🎋

Twain's comic discovery of a reified Europe rode a mounting tide of American travel
oriented more to sightseeing and less to personal cultivation.[56] With the Paris Exhi-
bition in full flower in 1867 (which Twain visited on his cruise), unprecedented numbers of visitors took advantage of lower steamship fares and faster, more comfortable
continental travel to visit Europe. Twain himself estimated the number of Americans traveling abroad in 1867 as nearly 100,000 per year.[57] More sober judgments set
the number at around 30,000 at mid-century, before the travel boom following the
Civil War.[58] Despite these numbers, however, Europe remained inaccessible for most
Americans: even a second-class cabin for a round trip between New York and
Liverpool cost at least $150, far beyond the means of even the middle class. The ex-
perience of Europe for most Americans came strictly at home, where they read popular
travel literature or viewed stereocards and chromolithographs of famous art works
and well-known European vistas and monuments.[59]

The near ubiquity of such writing points to the extent to which leisured travel in
the late nineteenth century represented as much an experience of reading as it did
one of moving. Travel writing, along with the complementary flood of promotional
literature, by identifying, describing, and even naming noteworthy attractions, did as
much to make possible and desirable the pursuit of touring as did improvements in
transportation and accommodations. John Sears, in his study of American tourist sites,
has highlighted the ways in which "the raw material of nature" discovered in the White
Mountains of New Hampshire, Niagara Falls, Yosemite Valley, and Yellowstone "was
rapidly transformed into a cultural commodity by reproducing and marketing verbal
descriptions and pictorial representations." Such places served as "cultural productions" for a nation "hungry for national icons and for places which symbolized . . .
exotic wonder."[60] As Twain understood and made clear in his book, the playful tensions between authentically "being there," on the one hand, and seeing where one
has been or will go, on the other, represented the shaping experience of modern travel.
Thus, accompanying his deconstruction of the rhetoric of travel experience was a
reconstruction of the discourse of travel.

Twain was not alone in grasping the tensions between experience and discourse:
despite its explicit use of the rhetoric of authenticity, popular travel writing also stimulated the textual consumption of culture. Even as authors sought "to make words a
substitute for pencil and palette," even as they struggled to "acquire the power of
bringing home to thousands of firesides clear pictures of the remotest regions of the
earth," the very intensity of the experiences they recorded merely underscored the
vicariousness of the reader's own cultural encounters.[61] "I cannot tell you," wrote

Beecher in a common rhetorical ploy, "who have not seen [these portraits], what it is that arrests the eye." Julia Ward Howe confronted the paradox more head-on: "Of the pictures it is little useful to speak. Your description enables no one to see them, and the narration of the feelings they excite in you is as likely to be tedious as interesting to those who cultivate feelings of their own."[62]

Twain seized on the paradox of presence and absence implicit in all travel writing only to invert the relative values conventionally attributed to the opposition. The essential site for modern culture, he realized, lay not "over there" in Europe, in some distant place of authenticity, but in the texts of travel that guided both traveler and reader. If, as Twain suggests in his book, the authentic—of which Europe is a sign—lies not in the original work of art, but in the discourse that represents that art in a frame of values and expectations; if, in other words, the "Old Masters," though they may make paintings, don't make Art, whereas guidebooks do; then, the newest guidebook, which is the one Twain himself writes, embodies the truest Europe, the most authentic cultural product. For Twain to "suggest" to his readers how they "would be likely to see Europe," as he does in his preface, is to intimate that they, too, would enter into an experience as mediated as the one they have while reading his book. If, as his humor implies, travel never escapes the text, then travel books like *The Innocents Abroad* take the reader over the same ground as that traveled by the tourist. Travel books like *The Innocents Abroad*, his humor implies, do not guide the traveler, so much as the tourist's experiences validate the pretext of travel.

Then what was the pretext of travel writing? How did it speak to an audience the vast majority of whom never had and never would travel abroad? Or, to put the issue in different terms, as writers recorded their experiences with authentic culture, how did these accounts manifest themselves as a cultural form itself capable of imparting its own experience? "What are paintings worth," asked one writer, "but for *the effects which they produce* on those who see them?"[63] Or, the writer could have asked, What is culture worth? What is the value of Europe as it emerges in such writing other than the effects it produced on those who wrote about it and read it? For, a surprisingly large percentage of the voluminous literature on European travel described natural vistas, whole cities, boulevards and back streets, even the people who inhabited these spaces, not as objects in themselves, but as catalysts for complex aesthetic experiences.

For the travel writer, each visit to a gallery, like each visit to a city or a cathedral, was part education and part pleasure, part private cultivation and part a public introduction into a shared body of cultural knowledge. Travel represented, in short, the conversion of wealth—the money it took to travel Europe—into what one writer called "a floating aesthetic capital"; that capital could later be invested as knowledge, as experience, but, above all, as taste—as a sense of distinction proper to one's money.[64] In one sense, travel writers sought, in effect, to spread this wealth, to democratize culture, to bring directly as possible to readers the substance of their cultivation. In another, such writing represented the most direct investment of cultural capital they could make: publishing a travel account allowed one to earn some money while at the same time documenting one's attainment of cultural distinction.

The most authentic cultural product of authentic cultural travel was thus the fully educated author/traveler who, as codified by Jarves in his widely read treatise on art appreciation, *The Art Idea* (1864), through "gradual mental growth and study," had successfully transformed initial expressions of "indiscriminate rapture or aversion . . . into an intelligent perception of art-motives" that recreated, as narrative, a conventional language of taste and "correct views."[65] Seldom did travelers cover the same psychic distance as that of Beecher, whose ravings at the Palace de Luxembourg were followed at the Louvre by the balanced "secondary pleasure of no small degree" of calmly developing his own hierarchies of taste. But even Grace Greenwood, after having wandered through the Louvre "astonished by its vastness and splendor," visits the Venus de Medici in Florence later on her tour equipped with a language that precludes any "heartiness of adoration." Instead, she faults "the insignificant character of the head," even as she finds its "form" "[e]xquisite, tender, and delicate beyond my fairest fancy."[66]

As it emerged in travel writing, the language of aesthetic appreciation both signaled the presence of authentic works of high culture and distinguished its user as a person of education and sensitivity. Moreover, in wedding artwork and observer in a ritual exercise of detached and disinterested taste, it suggested a "disposition," to borrow Pierre Bourdieu's term, appropriate to the proper enjoyment of art.[67] Aesthetic language thus inscribed in the drama of appreciation an implicit use for art that was individual in focus but social in implication. Noting the docility of crowds in public spaces like parks and museums, some people began to attribute to art itself a power to shape society. "Art is the surest and safest civilizer," wrote one traveler. "Open your galleries of art to the people [as the Europeans do] and . . . you give them a refinement to which they would otherwise be strangers, . . . [a] sense of the beautiful or the sublime" that, when accompanied by "a few salutary lessons on the necessity of submission to authority," will eventually leave Americans "as well-behaved as the people of France or Italy."[68]

Travel accounts did more than document the mutation of enthusiasm into evaluation, ignorance into knowledge; they stood as its final result. They offered their readers more than secondhand descriptions of culture; they suggested a language, a disposition, a set of expectations that allowed readers to maximize their own, presumably more meager, aesthetic capital by investing in good taste. Thus, the pretext of travel writing lay in the pretensions of taste and hierarchy implicit in virtually every episode of art viewing, pretensions that linked proper uses of culture with social hierarchies. The meaning of Europe emerged not in how texts represented its cultural wealth, but in how they dramatized travelers' reactions to that wealth.

Twain's consuming vision engaged this rhetoric on a number of different grounds. In displacing an aesthetics of appreciation with one of recognition, he implied that the acquisition of cultural capital lay not in collecting the authentic but in reflecting the conventional. The values of his culture lay not in distinction (between art works, between connoisseurs) but in indistinguishability (between originals, and between originals and their images). His was an aesthetics of mass culture, an aesthetics potentially outside the realm of taste, dramatized by the blissfully ignorant tourist vandalizing the hierarchies of culture.

This, in turn, was accompanied by another gesture of the touristic sensibility, one made by an author who could not reproduce without travestying the cultural assumptions and values inherent in any genre. For it was not in Europe that Twain played the American Vandal most successfully, but at home, where he could align the vision of the "uneducated" or "impartial eye" of the innocent abroad with the "mercenary eye" of the practicing author.[69] Twain took seriously the connection between capital and culture that lay only implicit in the writing of others; after all, he joined the *Quaker City* cruise as a celebrity humorist whose fare was paid by the newspapers that printed his dispatches.[70] But it was when he placed his book in the hands of Elisha Bliss's American Publishing Company that Twain entered a terrain of culture every bit as codified and canonized as that of Europe. As he did when a tourist, Twain traveled this new land as a vandal of good taste.

In part because of their commercial success, and in part because of the bald way they pursued that success, subscription publishers like Bliss drew a full measure of distrust and criticism from critics even as liberal as Howells. When, for instance, critics voiced their fears that "literature and art are . . . treated like common merchandise," when another argued in 1884 that "literature has been degraded from its place, and in its room we have piles of printed stuff, gaudily tricked out in the worst of the printers', and lithographers', and the binders' art to sell 'at slaughter prices' as so much table ornament and bookshelf furniture," they had in mind not just dime novels and the cheap story papers, but subscription publishers as well.[71] It was not only that Bliss and his peers produced writing aimed at the lowest taste of the market; they were also accused of distributing a kind of "false" culture. One writer fumed that subscription books "serve very much the same purpose that ornamental tablets do in the family mausoleum—and . . . they are read just about as often."[72] Another went even further in describing the typical sham of such books as "[a] gorgeous binding, usually in very bad taste, thick but cheap paper, outrageously poor wood-cuts, the largest type with the thickest leads, add up to a very big, gaudy book, which a glib tongue or persistent boring cheats folks into buying at five dollars, when the reading matter which it contains, if worth anything, would make about a dollar-and-a-half book in the regular trade."[73] His description was by and large accurate: subscription books *were* in fact big, gaudy, ornamental, and expensive. Publishers like Bliss worked hard to justify steep prices and high profits by making sure that the customer received as much physical book as possible. Yet such marketing succeeded not by duping customers, but by selling them images of a culture they could not otherwise acquire. Such books were *meant* to be put on coffee tables or displayed prominently on shelves, as much as they were meant to be read. Nor was this marketing strategy generated by any kind of a cynical affront to taste; it exploited an increasing propensity by the American middle class to judge a book—and its owner—by the cover.

Even as genteel critics in dozens of advice books outlined for their middle-class readers courses of reading for improvement, they also charted what can be characterized as an etiquette of book possession, implying that owning books entitled one to similar claims to distinction as reading them. As Lyman Abbott argued, "books are the most telling furniture which can be placed in a room . . . an opinion is formed at once, from them, of the taste and cultivation of the family."[74] Henry Ward Beecher echoed him: "Books are not made for furniture, but there is nothing else that so beautifully furnishes a house. The plainest row of books that cloth or paper ever covered is more significant of refinement than the most elaborately carved étagère or sideboard."[75] Subscription books thus took their place in the family parlor with similar forms of culture—not only copies of the original artwork that travelers like Twain went to see, but also pianos, divans, screens, and other furnishings.[76]

Bliss and his colleagues recognized the importance of this image-making process by offering buyers as elaborate a piece of furniture as they could afford, allowing them to build a public identity through consumption. As he instructed his door-to-door agents, "Books are seldom bought for what they are as a whole, but for some *particular feature* or *features* they contain."[77] A feature could be the text itself (as it was presented in abbreviated form in the prospectus), the author's name, the subject matter, the book's physical attractiveness, or it may actually lie in the experience of purchasing culture. Thus, the salesperson was advised that one of the most powerful selling tools was showing the buyer names of prominent local citizens who already had agreed to purchase a book. Adding one's name to the list allowed the customer to join, quite literally, a select group of cultural consumers. Done correctly, Bliss assured his agents, they would realize "a kind of mesmeric power" and "a tremendous leverage" over the customer.

The salesperson, in effect, offered his customer what Twain is offered to join the *Quaker City* cruise: an "authentic" image of Culture. Thus, when Twain opens his book with the travel prospectus, he literally offers "a text for this book," a guide to buying his book translated as a guide for his trip. Like the customer/reader, the narrator is mesmerized by a commodity notable for its discrete features: "Constantinople! Smyrna! The Holy Land! Egypt and 'our friends the Bermudians'!" And, like the customer, he also enters a list, "selected by a pitiless 'Committee on Applications,'" which includes celebrities like Henry Ward Beecher and General Sherman.[78] Twain thus locates tourist and reader on a cultural map of taste drawn as much by the pretexts of cultural and social consumption as by authentic experience. The buyer's ultimate reading of the text, like the tourist's visit to the Leonardo, can only confirm or deny the powerful expectations that frame the actual cultural product.

This is not to suggest that in travestying the distinctions of taste, in displacing the authentic with the reproduced, Twain rejects the value of culture altogether.

Rather, just as the tourist remakes Europe in his or her own image, so too does Twain strive to find new grounds for the uses of culture in its images. In effect, his readers get for their money the same thing the Twainian tourist gets for his: the momentary fulfillment of a desire to augment the self through consumption. This desire then represents what Jean-Christophe Agnew has called "a commodity aesthetic . . . a way of seeing the world in general, and the self and society in particular, as so much raw space to be furnished with mobile, detachable, and transactionable goods."[79] If culture is commodified, its acquisition does not represent "mere" consumption, the vulgar accumulation of goods and vicarious experience. Commodified culture represents neither the authentic nor the vicarious; rather, insofar as it orients readers and tourists toward, and places them in, the world at large, it defines a space of the socially reproductive. In this sphere Twain ultimately locates his own writing.

This dimension emerges in *The Innocents Abroad* most powerfully at precisely the moment when Twain grows most weary of the "shams" of tourism: during his pilgrimage through the Holy Land. The journey reenacts with greater intensity the experience in viewing "The Last Supper." If his visit to the painting promised a paradigmatic encounter with an authentic icon of high culture, the Holy Land promises contact with the origins of culture itself. It represents "the chief feature, the grand goal of the expedition"; the tourists' imminent arrival elicits "the wildest spirit of expectancy" (309). In traveling overland to Jerusalem, the pilgrims will touch the authentic sites of the Bible, the most powerful text in Western Christendom. They will walk the ground once "pressed by the feet of the Saviour" and gaze at the same vistas "that God looked on. . . . The situation is suggestive of a reality and a tangibility that seem at variance with the vagueness and mystery and ghostliness that one naturally attaches to the character of a god" (339).

Almost immediately, however, whatever expectations Twain entertains are dashed by the sheer absurdity of translating a text of religious miracles to a bare and ruined geography. No matter how much in disrepair was "The Last Supper," no matter how heavily framed it was by the glib tongue of a guide and the preconceptions of guidebooks, it existed materially. In the Holy Land, however, Twain finds himself often visiting sights with no site. Biblical towns survive only as impoverished hamlets or as "shapeless" ruins. The Sea of Galilee is a dreary stretch of water in a harsh landscape bereft of fishermen. He and his fellow tourists are shown the precise spot where Paul was blinded on the road to Damascus and where Joseph's brothers cast him into the pit, knowing full well that the locations are not only disputable, but, in fact, arbitrary.

This absurdity reaches its highest point at the pilgrimage's most sacred destination, the Church of the Holy Sepulchre in Jerusalem, where they enter both "the most sacred locality in Christendom" (405) and a Barnumesque stage for humbug. Under one roof, Twain visits Christ's grave, the hill at Calvary, the "true pillar of flagellation," and the spot where Christ appeared to his mother and Mary Magdalene after his crucifixion. This zealous marking of origins breaks all bounds of the believable when Twain also encounters Adam's grave and, next to it, a pillar marking the center of the earth, from which the dust was taken to form Adam. The authentic site of history and culture is at the same time its most thorough parody, composed of monuments that are pure images, signs with no referents. The obsequious rituals of pilgrims and monks, the vast ornamentation of the separate chapels, even the Church itself designates what is essentially an *image* of truth.

Out of this absurdity, however, emerges an unexpected epiphany. As he did in front of the Leonardo, Twain shifts his attention away from the source to the image, from the "rock" of the Church to its "illustrious edifice." This time, however, he does so not to initiate a play between image and site, but to locate the authentic in the image itself. Despite "its claptrap sideshows and unseemly impostures of every kind," Twain concedes that the Church is, "in its history from the first, and in its tremendous associations, [the] most illustrious edifice in Christendom" (414). Adam's grave may be no more "true" than the bushel of fragments of the "true cross" Twain has seen during his voyage, but neither one is a sham. The Church and its sacred filigree have accrued too much meaning throughout history to be dismissed as a fraud:

> [F]or fifteen hundred years its shrines have been wet with the tears of pilgrims . . . ; for more than two hundred, . . . gallant knights . . . wasted their lives away in a struggle to seize it and hold it sacred from infidel pollution. Even in our own day a war that cost millions of treasure and rivers of blood was fought because two rival nations claimed the sole right to put a new dome upon it. History is full of this old Church of the Holy Sepulchre.   (415)

In inverting the normal touristic relationship between the site and meaning (the church is not full of history, but "history is full of this old Church"), Twain explicitly relocates authenticity in the historical process that has designated the site as worth visiting, a process that as a tourist Twain affirms. Thus, the true site in the Church of the Holy Sepulchre, and, indeed, the true origin of historical and touristic authenticity, is the comically mistranslated sign that reads, "'Chapel of the Invention of the Cross'— a name which is unfortunate, because it leads the ignorant to imagine that a tacit acknowledgment is thus made that the tradition that Helena found the true cross here is a fiction—an invention" (411). Twain, of course, is one of those "ignorant": in this "invention," which has long since overwhelmed the integrity of the original, lies authentic fiction.

The image here, the designating marker, emerges not as a perversion of "true" culture, but as culture itself. If the innocent abroad never really leaves the domain of the mediated, if he is caught in an endless deferment of the authentic as he visits cities, churches, museums, shrines, and monuments, he nonetheless actively participates in making them "authentic." Moreover, it is in terms of this paradoxical situation that Twain's own text can be understood. Tourism, as he presents it, is an activity of reconstitution, of interpretation, and, finally, of writing. The final product of this imposture is *The Innocents Abroad*—itself an extended prospectus for culture. Thus, the book represents one more marker in the comic cycle of expectation and fulfillment that both Twain—as tourist and writer—and the consuming reader, reproduce.

III. The Magic of Composition: *Roughing It*

Years later, in his autobiography, Twain recalled a telling incident relating to the publication of his first book, when a friend asked, in Twain's words: "How did you come to steal Oliver Wendell Holmes's dedication and put it in your book?" And, in fact, to Twain's astonishment and shame, the dedications were indeed close. Feeling himself "a tough and unforgivable criminal," Twain promptly wrote Holmes to apologize. The latter replied, in Twain's words:

> that there was no crime in unconscious plagiarism; that I committed it every day, that he committed it every day, that every man alive on the earth who writes or speaks commits it every day and not merely once or twice but every time he opens his mouth; that all our phrasings are spiritualized shadows cast multitudinously from our readings; that no happy phrase of ours is ever quite original with us.[80]

Twain concludes his account of the incident by declaring that the experience of "thirty-odd years" since then has proven what Holmes wrote is true. Plagiarism, or copying—whether "unconscious" or not—played a central role in the way Twain figured his own writing.[81] "We mortals can't create, we can only copy" is the way he put it in an interview.[82] In many ways, the grounds for this pessimism over creativity lay in the publishing world he inhabited his entire life. As a young printer in his brother's shop in Iowa, and, later, as a journalist in Nevada and San Francisco, Twain was well aware of, indeed deft at, the common newspaper practice of copying articles from other sources, often with no acknowledgment. As a popular author struggling to protect his literary property against the encroachments of publishing pirates and his public reputation against impostors, as an amateur inventor eager to patent his ideas, Twain was also well aware of how difficult it was, even, ultimately, how fictional it was, to define, much less protect, intellectual property. If words and ideas could magically translate into hard cash, their value had to be protected by some form of legal authentification.

In his writing, however, Twain practiced a form of what he called literary "stealing" with a boundless energy. As a parodist, his very humor depended on his ability to cite, evoke, and mimic other texts clearly enough for his readers to recognize the parody. As a travel writer, his method skirted the line of plagiarism even more closely. In reviewing *The Innocents Abroad*, Bret Harte noted that "'Mark Twain' seems to have followed his guide and guide-books with a simple, unconscious fidelity. He was quite content to see only that which every body else sees, even if he was not content to see it with the same eyes. . . . His remarks might have been penciled on the margins of Murray."[83] And yet, as numerous commentators have noted, Twain's "fidelity" may not have been as "unconscious" as Harte assumes. As he did with virtually every travel book he wrote, in writing *The Innocents Abroad* Twain steeped himself in other travel books. While on board the *Quaker City,* he used Josis Leslie Porter's *A Handbook for Travellers in Syria and Palestine* (1858) not only to prepare himself for what he would see, but to anticipate how he would write about sites he had yet to visit. When revising his newspaper letters into book form, he relied on other travelers' published accounts to jog his memory.[84] He also composed his section on Paris, after having lost his original dispatches, relying more or less directly on *Galignani's New Paris Guide for 1867*.[85]

In part, such borrowing, credited and uncredited, was the result of Twain's efforts to shape his book to the subscription market; it not only supplied the facts his readers wanted, it also padded his books to the proper length.[86] More important, however, it points to the extent to which Twain's text was constructed not so much as an original work of culture, but as a kind of cultural interchange, a literary circuit, through which flowed an alternating current of poetics and economics. *The Innocents Abroad*, like his other travel books, was a web of old writing—his *Alta California* letters, his *Herald* and *Tribune* letters, published letters of other travelers, guidebooks, retold stories (he further padded the Holy Land sections by rehearsing biblical tales), and personal anecdotes. Twain composed not in the strictly literary sense, but in the sense he would have best understood it, as a compositor selecting phrases and paragraphs instead of premolded letters, to be printed on a page. A journalist who knew Twain in Washington, D.C., described the author at work in just these terms: "And there was Mark in a little back room, with a sheet-iron stove, a dirty, musty carpet of the cheapest description, a bed, and two or three common chairs. The little drum stove was full of ashes, running over on the zinc sheet; the bed seemed to be unmade for a week, the slops had not been carried out for a fortnight, the room was foul with tobacco smoke, the floor, dirty enough to begin with, was littered with newspapers, from which Twain had cut his letters. Then there were hundreds of pieces of torn manuscripts which had been written and then rejected by the author."[87] If the piece captures a furnace-like image of the bohemian writer at work—a pose Twain adopted in San Francisco but later discarded—it also identifies what would remain the characteristic tools of Twain as a writer: the pen and the scissors. Twain did not produce so much as reproduce; his writing cast shadows of his reading.

His compositional habits suggest, in turn, the larger, more complex cultural circuit defined by Twain's travel books. As a travel writer, Twain journeyed through Europe as a collector, gathering snippets of mediated impressions that would eventually be displayed in his cabinet of curios. As such, what separates him from his fellow passengers—the passionate pilgrims whom he ridiculed for destroying, in their eager hunt for souvenirs, the monuments they came to see—is merely the type of material he collected. His book functions quite literally as a postcard, a reified souvenir of the authentic experience of visiting. Just as sending a postcard certifies the traveler's experience as real, so too does publishing his book certify Twain's authority as a travel writer, as a privileged observer. Thus, what *The Innocents Abroad* truly documents is not, for instance, the authenticity of Adam's tomb and the Church of the Holy Sepulchre, but the circuit of culture that manages to bring Twain's account of his visit back to the reader.[88]

The writer as tourist is thus represented most persistently, both in the book and in Twain's composition, as a reader, of guidebooks, newspapers, tourist markers, of tourist sites: he is as caught in the web of "inauthentic" culture as is his customer reader. If such a circuit erodes the sanctity or "aura" of the original work of art—if it erodes Howells's distinction between productive culture and consuming amusement—it does so by reconfiguring it as what Jean Baudrillard has called the "practique" of consumption.[89] Reading and writing, in Twain's world, became a way of positioning oneself in a commerce of culture, of immersing oneself in the flow of reproductions by consuming images and, in turn, reproducing them in a newly commodified form for consumption. And reincorporation: for the ultimate destination of the subscription volume was the parlor, where the book took its place amid other books, furniture, chromolithographs, and stereocard collections as part of another cabinet of curiosities, an archive of the world that itself was a sign of familial taste.[90] Out of this process, Twain grew wealthy and famous; in short, he became an author.

The Innocents Abroad represents Twain's first effort to enter the promiscuous circuit of culture and the market—bound tightly as it was in the dual nature of the book as a commodity and as a text of language—that Howells struggled so valiantly to regulate. The logic of tourism was, for Twain, the logic of writing: both traveler and author functioned as recyclers, happily "unconscious" plagiarists who existed most fully only when they repeated the words of others. Therein lay the practice of writing: in visiting an "authentic" site, the tourist reproduced a sight; in representing such an experience, the writer reproduced representation. As Twain put it in paraphrasing Holmes's reply to his letter of apology:

> [N]o happy phrase of ours is ever quite original with us; there is nothing of our own in it except some slight change born of our temperament, character, environment, teachings and associations; . . . this slight change differentiates it from another man's manner of saying it, stamps it with our special style and makes it our own for the time being; all the rest of it being old, moldy, antique and smelling of the breath of a thousand generations of them that have passed it over their teeth before![91]

What Twain learned as a tourist was precisely the lesson he discovered in writing his book: originality and authenticity have nothing to do with the culture he produced. The magic of authorship lay in copying, and thereby altering and converting, authentic art into reproduced art—into a commodity.

Twain made another effort at closing the magical circuit of money and words in his second book, *Roughing It* (1872). For, if in *The Innocents Abroad* Twain sets off as a tourist to discover "authentic" culture only to find a wealth of commodified images, in *Roughing It* he heads west to prospect for wealth only to find culture. This narrative holds on two different levels. As an author anxious to follow the success of his first book, Twain from the beginning envisioned his second in the image of his first, as a travel book full of fact, fancy, and humor. As he puts it in his preface:

> This book is merely a personal narrative, and not a pretentious history or a philosophical dissertation. It is a record of several years of variegated vagabondizing, and its object is rather to help the resting reader while away an idle hour than afflict him with metaphysics, or goad him with science. Still, there is information in the volume; information concerning an interesting episode in the history of the Far West, about which no books have been written by persons who were on the ground in person, and saw the happenings of the time with their own eyes.

Once again, he presents the narrator as a surrogate for the reader, insisting on the authority of "personal" experience over "pretentious history" and philosophy. Once again, in his very insistence, in the hyperbole of the comparison between "narrative" and "dissertation," Twain suggests the same game of earnest naïveté and disillusionment, great expectation and mock fulfillment, that structured his earlier narrative.

Even his claim to unique experience is disingenuous, or at best a pretext for the book as a whole. For while he does write authoritatively about "the silver-mining fever in Nevada," his adventures as a miner comprise no more than a dozen out of seventy-nine chapters that carry him from Missouri to the Sandwich Islands. The vast bulk of the book, particularly that set in the continental West, concerns a region whose marvels and exotic sights by 1872 were at least as documented in travel and promotional literature as those of Europe. England, France, and Italy may have their cathedrals and museums, but in Yosemite Valley, for instance, writers like Josiah Whitney, painters like Albert Bierstadt, and photographers like Carleton Watkins had found a natural architecture that superseded in scope, size, and drama the human efforts of Europe and represented in its beauty the work of the hand of God. Most important, by right of possession, the West's geologic formations could be claimed as national treasures endowed with a kind of divine historicity. A tree dated in the Mariposa Grove of California, commented one writer, "antedates the foundation stone of the oldest Gothic spire of Europe."[92] Like Twain's comparison in *The Innocents Abroad* between Italy's Lake Como and California's Lake Tahoe ("how dull [Como's] waters are compared with the wonderful transparence of Lake Tahoe!" [146]), such comparisons express how deeply related were the touristic discourses of Europe and the West.

Twain draws on his readers' prior knowledge of the West almost immediately. Twain's brother, he tells his readers, has been appointed Secretary of the Nevada Territory, and Twain covets "the long, strange journey he was going to make, and the curious new world he was going to explore":

> Pretty soon he would be hundreds and hundreds of miles away on the great plains and deserts, and among the mountains of the Far West, and would see

buffaloes and Indians, and prairie dogs, and antelopes, and have all kinds of adventures, and may be get hanged or scalped, and have ever such a fine time, and write home and tell us all about it, and be a hero . . . What I suffered in contemplating his happiness, pen cannot describe.[93]

Once again, the narrator emerges in a litany of overinvested words as a creature of expectation eagerly anticipating the excitement of travel. So he decides to accompany his brother on what, for him, will be "a three-month pleasure excursion" (30) to a West as mediated by expectations as Europe. His first twenty-five chapters catalog his encounter with people and lands every bit as "foreign" as those in his previous book. The Mormons, the pony express riders, the vigilante Slade, are all devoured by "a consuming desire" to see. At times, these sights disappoint, as when Twain, "a disciple of Cooper and a worshiper of the Red Man," is disillusioned (in a reprise of comments he made in chapter 20 of *The Innocents Abroad*) by the "silent, sneaking, treacherous-looking" Goshute Indians (119, 118). At other times, Twain's expectations are met, as when he discovers "that mysterious marvel which all Western untraveled boys have heard of and fully believe in, but are sure to be astounded at when they see it with their own eyes, nevertheless—banks of snow in dead summer time": "Truly, 'seeing is believing'—and many a man lives a long life through, *thinking* he believes certain universally received and well established things, and yet never suspects that if he were confronted by those things once, he would discover that he did not *really* believe them before, but only thought he believed them" (85). In Rome, at the Church of the Holy Sepulchre, as in all of Europe and the Holy Land, Twain had carried the burden of the tourist visiting only what others had seen before him. Here, as he implies in his preface, he leads his readers on an expedition that smacks of discovery: he poses as a pioneer of authentic experience. Nonetheless, his is a tourist's reaction. What Twain believes as a tourist is, of course, all the previous accounts he had read as boy, accounts not just in guidebooks and "dissertations," but in the ephemeral stuff of pulp literature. This is the West that Twain travels, the West of stagecoaches, outlaws, the pony express, and Indians. The narrator literally re-presents this West: his own experience validates the truth of other representations.

Yet these representations themselves, unlike those of European guidebooks, prove inadequate to the task of encapsulating the West. In part, this is because, unlike the Church of the Holy Sepulchre, history is *not* full of the West—there is no tradition of travel writing to tie sight to site in any meaningful way. More important, unlike the Europe of *The Innocents Abroad*, the West has a distinctly indigenous language that, distilled in the numerous tall tales and vernacular idiosyncracies of its white inhabitants, challenges the certainties of aesthetic appreciation. The result is a text, as numerous critics have noted, that stages what is, in effect, a linguistic confrontation between rival points of view.[94] In the heat of this comic battle, the West of *Roughing It* emerges, in Lee Clark Mitchell's words, not as a geographically defined region, but "first and foremost [as] a verbal construct." With its "looser attitude . . . toward truth and falsehood, word and referent, . . . the West becomes an occasion for all sorts of uncertain claims." (To borrow Twain's words, closing the fantasy of his brother's Western adventures: "pen cannot describe" the West.) Thus, the text enacts beneath its humor "a serious inquiry into the process of how things happen to be put in words."[95]

Nor does this inquiry unfold at only the epistemological level. For, as Twain puts it in his preface, his is "a personal narrative" constructed loosely around the adventures of an Eastern "tenderfoot," (to borrow Henry Nash Smith's use of the term), who is himself the bearer of the conventional idiom of aesthetic appreciation and who must learn to shift for himself in the world of tall tales and extravagant claims.[96] This narrator, however, is less Sam Clemens, the young enthusiast, than it is Mark Twain, the author of *The Innocents Abroad* and "The Jumping Frog of Calaveras County" (1865), the platform performer and journalist who was shrewd enough to exploit his popularity by publishing in 1871 (just prior to *Roughing It*) his *Burlesque Autobiography*.[97] Twain, in fact, ends his narrative, which ultimately carries him from the silver fields of Nevada to the Sandwich Islands, where he first tried his hand at travel writing, as the writer who "went away and joined the famous Quaker City European Excursion and carried my tears to foreign lands" (422). What emerges is not just a portrait of a young humorist uncovering the distinctive energy of the tall tale, but a text more explicitly concerned than the first with narrating the emergence of a public authorship and describing the conditions that make possible that emergence. The naïve visionary whose jealousy of his brother's opportunity to write about authentic experience (what could be more authentic than death?) emerges in the course of the narrative as the comic celebrator, indeed, the producer of consumption—the character whose vision makes possible both *The Innocents Abroad* and *Roughing It*.

In the midst of Twain's opening delirium about his brother's adventures in the West, he imagines himself visiting gold and silver mines: "and maybe [he would] go about of an afternoon when his work was done, and pick up two or three pailfuls of shining slugs, and nuggets of gold and silver on the hillside. And by and by he would become rich." The fantasy not only reiterates what Twain in his preface promised as distinctive about his book, it also prefigures, in the mode of pitched expectation that recalls the tourist, what serves in *Roughing It* as the central trope of Twain's autobiography of authorship. Nor is this the only way in which tourist and prospector coincide. Just as the tourist travels Europe in search of authentic sites, so the prospector searches the mountains for the authentic wealth of precious metals. And just as the announced itinerary grips the naïve tourist with unbearable anticipation, so too is the prospector smitten with "silver fever" (151), brought on by the dazzling promise of wealth that fills the atmosphere of the Nevada territory:

Every few days news would come of the discovery of a brand-new mining region; immediately the papers would teem with accounts of its richness, and away the surplus population would scamper to take possession. By the time I was fairly inoculated with the disease, "Esmeralda" had just had a run and "Humboldt" was beginning the shriek for attention. "Humboldt! Humboldt!" was the new cry, and straightway Humboldt, the newest of the new, the richest of the rich, . . . was occupying two columns of the public prints to "Esmeralda's" one.   (152)

Like the prospectus in *The Innocents Abroad*, newspaper accounts describing the mountains as "gorged" with ore (153) serve as the "text" for his second book. But it is not only the claims of wealth that possess Twain's imagination, it is the sight of it as well. "I would have been more or less than human if I had not gone mad like the rest. Cart-loads of solid silver bricks, as large as pigs of lead . . . gave substance to the wild talk about me. I succumbed and grew as frenzied as the craziest" (152).

Twain's frenzy continues as he sets out on a prospecting expedition: "I expected to find masses of silver lying all about the ground . . . glittering in the sun on the mountain summits" (160). Once there, "brimful with expectation," he scrambles across the slopes in "a delirious revel" of almost "unmarred ecstasy" searching for his fortune. When, however, he proudly carries a nugget back to camp only to discover that it is nothing more than a conglomerate of granite and mica, his dreams of easy wealth melt away and he is left "stricken and forlorn" (162). Prospecting, the more experienced member of his expedition tells him, is a drudging life of toil promising only modest gains; only the rarest claim amounts to a profitable strike, much less a fortune.

Twain's initial experience with mining recapitulates the comedy of expectation and disillusionment of his earlier travelogue. It is his lot to move in a world where the promise of instant wealth is tantalizingly close—the narrative is studded with stories of fortunes both found and lost through chance—but that nonetheless remains beyond his grasp. His failure, however, has less to do with poor luck than with his refusal to work for his ore. Wealth must come easily, it must come suddenly, it must come in a way that will perfectly fulfill his naïve dreams, or it is not wealth. The silver ingots he originally saw haunt him with their reified beauty; the fact that they are the products of hard labor carried out, as he finds later, not by prospectors, but by miners in the employ of large companies, remains irrelevant to his definition of success. This fundamental contradiction between the facts of labor and the dreams of wealth structures not only the comedy of the mining episodes, but the implicit autobiographical tale as well. For prospecting is but one episode in a larger narrative of Twain's learning "to shift for myself" (221), to earn a living without working. He had studied law for a week but had "given it up because it was so prosy and tiresome." He tried blacksmithing, but had "wasted so much time trying to fix the bellows so that it would blow itself, that the master turned me adrift in disgrace, and told me I would come to no good. I had been a bookseller's clerk for a while, but the customers bothered me so much I could not read with any comfort, and so the proprietor gave me a furlough and forgot to put a limit on it" (221).

Initially, Twain's disillusionment in mining seems to repeat that of his earlier "careers," but as he quickly discovers, he is not alone in his fantasy: like him, his fellow prospectors soon forsake the struggle to dig shafts into hard rock. Instead, "[p]rospecting parties swarmed out of town with the first flush of dawn, and swarmed in again at nightfall laden with spoil—rocks. Nothing but rocks" (166). These rocks are then assayed as samples that suggest remarkable wealth. The result is a "beggars' revel" as the miners immediately turn, "stark mad with excitement," to bartering shares in their future mines. The lodes of ore remain buried deep in the Nevada mountains while the prospectors bask in their "mountains of prospective wealth": "There was nothing doing in the district—no mining—no milling—no productive effort—no income—and not enough money in the entire camp to buy a corner lot in an Eastern village, hardly; and yet a stranger would have supposed he was walking among bloated millionaires" (166). This experience leads Twain to discover "the *real* secret of success in silver mining—which was, *not* to mine the silver ourselves by the sweat of our brows and the labor of our hands, but to *sell* the ledges to the dull slaves of toil and let them do the mining" (168).

Twain's recognition recapitulates the discovery he made at the Church of the Holy Sepulchre: just as the value of the tourist site lies in its quality as a sight, the value of a mine lies not in what is in the ground, but in its stock:

> Every one of these wild cat mines—not mines, but holes in the ground over imaginary mines—was incorporated and had handsomely engraved "stock" and the stock was salable, too. . . . You could go up on the mountain side, scratch around and find a ledge . . . , put up a "notice" with a grandiloquent name in it, start a shaft, get your stock printed, and with nothing whatever to prove that your mine was worth a straw, you could put your stock on the market and sell out for hundreds and even thousands of dollars. To make money, and make it fast, was as easy as it was to eat your dinner.   (231)

That mining "stocks" bear little resemblance to the real value of a claim is, quite literally, immaterial: if circulated feverishly enough, they magically become an authentic currency.

Despite the promise of easy wealth, this speculative economy proves too unstable for Twain; failing as a prospector, he finds his way onto the Virginia City *Daily Territorial Enterprise* as a reporter. However, far from removing him from the fever of prospecting, his new job thrusts him to its center. As his editor tells him, his goal is not so much to report the news as it is to create "confidence" (223) in his readers, and quickly he plays a key role in maintaining the fictional economy. In effect, as a reporter he acts as an adjunct to the assay office: in exchange for shares in a "mine,"

Twain legitimates their value by publishing notices that resemble the very articles that had fed his fantasy earlier:

> If the rock was moderately promising, we followed the custom of the country, used strong adjectives and frothed at the mouth as if a very marvel in silver discoveries had transpired. If the mine was a "developed" one, and had no pay ore to show (and of course it hadn't), we praised the tunnel. . . . We would squander half a column of adulation on a shaft, or a new wire rope, or a dressed pine windlass . . . (231–32)

Thus, as a reporter, Twain finally finds his "career" as a prospector; his published "claims" not only fuel the speculative fever of discovery ("There was *nothing* in the shape of a mining claim that was not salable"), they bring him a treasure chest of silver—at least as it is represented by stock certificates. In this sense, writing literally allows Twain to make money without labor. His newspaper articles at once present an image of real wealth and, insofar as they are "encouraged" by the gift of mining shares, embody money by virtue of their being exchangeable in their own right for other printed images of wealth.

Twain thus locates the beginning of his career as a writer, a career that is fulfilled so far by the appearance of his first two books, in a fevered game of confidence. Writing, in the world of Virginia City, files an undeveloped claim; both author and reader emerge as prospectors caught in a comically reified world of unlimited expectation. The writer assures himself a position in this world by giving these claims a kind of "currency": by publishing them as current news and by creating a communal confidence in their value. The exchange of this currency, in turn, sustains an economy of expectation, while the very existence of that economy keeps alive the fantasy of wealth without labor. Thus, the author does not so much produce narratives, as he reproduces other tales—especially if, like Twain, he is intent on writing as big a book as *Roughing It*. His episodic presentation of a seemingly endless procession of tall tales like the ride of Horace Greeley, which Twain hears "four hundred and eighty-one or eighty-two times" (124), or Jim Blaine's endless "Story of the Old Ram," function as a kind of social currency traded as hoaxes, shams, jokes, and impostures from one Westerner to another, and, finally, from Twain to the reader. As Twain figures it, authorial success, the creation of value, depends not on the painful digging for precious metal, the actual labor for the authentic—a labor Howells would typify as "realism"—but on one's ability to negotiate a world of signs.

This is not to say that he dismisses altogether the "real" work of mining. For beneath the "riot" of speculative prospecting, "down in the bowels of the earth, where a great population of men thronged in and out among the intricate maze of tunnels and drifts, flitting hither and thither under a winking sparkle of lights" (283), the "substantial business" of industrial mining pursues its own ends. This arcane world, whose "vast web of interlocking timbers" not only holds "the walls of the gutted Comstock apart," but also figuratively supports, and finally marks a limit to, the speculative fantasies of investment.[98] After all, it is this kind of drudging toil that produced the ingots that in the first place "gave substance to the wild talk" that so captured Twain's fantasy. But this kind of work does not fit Twain's narrative, as he acknowledges in the opening to his chapter that describes such operations: "Since I desire, in this chapter, to say an instructive word or two about the silver mines, the reader may take this fair warning and skip, if he chooses" (281).

Or does it? For it is precisely these "instructive" words that Twain uses, to borrow his own word of advice, as the "sauce" for his subscription books. In the hands of the speculative author, the "dry statistics" of industrial labor ("All the bullion was shipped by stage to San Francisco . . . and the freight on it (when the shipment was large) was 1¼ per cent of its intrinsic value" [282]) "g[i]ve substance to the wild talk" of his narrative. Or rather, like the Europe of *The Innocents Abroad*, the substance of precious metals, or, in a larger context, the substance of Twain's experience in the West, gave him the pretext for writing a text which, in the very heterogeneity of its language and structure, refused the Howellsian distinction between market and culture. For Twain, writing was "money got for nothing" precisely because, for him, money and writing worked in the same way: they represented value. It was not simply a matter of writing for the market; rather, the literary market made possible, because it gave value to, writing, just as writing made possible, because it realized value for, the literary market.

Thus, in his first two books Twain constructs an authorial persona that, in its comic celebration of spectacle, differs radically from Howells's vision of the author in the market. The Howellsian writer works as a combination of artisan and professional. As artisan, he independently produces a work of art that he then sells on the market. As professional, once he is in the market, he maintains a qualified autonomy by asserting a distinctive authority over a domain of expertise defined loosely as "the real." Cultural products and economic commodities, segregated in their separate spheres of intention and carefully proscribed uses, circulate in an uneasy relationship to one another—at times antagonistic, at times complementary. In contrast, the Twainian writer remains, in all senses of the word, fully invested in a comic world of spectacle and consumption that refuses such essential differences. Freed from the necessity of work, captivated by the magic of turning words into money, the writer emerges as a speculator powerful enough to transform the "false" hopes of instant wealth into a currency of fiction and "confidence."

It is tempting to dismiss Twain's comedy of commodification in these early books in the face of Howells's more sober search for material grounds of a writer's labor. But, as Georg Lukács has argued, reified consciousness if predicated precisely on the illusion that one can step out of the dominant relations of production.[99] What Twain discovered in his entrance into the cultural marketplace was what can be termed a labor theory of cultural value. No cultural product carries in itself an intrinsic value; rather, value is precisely what is produced by representation and its uses. He could turn fiction into money because fundamentally money was a form of fiction. It was both the attachment of these fictions—to gold, to the Church of the Holy Sepulchre—and the way in which these fictions were circulated, elaborated on, and consumed that made authentic culture. The tropes of a commodified world of fictional spectacle that he employed in his early books—tourism and prospecting—would reappear only sporadically throughout the rest of his writing. But his understanding of how the promiscuous mix of culture and economics set social values would never cease to shape his best work.

THREE

❦

A "Rightly Constructed Boy's Life"

The Adventures of Tom Sawyer

I. NOSTALGIA AND PLAY

While preparing *The Adventures of Tom Sawyer* for publication in 1876, Twain paid special attention to the book's illustrations. He was already aware of how important they were in selling his books, appearing as they did as one of the chief attractions of the prospectus, and adding enough to the written text to give each book its heft. In this case, he was even more concerned than usual, because Twain's first novel (he had cowritten *The Gilded Age* [1873] with his neighbor Charles Dudley Warner) weighed in far below the usual 600 to 800 pages needed for subscription books. He had been dissatisfied with the illustrations of his earlier books, but when he saw those of the artist True Williams he was pleased, regarding "many of the pictures . . . [as] considerably above the American average, in conception if not in execution."[1] He did, however, take the liberty to suggest, and very likely to execute, two other illustrations that appeared in the final volume. One presented, in "painfully scrawled" script, the text of Tom's written oath of silence about Dr. Robinson's murder. The other was Tom's "dismal caricature" of a house flanked by stick figures of a boy and girl drawn to amuse and impress Becky Thatcher. The latter illustration was crudely boxed on the page and captioned "Tom as an Artist."[2]

Their blatantly amateurish quality—unabashedly admired by both Huck and Becky—suggests a complex relationship between author and character. On one hand, the illustrations represent a signature of Tom's boyish immaturity: the scrawls stand in comic contrast both to the work of the "artist" Williams and to the justified type on the page of the book. On the other, they represent a disfigured signature of Twain himself, who reaches through his character with a ghostly hand to leave his only "true" mark in the text in Tom's handwriting. "Tom As an Artist" represents Twain the ventriloquist projecting his voice through the mouth of his character.

There is much evidence to support a reading of Tom as a characterized rendition of Twain the writer.[3] Tom's overwhelming penchant for performance, his need for an audience, and, most significantly, his rejection of work for a fantasy of play, recall

Twain both as a platform humorist and as the "shifty" wealth-seeker of *Roughing It* (1872). The way in which Tom executes his drawing—asking Becky step by step for suggestions about what to add to it, provoking her with its domestic fantasy to acknowledge her feelings for him even as he expresses his for her—recalls the performative dynamics that Twain would later describe in "How to Tell a Story" (1897). Moreover, like both the tourist and the prospector, Tom lives in a world of expectation brought to a pitch of fantasy. Taking literally the minister's allegorical sermon on the lion and the lamb, believing wholeheartedly in the superstitions of boyhood, Tom is able to transform his world into a pleasure ground, seemingly immune to the encroachments of work. More important, Tom represents an eloquent broadening of what Henry Nash Smith has labeled "The Matter of Hannibal," the autobiographical vein of Mississippi life that Twain had first struck in "Old Times on the Mississippi" (1874), and which shaped the figure that would eclipse the innocent abroad as his most popular public image.[4]

Twain acknowledges this autobiographical connection in his preface, insisting that most of what he narrates "really occurred; one or two were experiences of my own, the rest those of boys who were schoolmates of mine." Yet this gesture simultaneously introduces another presence that qualifies whatever identity Twain may share with his protagonist: that of "The Author," as Twain signs his preface, who claims Tom as his fiction, "a combination of the characteristics of three boys whom I knew, [and who] therefore belongs to the composite order of architecture." The word "composite," hovering as it does between three different "orders" of making—architecture, printing, and writing—suggests that this voice represents a facet of the author every bit as important as Tom. Just as Tom invites Becky to admire his artistry, "The Author" invites admiration of his artistry in limning Tom: if Tom is an autobiographical character, "The Author" is his biographer. Such doubling, in turn, suggests that Twain figures his authorship in the dialogic tensions between "composite" boy and composing "Author" the Twainian public humorist of stage, press, and travel books, is condensed into boyhood, creating a voice ready to set the stage for Tom's antics. If what Twain calls the "rightly constructed boy's life" (175) is the product of the "artist," "The Author" is the product of that boy's construction.

This formal splitting of protagonist and narrator signals a change from his earlier use of the first person voice—indeed it distinguishes his first novel from the bulk of his writing—and raises a number of questions essential not only to the text, but to Twain's strategies as a writer. What prompted such a change? Given that, upon finishing his book, he ruled the use of a distinct narrator a mistake; given that he takes pains in his preface to claim the story as, once again, part of his "personal history," why does he abandon the explicitly autobiographical mode that had proven so successful? Why, for that matter, does he choose a boy both to represent and to mask his own artistry? Or, to put the question differently, what is it about boyhood that makes Tom such a compelling representative of Twainian performance even as it proves inadequate to rendering Twainian authorship?

The answers to such questions lie in the tropes of building ("composite order of architecture," "rightly constructed boy's life") that Twain employs to describe what he does as a writer. For Twain, the novel presents a problem of defining the labor of play or, as he puts it in his preface, of "entertainment." Implicit in the "rightly constructed boy's life" is a theory—or, to put the case less grandly, a knot of assumptions and expectations—about the right construction of fiction enacted by the text. For at the heart of the novel lies a homology between the imaginative labor that allows an adult man to render his own boyhood as a separate state of existence and the social labor that makes that fictional separation possible even as it insists on an essential connection between boy and man. Tying together these two forms of labor is Twain's recognition of the important role fiction plays in making boys into men. It is on the foundation of this cultural work that he builds his own edifice of the authoritative author.

The dialectic between "The Author" and his creation posited in the preface continues in the narrative itself, in the play between narrator and protagonist. Stung by Becky Thatcher's rejection of his attentions, Tom marches out of the schoolhouse "over the hills and far away" (62) in anguish. He finally stops on "a mossy spot under a spreading oak" and gives himself up to a flight of sentimental fantasy:

> He sat long with his elbows on his knees and his chin in his hands, meditating. It seemed to him that life was but a trouble, at best, and he more than half envied Jimmy Hodges, so lately released; it must be very peaceful, he thought, to lie and slumber and dream forever and ever, with the wind whispering through the trees and caressing the grass and the flowers over the grave, and nothing to bother and grieve about, ever any more. . . . Ah, if he could only die *temporarily*! (63–64)

The passage opens with a kind of spectatorial distance: Tom is the object of a gaze that grows increasingly ironic as his "grief" emerges in a string of clichés akin to those of the ecstatic tourists in front of "The Last Supper." Yet here there is no need for the "corrective" vision of the naïve tourist; the indirect discourse frames Tom's musings with an irony even as it invites a kind of nostalgic indulgence in the naïveté of youth (Tom believes his clichés). The result is a writing that, in effect, produces two characters—the youthful victim of borrowed fantasies and the sophisticated, worldly narrator.

Or, we should say, three characters. For Twain here writes in much the same mode as would inspire his Whittier Birthday Speech. Just as his banquet audience's recognition of the humor in his talk depended on their knowing the source of the texts he parodied, so too here does his irony depend on his reader's recognizing the sentimental clichés. In his novel, however, the polarities are reversed: its language is saturated not with fragments of literature, but with fragments of the sentimental. Moveover, these hierarchies are much less stable than they are in his speech. As Tom continues to brood, his maudlin fantasies modulate from the sentimental to the sensational: he will avenge himself by running away. In a manner that recalls Twain's career meditations in *Roughing It*, Tom considers a life as a clown, as a soldier, and as an Indian, finally settling on piracy:

> How gloriously he would go plowing the dancing seas, in his long, low, black-hulled racer, the "Spirit of the Storm," with his grisly flag flying at the fore! And at the zenith of his fame, how he would suddenly appear at the old village and stalk into church, all brown and weather-beaten, in his black velvet doublet and trunks, his great jack-boots, his crimson sash, his belt bristling with horse-pistols, his crime-rusted cutlass at his side, his slouch hat with waving plumes, his black flag unfurled, with the skull and cross-bones on it, and hear with swelling ecstasy the whisperings, "It's Tom Sawyer the Pirate!—the Black Avenger of the Spanish Main!"   (64)

Again, the irony continues, this time in the comic contrast between the hyperbole of Tom's immature sexualized musings and the deflated return to the Sunday school: we are not to forget this is a boy's fantasy. At the same time, however, the very exactness of the description, its "swelling" rhythm, gives the passage a rhetorical momentum that qualifies its parody. The language is no longer strictly indirect; the ironic frame dissolves as the narrator invites delight in the very fantasy of melodramatic possibility it parodies. Boy protagonist and adult narrator come into comic complicity.

This collusion continues on a larger scale as Tom's subsequent adventures actually fulfill his fantasies. After reveling in an imaginary life of piracy, he, Huck, and Joe travel to Jackson's Island as "pirates" commanding their own "ship." While there, they assume the roles of circus clowns and Indians. Most spectacularly, Tom even realizes his ambitions to "die *temporarily!*" not once but twice, by appearing at his own funeral and by returning in triumph from the cave after he and Becky have been given up for lost. With this, the text takes a decidedly performative shape; Tom and the narrator form a comic team that seemingly victimizes both the reader and the repeatedly astonished citizens of St. Petersburg. Tom's appearance at his own funeral, his emergence with Becky from the cave, unfold under a veil of secrecy drawn as much by the narrator as by Tom. The reader, who has only watched Joe and Huck greet Tom's "splendid" plan with "a war-whoop of applause" (122), enjoys its unfolding as a happy victim who, like the congregation at Tom's "funeral," "would almost be willing to be made ridiculous again" to experience the release of surprise (131–32).

As such, Tom's boyishness authorizes a kind of narrative irresponsibility, an immersion in fantasy that upends the hierarchy of voices, collapsing the distinction between reserve and investment that the narrator's irony invites. The narrative's episodic form, the ease with which the subplot of Injun Joe's murder is dropped and taken up again, the absurd pattern of coincidence that brings the story to a close, all suggest a text every bit as "harum-scarum" as Aunt Polly declares Tom to be (116). Thus, if Tom plays the straight man for the narrator's irony, the narrator plays the straight man for Twain, who, partially masked as Tom, can qualify and burlesque the ironic voice of "The Author." Yet the specular distance never quite succumbs to the carnivalizing plotting of the comic team. Tom is, after all, only a boy; his triumphant performances unfold beneath, as it were, a dialogue of ironic nostalgia between narrator and reader that takes place over his head. Indeed, for all of the comic collusion, it is the essential incompatibility of these two dialogues that most powerfully structures the fiction. Twain seems to be writing two novels in the same text: one, a fantasy-laden quest for the "glory and eclat" of performance; the other, a narrative representation of that performance.

Such a division of purpose is hinted at in the preface, where "The Author" urges his book on two groups of readers: "Although my book is intended mainly for the entertainment of boys and girls, I hope it will not be shunned by men and women on that account, for part of my plan has been to try to pleasantly remind adults of what they once were themselves, and of how they felt and thought and talked, and what queer enterprises they sometimes engaged in." As it stands, the preface is a little disingenuous here: in writing the book, Twain from the beginning had intended to address adults, changing his mind only when Howells, who read the manuscript, convinced its author that he could increase his market by including children as part of the audience.[5] As late as 1871, just eighteen months before he began *Tom Sawyer*, Twain had dismissed children's writing as "wholly worthless, for I never saw [any] that I thought was worth the ink it was written with. . . . I have no love for children's literature."[6] Such writing smacked of didactic tedium, a solemn piety that he had already burlesqued in two sketches. The first, "The Story of the Bad Little Boy" (1865), parodied Sunday-school books—"those mild little books with marbled backs"—by telling the story of Jim, a selfish, mean-spirited boy who, despite his long career of mischief, escapes punishment and grows up to be a respected legislator. Five years later, Twain published "The Story of the Good Little Boy," which predictably detailed the career of a Sunday-school-perfect Jacob Blivens who, like Jim, "didn't come out according to the books"—his moral piety leads him to a spectacular and sudden death that leaves him no chance to voice the obligatory dying speech of self-justification.[7]

In writing "mainly for . . . entertainment," Twain clearly distinguishes his fiction from the moral didacticism he disliked. Elements of his earlier parodies resurface in *Tom Sawyer*: one of the model boys in the Sunday school is reduced to "little better than an idiot" (30) after reciting 3,000 Bible verses, while Tom thrives despite—indeed, because of—his pranks and his deep immersion in dime-novel fantasies of piracy and Robin Hood. Yet what links Twain's novel with his earlier sketches is not so much its parody of a moral universe of good and bad as it is the shared assumption that texts play a powerful role in shaping that universe. After all, in his ability to invest himself fully in the language of the sentimental and sensational, Tom has more in common with the unfortunate Jacob Blivens than with Jim. The latter is merely a bad boy, the former a naïve reader who not only believes what he reads, but, like Tom, yearns literally to enter that fictional world. Tom aspires to be a pirate or Robin Hood, while "Jacob had a noble ambition to be put in a Sunday-school book. He wanted to be put in, with pictures representing him gloriously declining to lie to his mother, and her weeping for joy about it."[8]

Taken together, Tom and Jacob live their lives as young innocents at home in their fictions. Like the tourist who looks only to confirm what he has read, their worlds are not real until they act "by the book" (67); both boys project themselves into architectures of mass-produced fantasies—stories without authors, without sources, internalized as quickly as they are read. What distinguishes Tom from Jacob is not their relative goodness, but the degree to which Tom is able to realize his fantasies, to make them work not only for himself, but for the town as whole and, in a qualified sense, for the reader.

In this light, "Tom as an Artist" represents the innocent at work, the famous author Mark Twain who recycles the fictions of others into his own fictions, inducing his audiences, in turn, to adopt the recycled fictions as their own. The child reader is that reader ready to enter this circuit wholeheartedly, to give himself or herself up to the "consuming passions" of mass culture. Yet once again, it is precisely such naïve reading that the narrator's specular irony suspends. Tom, we are never allowed to forget, is, after all, merely a boy, a (happy) fool to his own fantasies, which are comically realized only in his own imagination. "The Author," on the other hand, stands outside of this closed circle, appealing to another class of readers who are removed enough from such naïveté that they can only be "pleasantly remind[ed]" of the "queer enterprises they sometimes engaged in." As such, Twain does not write so much "for . . . entertainment" as he does *about* entertainment. His doubled voice may remind mature readers of the queer business of fantasy; it may, in fact, allow them to immerse themselves if only momentarily in naive reading; but it also inscribes a vast distance between the authorless imagination of youth and the composed fictions of adulthood. Such a tension between distance and investment suggests that in his first fiction Twain sought to authorize a new, more complex basis for his own authorship.

There is yet one more disingenuous note in Twain's preface. It is not men and women whom "The Author" addresses, it is men; nor does he remind them strictly of childhood, it is boyhood. The narrative voice signals this dimension early, entreating readers to recover the lost novelty of the "strong, deep, unalloyed pleasure" of boyhood, which is found in such simple acts as whistling: "the reader probably remembers how to do it if *he* has ever been a boy" (5) [emphasis added]. Throughout the text, the nostalgic mode sounds in the key of the masculine: Tom's piracy fantasies, his romance with Becky, his wounded pride at her rejection and at Aunt Polly's false accusations, his pursuit of buried treasure, his escape to Jackson's Island—all delimit a world of essential boyhood. For, if Tom resembles the innocent tourist, the objects of his "consuming desire" have little to do with cultural distinction, nor do they involve much deferred gratification. Tom's rage for fulfillment is willful, anarchic, and undiscriminating: it focuses with equal energy on jam, bugs, fruit, Cardiff Hill, Becky Thatcher, a dead cat, or gold. Even a fly on a church pew "torture[s]" him; his hands "[itch] to grab for it" (40). The energy of naïve sensuousness establishes a "pattern" of boyhood—"restless, noisy and troublesome" (30)—that invests itself in a litany of physical objects from the underground economy of boy culture: "twelve marbles, part of a jewsharp, . . . a spool cannon, a key that wouldn't unlock anything, a fragment of chalk, . . . a tin soldier, a couple of tadpoles, six fire-crackers, a kitten with only one eye, a brass doorknob" (15). These objects, in turn, are animated by a world of mysterious spells and occult beliefs inscribed in equally mysterious phrases like, "Barley-corn, barley-corn, injun-meal shorts, / Spunk-water, spunk-water, swaller these warts" (50).

On this fundamentally inscrutable world of boyhood, built out of the familiar universe of the objects and institutions of domestic life, Twain builds a nostalgia so complete that the town of St. Petersburg itself seamlessly merges with the idyllic rhythms of summer, the pastoral splendor of Jackson's Island, and the woods of Cardiff Hill. There is no main street, no commercial life, no steamboat traffic: the adult world of work is altogether excluded from the village. The church, the parlor, Tom's bedroom, the school, Jackson's Island: these locations refer to a town without really constituting one. This geographical and sociological indeterminacy meshes with a powerful timelessness that converts each Sunday into every Sunday, each school session into all others. Notwithstanding the prefatorial remark that sets the time "thirty or forty years ago," St. Petersburg floats in a quasi-millennial space of boyhood, where each morning "The sun rose upon a tranquil world, and beamed down upon the peaceful village like a benediction" (26).

The very comprehensiveness of this idyllicism suggests that Twain's nostalgia is calibrated not in decades, but in the gulf separating manhood and boyhood. This distance is acknowledged more explicitly in Twain's terse conclusion, where he writes: "So endeth this chronicle. It being strictly a history of a *boy*, it must stop here; the story could not go much further without becoming the history of a *man*" (260). The ending is abrupt, fencing off the idyllicism of boyhood with the stark shadow of a manhood that threatens to transform the novel. The awkwardness of the conclusion may reflect Twain's decision to abandon his earlier plans for carrying his novel well into Tom's manhood, loosely structured as a picaresque bildungsroman. But this too only further emphasizes how indelibly linked and yet fundamentally antagonistic are boyhood and manhood in the novel. Men are judges, teachers, and ministers; together they enforce a moral universe of absolute right and wrong, deferred pleasure and certain retribution. They ceaselessly rehearse this authority by disciplining boys, who "itch" and "rage" and doff their clothes at every chance, while adults labor to dress their exuberant bodies in propriety. Tom must attend Sunday school with "his neat roundabout [buttoned] up to his chin," looking "exceedingly improved and uncomfortable": "he was full as uncomfortable as he looked; for there was a restraint about whole clothes and cleanliness that galled him" (29). There he is urged "'to sit up just as straight and pretty as you can and give me all of your attention'" by a Sunday school superintendent whose collar forms "a fence that compelled a straight lookout ahead, and a turning of the whole body when a side view was required" (32). Examination Evening at school subjects Tom and his peers to the "tyranny" of a schoolmaster who produces marionette-like students out of boys. One scholar delivers his recitation while "accompanying himself with the painfully exact and spasmodic gestures which a machine might have used" and finishes with a "manufactured bow" (155).

Such adult victories, however, are only temporary; the interior spaces of the parlor, the school, and the church can do little to contain the restless enthusiasm of boys. Tom and his friends play hooky from school, run away from home, and find any diversion at hand to relieve the tedium of discipline. At times, resistance turns into revenge, as when the schoolboys strike back at their teacher by exposing his gold-painted head to the audience on Examination Evening. This planned escapade, however, is an exception. For it is not the mind, but the fundamentally illogical physicality of boyhood itself, with its "natural" cravings, that fuels Tom's resistance and escape into fantasy worlds of violence and superstition. Yet boys, as Twain backhandedly acknowledges in his conclusion, must become men—"pretty grave, unromantic men, too, some of them" (254)—who will presumably embody the self-controlled lives they once rebelled against. Tom "would be President, yet, if he escaped hanging" (173), the narrator tells us, and it is this anxiety of the future, the sense that the end of childhood will transform Tom utterly into the embodiment of authority or criminality, that suffuses Twain's conclusion.

The problem grows all the more pressing given that, fundamentally, *Tom Sawyer* is precisely "a history of a *man*." To remind (male) readers of their past is to encourage an act of remembering, to reconstruct the child in the adult and the adult in the child. If Twain's idyll of boyhood is everywhere circumscribed by adult manhood, if the border of his fictional imagination is marked by some mysterious metamorphosis of boy into man, his "rightly constructed" boy is built out of—and is an inverted reflection of—the very masculinity the text tries to postpone, deny, erase. Nowhere is this line drawn so firmly, and questioned so thoroughly, as between the narrating author and the performing protagonist. Simply put, it is a question of labor. Tom may serve as yet one more figure of the artist as "image-breaker," an iconoclast ready to break the work ethic of productive writing, but it describes only a part of Twain's labor as "The Author" of his text. While Tom's antics make ridiculous masculine injunctions to socialization, Twain must work as an artist of "composite order." The covert complicity between narrator and protagonist allows him to negotiate this contradiction to some extent, but this only reinscribes the problem at a more pressing level. For the narrator himself is an adult, a member of the community against which Tom struggles; the narrative effort to "rightly construct" Tom as the fictional object of adult nostalgia is implicated in the communal effort to construct Tom rightly as a man. The unfortunate students who mechanically mouth "compositions" at Examination Evening are no more "marionettes" than is Tom, who voices not the language of childhood, but the "composite" language of manhood's vision of childhood.

Central to Twain's project, then, lies a creative contradiction that implicates the making of Twainian fiction in the socialization of boys into men. To become a man in the world of *Tom Sawyer* is to forego the pleasures of naïveté, to cross a gap of maturity so wide that one can return to it only with the specular irony of nostalgia. Yet it is also to cross the line from marginal fantasy to authored narrative. When Aunt Polly tells Tom of the pain he caused her by running away to Jackson's Island, he can only reply: "'I know now it was mean, but I didn't mean to be mean. I didn't, honest'" (145). To recognize meaning in this world is to recognize meanness, to take responsibility—in short, to become an author who must compose in order to play.

Thus, to become an author, to grasp the meanness, the power, of meaning, one must become a man. This is true both in the world of *Tom Sawyer* and in the world of Gilded Age culture. As the controversy over the guest list to Whittier's birthday celebration would soon confirm, in the literary and social clubs in Boston and Hartford, in the editorial offices and publishing houses of New York, in the more bohemian circles of San Francisco, on the newspaper staffs and in the bookstores, authors in Gilded Age America were men.[9] To be sure, women wrote: they dominated bestseller lists and accounted for nearly three-fourths of all the novels published during the 1870s; they appeared as valuable contributors in the most prestigious and most popular magazines; they commanded the attention of editors, reviewers, and publishers; they even edited some of those magazines themselves. Moreover, the vast majority of the audience for any work of fiction was decidedly female. But even the most successful women writers, as Mary Kelley has demonstrated, retained a sense that in assuming a public authorship, in building a career in the public eye, in aspiring to literary recognition, they were treading on decidedly masculine terrain.[10] In part, this anxiety stemmed from the fact that, in most cases, the organs of literary dissemination were dominated by men who edited, published, reviewed, publicized, and profited from the efforts of women. More pervasively, the sense of feminine transgression in writing for a public stemmed from the way literary authority reproduced a certain kind of masculine authority. Successful authors who had made their marks *in* culture were expected to assume an authority *over* culture as well. As Twain's career makes clear, literary celebrities were not only interesting as celebrities, they were empowered to speak out on a range of subjects, to move as "statesmen without salaries" whose pronouncements bore the weight of public opinion.[11] With obvious exceptions, which only prove the rule, public authorship was shaped by gender ideologies that hindered, if not precluded, women—and encouraged, if not guaranteed, men—from attaining a public "presence," to use Howells's word.[12]

This masculine hegemony, however, did not prevent male writers from anxiously exploring their own gendered identities (in fact, it may have encouraged them to do so). After all, novel writing was a notoriously "sexually ambiguous" career, thrusting women out of the domestic sphere into a public spotlight and associating men with the traditionally feminine world of emotion.[13] When Howells characterized the poet who "must use his emotions to pay his provision bills" as "ridiculous . . . repulsive . . . shabby," his sense of outrage stemmed not just from the exploitation of the market, but also from the way the market feminized the male writer.[14] His solution, as Michael Bell has argued, lay in seeking a "manly art" of writing through his campaign for an ostensibly antiliterary realism. The "real" realist, like the "real" man, eschewed the "preening and prettifying . . . of literary men" in pursuit of a more republican productivity, "employing language as [he] would have employed any implement, to effect an object."[15] This artisinal construct of manhood was, in turn, enmeshed in a vocabulary that linked the writer with masculine professionals known for the exacting authority of their language: the scientist, the doctor, the lawyer, the judge.[16]

Twain retained traces of this republican craftsmanship in his oft-repeated insistence on the "difference between the *almost right* word and the *right* word."[17] More essential to his sense of masculinity was the language of the literary entrepreneur who cornered markets and waged military marketing campaigns. (Behind this language often lay a barely acknowledged sense of rivalry with his Hartford neighbor Harriet Beecher Stowe, whose *Uncle Tom's Cabin* [1852] remained for Twain a benchmark of popularity he would never approach.)[18] Common to all of these figurations of authority was the same concern for the control—indeed, the domination—of an audience that characterizes Twain's discussion of the art of humor in "How to Tell a Story." Like Tom's artistic seduction of Becky, the male platform humorist realizes a kind of sexual mastery as he arouses and provokes his female listeners. (The same dynamics may account for Twain's habit of reading his book manuscripts aloud to largely female groups of listeners that included most often his wife and children.)[19]

In chapter 1, I noted how Twain's tropes of castration and death characterized his sense of the contrast between speech and writing. I want here to return to this sexualized phallic power as it was manifested in his particularly vivid account of an all-male evening of dinner and speeches. Describing the speeches he heard at the Grand Reunion of the Army of the Tennessee held in Chicago in 1879, he wrote to Howells, "How pale those speeches are in print—but how radiant, how full of color, how blinding they were in the delivery!" Printed in the paper next morning, they "don't seem the same—their still sentences seem rather the prone dead forms of a host whom I had lately seen moving to the assault in the fire & smoke & tumult of battle. . . . Lord, there's nothing like the human organ to make words live & throb, & lift the hearer to the full altitudes of their meaning."[20] He was even more explicit in writing to his wife, Livy, commenting on one speaker, "how handsome he looked, as he stood on that table, in the midst of those 500 shouting men, and poured the molten silver from his lips! Lord, what an organ is human speech when it is played by a master!"[21] The masculinity of the speaker lay in the potency of his spoken language, itself confirmed by its power to move literarily and literally (bring to its feet) an audience.

It was this kind of manliness, as Twain's letter to Howells reiterates (recall his letter to Edward Bok), that writing threatened. It may be that Twain's energetic pursuit of the business of authorship represented some sort of compensating attempt at restoring such control. But such a formulation tells only half the story. For Twain's performative manhood was shaped as much by his willingness with his humor to put at risk—indeed, to expose and even ridicule—that manhood, as it was by a will to dominate. To be sure, as his self-styled humiliating "failure" at the Whittier banquet made clear, the stakes of such risk could be very high. Nonetheless, all cultural pretensions aside, for Twain, a humorist was required "to paint himself stripéd & stand on his head every fifteen minutes."[22] He developed this image more fully in *Huckleberry Finn* (1885), where the Dauphin appears on stage "a-prancing out on all fours, naked; and he was painted, all over, ring-streaked-and-striped, all sorts of colors, as splendid as a rain-bow. And—but never mind the rest of his outfit, it was just wild, but it was awful funny. The people most killed themselves laughing."[23] The farce, itself a "pale" version of a more ribald, and explicitly priapic, tale that Twain knew as "The Tragedy of the Burning Shame," succeeds only at the cost of humiliating exposure—not just of the performer's body, but also of the lengths to which he will go to win laughter from his audience.[24] In the end, however, unlike the Whittier banquet, it is the audience that is "most killed" as the confidence men have the last laugh when they swindle the audience of its money.

Like the Dauphin, Twain often achieved his most potent effects by burlesquing the very masculinity he elsewhere celebrated. His speech at the reunion, for instance, greeted, in his words, by a "tornado of applause and laughter," invited his listeners to imagine General Grant (whom Twain characterized to Livy as that "iron man")[25] as a baby "trying to find out some way to get his big toe into his mouth." In short, the speech exercised its power by deflating the military masculinity that the banquet celebrated: "When the thunders of war were sounding in your ears, you set your face toward the batteries, and advanced with steady tread; but, when [the baby] turned on the terrors of his war whoop, you advanced in the other direction—and mighty glad of the chance, too."[26] In cases like this, Twain wielded his humor, like speech itself, as a "dangerous weapon." Like the Dauphin's audience, Twain's listeners, in laughing, were provoked into acknowledging their investment in and anxiety over the very humiliation Twain risked with his burlesque.[27] Twain based his manly art of humor not on phallic dominance, but on the anxieties that both motivated and curtailed that dominance.

In doubling his authorial presence in *Tom Sawyer*, Twain is able to indulge more directly than in his earlier narratives his phallic fantasies of humorous domination by presenting them as the antics of (merely) a boy, without risking humiliation as a narrator. Tom's pirate fantasies return him to Sunday school, precisely that stage he tried unsuccessfully to seize by presenting his illegitimately accumulated reading tickets for a Bible, only to identify the first two apostles as David and Goliath. This humiliation, however, represents only a temporary setback. His pirate fantasy of shocking his audience into admiration is realized when he appears at his funeral service, after he testifies as a surprise witness at the murder trial, and after he escapes with Becky from the cave. At the same time, in framing these escapades with the nostalgic voice of the narrator, Twain places "The Author" outside the excesses of masculinity, able, in effect, to escape and even reflect on the anxieties of performance to which he nostalgically returns. If Tom were allowed to mature into manhood, he would have to confront these same anxieties.

That Tom could provide Twain with a safe "platform" (to use the word that commonly referred to the lecture stage) on which to perform phallic fantasies suggests the extent to which boyhood served the writer as a privileged state of manhood. But the question remains: what was it about boyhood that not only made it seem safe, but made the combination of fantasy and safety seem an appropriate topos for the construction of authorship? Twain, himself, certainly found the lure of boyhood almost irresistible. What he would later call his fictional "hymn" to boyhood grew out of a lifelong conviction that "the romance of life is the only part of it that is overwhelmingly valuable, & romance dies with youth. After that, life is a drudge, & indeed a sham. . . . I should greatly like to re-live my youth, & then get drowned."[28] As an author, he came as close to this wish as possible. *Tom Sawyer* initiates a string of texts—including *The Prince and the Pauper* (1882), *Huckleberry Finn, Joan of Arc* (1896), and *The Mysterious Stranger* (1916), not to mention such sequels as *Tom Sawyer Abroad* (1894) and *Tom Sawyer, Detective* (1896)—so rooted in childhood that at one point Twain would feel moved to apologize for his obsession: "I confined myself to the *boy*-life out on the Mississippi because that had a peculiar charm for me, and not because I was not familiar with other phases of life."[29]

As personal as this charm may have been, it was but one note in a sustained chord of adulation for the child during the decades following the Civil War. Driven by a century-long interest in childhood sparked by the Romantic celebrations of youthful innocence by Jean Jacques Rousseau and William Wordsworth and fueled by the growing efforts of educators to shape malleable youths into adults, modern interest in childhood had, by the 1870s, taken a distinctly sentimental turn.[30] *Tom Sawyer* entered a popular reading market for and about children, one shaped by pleasure fiction, textbooks, didactic works, and magazines like *St. Nicholas* and *The Riverside Youth Magazine*. The assumed audience was the male reader who, in the words of a contemporary reviewer, "look[ed] back to his childhood, as to the paradisaical period of his life, his Eden before he was driven into the world by sin."[31] Two examples of relatively popular narratives give a good idea of the cultural tenor of this celebration. In

1869, Thomas Bailey Aldrich published his immensely popular boyhood reminiscence, coyly titled *The Story of a Bad Boy*, which celebrated a forever-lost "[h]appy, magical Past" in which even a boyhood enemy is transfigured into a Wordsworthian angel "with a sort of dreamy glory encircling his bright red hair!"[32] Several years later, Charles Dudley Warner, Twain's coauthor of *The Gilded Age*, predicated his widely read fictional memoir, *Being a Boy* (1877), on the simple premise that "[o]ne of the best things in the world to be is a boy."[33]

Like much of the less didactic children's writing emerging during the late century, these texts share with *Tom Sawyer* a common nostalgia for a boyhood that is admittedly lost forever, thus reinscribing the gap between adult and child they seek to bridge. This tension is most apparent in Aldrich's narrative, a text often cited as a direct precedent of Twain's, where the author makes it clear in the beginning that his account is at least partially autobiographical: "This is the Story of a Bad Boy. Well, not such a very bad, but a pretty bad boy; and I ought to know, for I am, or rather I was, that boy myself."[34] The discomfort with linking boy and man registered in the indeterminacy of Aldrich's "I"—"I am," or "I was" that boy—is reinforced by the fact that Aldrich, like Warner, does not carry his protagonist any further toward manhood than does Twain.

Surveying such writing, Daniel Rodgers has characterized popular boys' fictions as regressive fantasies shaped by contemporary anxieties about modernization: "Retreating to preserves of the imagination or to rural and child-centered oases of boyhood memory, children's writers tried to carve out a place unviolated by . . . industrial society."[35] Aligned as such fictions were in a historical narrative extending from rural to modern, the gap between boy and man registered a sense of lost horizons, even historical inevitability; it helped readers accommodate to an alienating and reified present they did not understand. In this light, the fictional child functioned, in the words of T. J. Jackson Lears, therapeutically; it offered "a vision of psychic wholeness, a 'simple, genuine self' in a world where selfhood had become problematic and sincerity seemed obsolete."[36]

Such readings persuasively account for the resilient link in such writing between childhood and pastoral settings in idyllic small towns and villages. (Howells, reviewing Aldrich's and Twain's books together in the *Atlantic Monthly*, noted the relationship of setting to character in both books, commenting particularly on Tom's "fidelity to circumstance.")[37] More ambitiously, they also suggest that authors produced such escape fantasies for the same reasons that they were read: to objectify yearnings for cultural homogeneity and tradition by celebrating a simpler past. Like the era's political oratory, like the flowering of antiquarian history and regionalist writing, boys' books enacted a "sentimental regression" from a disturbing present.[38]

Yet the "oases" of boyhood that most readers knew lay not in the antebellum idyllicism the authors evoke, but rather in the middle-class home. To frame nostalgically the play of boys, to isolate them from manhood, was to reproduce figuratively the aspirations and the experiences of a middle class overwhelmingly absorbed in forming the home as a "haven in a heartless world," a private environment dedicated to cultural preservation and emotional redemption—a therapeutic preserve for child-like innocence.[39] It was in the home, under the care of a mother who was assumed to be free from nondomestic labor, isolated from the threatening public sphere of strangers, work, and the temptations of vice, that boys were allowed to enjoy an innocent prelude to adulthood. Yet this isolation had more than a strictly therapeutic dimension. Sequestered in a world of loving personal relations, the young boy was "rightly constructed" by a moral education designed to form an internal character that would allow him to negotiate as an adult the very public life from which he was protected. By the 1870s, the home had assumed, along with schools and youth organizations, a preeminent role as one of the era's "man-making" institutions.[40]

These twin purposes, however, spawned a paradox: as boys were isolated in environments of preservation, the relationship of boyhood to adulthood grew increasingly problematic. For boys became men only by crossing a clearly demarcated line between feminized domestic privacy and a masculinized world of public labor. The uncertainties of this passage led men to register extraordinary concern for evaluating and reaffirming their "manliness."[41] Even as boys became the objects of increasing institutional and familial care, men flocked to secret fraternal orders like the Odd Fellows and the Freemasons, where they dramatized in elaborate rituals a transition of naïf into initiate, boy into man.[42] Expected to embrace a "battlefield code" of vigor and prowess, they learned "to transform fears of vulnerability or inadequacy into a desire for dominance," to shun any signs of "weakness and effeminacy."[43] It was precisely the feminine that many liminal activities, from secret rituals to sport, from sexual abstinence to protracted labor and capital accumulation, were designed to expunge. Still, beyond any sense of adult autonomy, no matter how "self-made" any successful man may have claimed to be, lay the fact that he was "rightly constructed" as a boy, rightly prepared for his world by women in the home.[44]

Fictional "oases" such as Twain's thus not only represented fantasy retreats from the contradictions of a modern masculinity, they also affirmed and even perpetuated the very privatized domestic culture that so powerfully shaped gender roles. Even as Tom's phallic fantasies, his resistance to the socializing incursions of adulthood, give voice to Twain's own masculine anxieties, his novel's unremittingly idyllic domesticity gives eloquent and coherent expression to what Eli Zaretsky has called the middle class's signature fantasy "that humanity can pass beyond a life dominated by relations of production."[45] Harbored in the safe confines of domestic fantasy, free from the encroachments of adult life, Twain's "rightly constructed boy's life" stands as the inverted image of "The [self-making] Author"; it affirms the power of domesticity and legitimates the middle-class practice of distinguishing between "productive" and "reproductive" labor.

With *Tom Sawyer*, Twain redraws the social map on which he had earlier situated his fictional labor—a map hitherto divided into the seemingly antagonistic, yet ultimately complementary, spheres of culture and capital—to include the domestic world. Not that this world had been absent in his earlier conception. As the material destination for his subscription books, the family home served as the ultimate site of consumption, the space where finally capital was exchanged for culture and put to use as cultural capital in the formation of distinction. But, in writing a book about boys, in ostensibly writing it for children as well as adults, and in telling that story in the voice of an adult male narrator, Twain implicitly recast the domestic sphere as a site for the right construction of boys. In essence, he invited "The Author" and his text into the home as a major player in the drama of social reproduction. In one sense then, this entailed an act of literary fathering. However, insofar as that fathering took place only through the written word, it also entailed an act of literary authorization that situated the male writer on boyhood as an expert, a self-proclaimed "philosopher" of the feminized domestic sphere. Just as traveling served *The Innocents Abroad* less as a material "context" than as a pretext for Twain's engagement with the cultural pretensions of travel writing, family life offered Twain a particularly volatile site on which to engage what Steven Mailloux has called the "cultural rhetoric" of the literary: a discourse that "enables and constrains the interpretation and use of fiction."[46] It was this discursive confrontation that enabled Twain to continue the "building" of his authorship.

II. Rightly Constructing Boys

When Tom Sawyer completes his first public confidence game, in which he fulfills Aunt Polly's grudgingly administered punishment by enticing his friends to white-wash the fence in exchange for their pocket wealth, the narrator closes the chapter with a "lesson":

> [Tom] had discovered a great law of human action, without knowing it—namely, that in order to make a man or a boy covet a thing, it is only necessary to make the thing difficult to attain. If he had been a great and wise philosopher, like the writer of this book, he would now have comprehended that Work consists of whatever a body is *obliged* to do and that Play consists of whatever a body is not obliged to do. (16)

It is not so much "things" that boys and men covet in the world of *Tom Sawyer*, but "the glory and the eclat" (31) of performance. Tom converts the "things" he has conned his friends out of into the Sunday school tickets that would allow him to receive a Bible and, more important, the wonder and envy of his peers. Yet the narrator here is more interested in distinctions than resemblances. Not only do boys play while men work, boys have no philosophy, no sense of obligation, no larger horizon of knowledge that transforms play into work. English gentleman, continues the narrator, ride their coaches twenty miles a day "because the privilege costs them considerable money; but if they were offered wages for the service, that would turn it into work and then they would resign." Boys, as little aristocrats, pursue their pleasure indiscriminately, submitting themselves to the "labor" and "industry" of digging for gold as they seek to fulfill their "raging desire . . . for hidden treasure" (175). They play Robin Hood "'by the book,' from memory" (67)—even though Tom cannot manage memorizing a few Bible verses. Work can become play and play can become work: when Tom and Joe dispense with the book they "'go it lively!'" with their swords, "panting and perspiring with the work" (67). Boys play because there is no end to their activity, no means for that matter, no explicit goal and no strategy, no single object of desire. School will not last for ever, but summer will; night, with its illicit freedoms, must end, but there is always another.

The narrator, on the other hand, "great and wise philosopher" that he is, is burdened with work; he comprehends great laws enough to encapsulate them in handy aphorisms. He has mastered them enough to parody them or, at least, to mock his mastery of them. More important, unlike Mr. Dobbins, unlike the Sunday-school superintendent, the minister, the judge, unlike even Aunt Polly, the narrator comprehends boyhood. To Aunt Polly, Tom is "harum-scarum"; to Judge Thatcher, who thinks strictly in terms of means and ends, Tom's future teeters between the presidency and hanging; to the other adults, the restless pattern of boyhood threatens to disrupt their own almost pathological needs for order and control. They try to master boyhood by punishing it, whipping it, humiliating it. The narrator, on the other hand, knows boyhood because he remembers it ("Most of the adventures in the book really occurred," he avows in the preface); he has mastered its fantasies, its sense of play, its language; he knows what it means to "covet a thing."

The adult mastery of boyhood is very much at stake in *Tom Sawyer*. The book opens with Aunt Polly poking a broom under the bed, trying to drive Tom out of his hiding places, to "arrest his flight" (2), and bring him into the light where she can see him. It ends with Huck Finn, "the juvenile pariah of the village . . . cordially hated and dreaded by all the mothers" (47), suffering mournfully under the benevolent care of the Widow Douglas. What do these adults want with these boys? "Well, I lay if I get hold of you I'll—" (1): Aunt Polly never finishes her threat to Tom, but the intention is clear. She will beat some sense into the boy, teach him some philosophy. But this is easier threatened than done. For even Aunt Polly, who comes closest to exercising some sort of control over her charge (it is after all Tom's guilty memory of her that eventually draws him home from Jackson's Island), cannot bring herself to punish him when he needs it most. "I can't hit him a lick," she muses. "I ain't doing my duty by that boy, and that's the Lord's truth, goodness knows. Spare the rod and spile the child, as the Good Book says. I'm a-laying up sin and suffering for us both, *I* know. He's full of the Old Scratch, but laws-a-me! . . . I ain't got the heart to lash him, somehow" (2–3). The men can lash him, but Tom takes his lickings as a matter of course; he even takes advantage of them to win Becky's heart.

Nonetheless, Tom is not as wild as he could be (nor is Huck for that matter). He does, after all, have a conscience, one that appears to him as an anonymous "intruder" (105)—an external but powerful voice of guilt that threatens thunderbolts from heaven and leads him to tortuous distinctions between stealing and borrowing—and allows him to brave Injun Joe by testifying against him at the murder trial. Conscience forms some rudimentary element of philosophy; it keeps Tom from the "carnival of crime" Twain enjoys in the story he wrote by that title in 1876.[47] In nineteenth-century terms, Tom is a character with character; he possesses that "portable parent," an internalized control shaped in the confines of the home, which the best children were expected to have.[48] But Tom has no parents; Aunt Polly, for all of her love, is well aware that she remains too suspended between a painful conscience and a soft heart to guide him. Then where does he get this conscience? From whom will he learn the philosophy of manhood; how will he comprehend the obligation of work? Certainly not from Mr. Dobbins, nor from Aunt Polly. For what Tom needs is a father, a figure of masculine authority, a role model who understands how a boy becomes a man. As Aunt Polly puts it, "[M]an that is born of woman is of few days and full of trouble" (3).

Instead, men must be born of men. At least this was the lesson thousands of boys and parents learned from the fictional adventures of a five-year-old boy named Rollo. Compare, for instance, the narrator's "lesson" about work with that intoned by little Rollo's father: "Work . . . is when you are engaged in doing any thing in order to produce some useful result. When you are doing any thing only for the amusement of it, without any useful result, it is play."[49] The passage comes in Jacob Abbott's *Rollo at Work* (1853), the second of twenty-eight volumes that detail Rollo's earnest, if often wayward, attempts at learning to become a man. Originally appearing in the 1830s, these texts, which one reviewer labeled "a saturnalia of common sense," became by far the best-known didactic boys' books of the century.[50] Rollo is the Model Boy that Tom is not; Abbott's books are those "marble-backed" volumes that so mislead Jacob Blivens. They also presumably misled the Clemens daughters, for whom their father bought them. They also account for at least some of Tom's waywardness: Twain, at one time, considered introducing young Rollo to Tom and Huck in a later novel.[51]

Rollo's father knows the philosophy of work and never misses a chance to communicate it to his son. Why, asks Rollo, cannot the family's colt Elky be hitched to the wagon? His father replies, "Elky is not old enough to work." While the colt may have the strength for the task, it "has never learned to work yet": "he has something more to do than merely pull; he must pull right, and he must be taught to do this. Besides he must learn to obey all my various commands. Why, a horse needs to be taught to work as much as a boy" (*Work*, 10–11). Rollo is at least as eager a student of work as a horse, but as he and his friend James set out on their appointed tasks, they fall happy victims to diversions, quarrels, and boredom. After each episode, Father patiently adds to his son's knowledge of work. Labor is more "solid," it demands that one go "directly forward . . . , without stopping to rest, or to contrive new ways of doing it, or to see other people, or to talk" (*Work*, 44). But work is a hard concept to grasp; it involves more than exertion. As Father puts it, "boys *play* hard, sometimes, as well as work hard" (*Work*, 74). In order to become "a faithful and efficient little work*man*," a boy must learn to recognize the larger satisfactions of deferred gratification (*Work*, 58; emphasis added).

Oddly enough, it is in *Work*'s companion volume, *Rollo at Play* (1853), that the boy learns the philosophy of work.[52] When Rollo complains about his father's cancellation of an eagerly anticipated blueberry-picking trip because of rain, he receives a stern lecture: "In a few days there will be thousands and thousands of dollars' worth of fruit and food more than there would have been without this rain; and yet you are very unwilling to have it come, because you want to go and get a few blueberries!" (*Play*, 81–82). Rollo's grumbling poses not just a domestic problem, but a crime against the economic welfare of the family and, as his father goes on to explain, even a sin against God. Rollo learns his lesson and accommodates himself, at least temporarily, to this cosmology of filial piety, self-control, and productive labor. Despite his subsequent, indeed interminable, need for education in the following twenty-six volumes (*Rollo Learns to Read*, *Rollo Learns to Write*, *Rollo at School*, etc.), Abbott leaves little doubt that his protagonist will mature into an image of his father and reproduce the stable social world of the ordered family and the productive Jeffersonian farm.

Certainly Rollo's father knows the philosophy of manhood that can differentiate play and work; but how well does he know boyhood? As he communicates it to his son, boyish play represents nothing more than the negation of manhood, an idle absence that must be filled with knowledge. Without that knowledge, the child is not only wayward, he is an affront to the father's (and God's) authority and a threat to the text's gracious agrarianism. Abbott, on the other hand, seems to know boyhood quite well. For his texts work not just to represent the right construction of boys into men; they also aspire to represent that construction to boys. What better way to do so than appealing directly to the very waywardness, the need for pleasure, that the father would channel into work?

Thus Abbott's philosophy of manhood depends on a complementary philosophy of reading. The didactic fiction for boys that the Rollo books exemplify sought to effect in the reading process itself the very transformation of boy into man they represented; they offered the Jacob Blivens of the world the fantasy material they so craved. Maria Edgeworth, whose children's fiction had proven immensely popular since its appearance at the turn of the nineteenth century, set the formula early, in the preface to *The Parent's Assistant* (1800): "To prevent precepts of morality from tiring the ear and the mind, it was necessary to make the Stories, in which they are introduced, in some measure dramatic; to keep alive hope, and fear, and curiosity, by some degree of intricacy."[53] Abbott, too, sought to direct the young reader to moral ends by offering the pleasures of fiction. As he puts it in his "Notice to Parents" in his first volume, in terms Twain would echo in his own preface forty years later, while his texts "are intended principally as a means of entertainment for their little readers," they also aspire to more "useful purposes": educating children in reading, exercising their powers of reason, and offering an image of a "quiet virtuous life" worthy of imitation.

What Abbott's texts offer then, in lieu of work or play, is an amalgam of both—"safe amusements," as the subtitle for *Rollo at Play* puts it.

These "safe amusements," or, in Twain's language, "entertainments," occupy a middle ground between work and play, boy and man; they define a kind of adolescent stage in the philosophy of manhood. Like adolescence, they embody an uneasy mix of contrarieties that call for the careful management of pleasure. For work does not obviate pleasure, it defers it; its pleasure emerges retrospectively, ultimately in the satisfaction of a stable social order. Abbott manages this economy by depicting Rollo playing at tasks that resemble little more than work: constructing a box, building a wigwam, planting a garden. But boys must be offered immediate pleasure in order to be taught, a pleasure that can threaten the reserve of "safe amusement." This is what Rollo discovers when the rain passes and he is finally able to go blueberry picking. There he encounters three "bad" boys with whom, contrary to his father's explicit warnings, he strikes up a conversation. Quickly—indeed, almost despite himself—Rollo finds himself fascinated with them, especially Jim, a "ragged and dirty-looking boy" who, with the others, "used language which Rollo knew was wrong" (*Play*, 167, 168). Wrong as it is, the language grips the boy's attention as tightly as Huck's does Tom: "The boys went on talking to one another and to Rollo, telling various stories about their running away from school, stealing apples, and such things. Rollo was much interested in listening to them, though he knew, all the time, that he was doing wrong. But he had not the courage to leave them abruptly, as he ought to have done, and go back to his father" (*Play*, 169). Rollo's encounter with delinquency is summarily resolved by yet another lecture and a vanquishing of the bad influences: it is just this sort of behavior from which Father hopes to steer his son. At the same time, however, the fact that this tantalizing glimpse of a life beyond the margins of order registers so strong an impression on Rollo as *stories* suggests that Abbott comes to "know" childhood in offering boys the pleasures of potentially wayward imaginative fiction.

Twain's aversion to such didacticism notwithstanding, the shared philosophy of work and the parallels between the two prefaces suggest that Twain borrowed from as much as he parodied Abbott's texts. Certainly for readers in the 1870s, and for many in earlier decades, Abbott's agrarianism represented as much a nostalgic idyll as did Twain's rendering of small-town boyhood. More important, the absence of a father in *Tom Sawyer* objectifies what the Rollo volumes suggest: that a knowledge of childhood comes not from a patriarchal philosophy that segregates work from play, but from a controlled indulgence in the fantasies of boyhood.

This is what Abbott advocated in his childrearing manual, published in 1872, in which he condensed the experience and knowledge gleaned from decades as an educator and an author. Arguing that "children are not generally indulged enough," he instructed parents to practice a program of *Gentle Measures*, as his book was titled, rather than punishment, in socializing their young.[54] Excessive corporal punishment very often indicated that the parent was failing his or her duty. After all, he argued, children were as instinctive as animals: "nine-tenths of the whispering and playing of children in school, and of the noise, the rudeness, and the petty mischief of children at home, is just this hissing and fizzling of an imprisoned power, and nothing more" (or, as Aunt Polly puts it, boys like Tom are "only just giddy, and harum-scarum").[55] The goal of right parenting was not to break a child's will, but to channel this innate energy into the formation of a proper character.

As such, Abbott's advice recasts parental authority in terms that render the men in *Tom Sawyer*, no less than Rollo's father, anachronistic, even absurd, in their absolutism. By the 1870s, patriarchal forms of childrearing that entailed punishment and fatherly confrontation had long since been written out of the literature of middle-class domesticity.[56] As early as the 1830s, in seeking to address "the wants of the middling class in our own country," writers regularly assumed the absence of fathers, who "in the rush and whirl of business, . . . forget their obligations to their children."[57] The "gentle measures" advocated by Abbott and his peers were tailored for the mother at home, whose parenting was presumably guided more by the heart than the hand.[58]

Abbott's text is often cited as the capstone of a fifty-year trend in the liberalization of childrearing.[59] Yet this tells only half the story of Abbott's advice. For Abbott writes not to help shape happier children—they would presumably find their own pleasures—but to establish a rational basis for the maintenance of parental power. "The only government of the parent over the child", he insists, "that is worthy of the name is one of authority—complete, absolute, unquestioned *authority*." "Gentle measures" thus represent "the easiest and most effectual means for establishing and maintaining that authority in its most absolute form." If parents allow "the freest indulgence of children" in play, they do so only, on the one hand, by guiding that energy into acceptable channels and, on the other, by rationalizing punishment: "It is in all cases the certainty, and not the severity, of punishment which constitutes its power."[60]

The basis for this rational authority was knowledge. To raise children "on the right principles" parents must "rightly . . . understand the true nature of that extraordinary activity which is so noticeable in all children." Thus, "it is necessary to turn our attention somewhat carefully to certain scientific truths in respect to the nature and action of force in general . . . which throw great light on the true character of that peculiar form of it which is so characteristic of childhood."[61] Abbott's emphasis on such knowledge echoed that of thirty years of advice urging parents to "study childhood"; Jacob's brother John, in one of the most popular advice manuals during the middle decades of the century, argued that "unless we are willing to think ourselves; to study the disposition of our children; to watch the influence of the various motives we present to their minds, many faults will pass undetected, and we shall lose many advantages we might otherwise have obtained." Deploring the ignorance of mothers, another writer urged that they "must watch the peculiarities of the disposition of [the] child."[62] Such prescriptions envisioned parenting less as a process of direct intervention than as a complex practice of observation and management. A carefree childhood depended on "the watchfulness of parents"; the model mother would shed "over all the play, infusing into all the glee, a certain sober and thoughtful look of character and principle."[63]

Thus, didactic and nostalgic boys' fictions joined with the vast flow of prescriptive and advice literature to isolate the boy as the subject of a form of knowledge, itself the basis for a discipline that would keep children in "safe amusement" and allow them to eventually internalize a mature philosophy of work, restraint, and obligation—in sum, a conscience. Certainly, by the 1870s, many boys were brought up along just these lines, in many cases by families who consulted such literature for practical guidance. At the same time, however, the very process of representing boys implied a certain authority, a parental authority no doubt, but also a larger expertise embodied in a rhetorical authority that reached beyond the immediate concerns of day-to-day family life. For a philosophy of boys authorized advice writers, just as it empowered Rollo's father, to voice larger social philosophies that placed the right construction of boys at the center of a future world of social stability.

Perhaps the most vigorous aspirant to such authority was Horace Bushnell, the widely popular Hartford theologian—and, until he died in 1876, a prestigious member of Twain's social circle—whose *On Christian Nurture* ran through numerous editions after it initially appeared in 1847.[64] There he couched his advice in a utopian vision of the family reforming with its Christian sons a world that has lost direction, one where "modern notions and speculations have taken a bent toward individualism" and where Americans have lost any sense of the "organic" relations between state, church, and family.[65] Forged out of the properly regulated day-to-day "transactions and feelings" of private family life, a public environment will emerge that best fosters "a common character" to the republic as a whole. The sons responsible for carrying on this tradition will, as they mature, exude an "odor of the house": "And so it comes to pass that a son, grown almost to manhood, will gladly serve the house, and yield to his parents a kind of homage that even anticipates their wishes, just because he has learned to be in subjection, with all gravity, under restrictions that were once a sore limit on his patience."[66]

Bushnell not only distills the tone of many of his peers in the science of boyhood, he crystallizes the ways in which such writing aspired to establish a public rhetoric of order and social authority with boys as the subject and the family as the object of attention. Writers about boys helped provide the means by which Americans could understand social conformity as adult masculinity and social deviance as a form of boyish behavior; they interpreted the methods by which deviance was disciplined and socialized as a process of "natural" growth and education. More specifically, as authors of advice manuals for young men, childrearing guides, and didactic children's literature sought to offer practical advice to parents intent on preparing their children for a modernizing world, they also established a public rhetoric that allowed them to link the day-to-day concerns of childrearing and family life with broader aspirations of social order and class success. The way in which the century's advice literature characterized the boy and figured his transformation into a man served as the linchpin in an elaborate historical narrative of class reproduction and hegemony that bridged a disordered present by linking an ordered past with a utopian future.

As such, boys were as much the creatures of the vast flow of prescriptive writing—printed sermons; magazines on mothering and home life; didactic fiction of all kinds; publications on medicine, ethics, religion, and etiquette—that comprised what Daniel Walker Howe has called the "communications system" of mid-Victorian America, as they were of the home.[67] As subjects of advice, they became one of the means whereby the purveyors of that knowledge could establish their authority. For knowledge, as boy experts were well aware, had no value unless it was disseminated. Even as John Abbott enjoined his readers to observe boys, he urged them to put their findings in writing where, "through the pages of some religious magazine, [they could] be circulated to the farthest parts of our country, and [exert] a powerful influence on the hearts of mothers."[68] As such, Abbott advised mothers to assume the same cultural role as he did in publishing his lectures to his parishioners for general consumption. He and his colleagues aspired to establish what one author called "a system for the mass of the people" by disseminating information in the form of philosophy, observation, anecdote, science, and medicine, all of which formed the knowable subject of the child.[69]

Advice manuals voiced a remarkably explicit sense of a cultural authority that anticipated and echoed that of professional lawyers, doctors, and, finally, authors. Writers of conduct guides addressed to young men explicitly offered their texts as surrogates for fatherly advice, adopting a voice of tradition, experience, and continuity.[70] For instance, in his immensely popular *The Young Man's Guide*, which went through twenty-one editions between 1833 and 1858, William Alcott urged his "young friends" to talk whenever possible with their elders. But when such contact is not possible, "there is one method besides conversation, in which you may come at the wisdom of the aged; and that is through the medium of books." In books like Alcott's, the text implies, the youth would find the "valuable information and useful advice" he could not otherwise acquire.[71]

One of the most elaborate dramatizations of such intentions appeared in Ann Porter's *Uncle Jerry's Letters to Young Mothers* (1854). The book opens with a young mother, confronted with the difficulty of raising children, recalling the words of "an aged mother to a younger sister" urging her to "[o]btain and keep the confidence of your children." The writer laments: "O for the secret how to do this!" "[P]ainfully conscious of [her] ignorance," she yearns for advice from more experienced elders: "How often young mothers wish they could know if others have the same perplexities and the same painful sense of difficulties as themselves!" Like her peers, she has "read many books on family government and the training of children," but they have been to no avail: "there were many difficulties I could not solve, many spots where I needed a guide," especially with the "scanty aid from a husband whose business left him few hours of leisure during the week." So she writes her uncle and aunt ("I need help in my ignorance—the experience of a wiser person than myself"), who reply in a series of instructive letters.[72]

While more explicit than most, *Uncle Jerry's Letters* fashions a drama of historical disjunction and cultural revitalization common to many advice manuals. In the voice of doting elders, the author offers her advice disguised as a male voice of tradition. As tortured as this conceit is, it gives a good indication of how, beyond giving practical advice, such prescriptive literature reconstituted the absent patriarch in the text itself through a knowledge of boyhood.[73] It offered a bargain: ushering the father out the front door on his way to work, it reintroduced male authority through the back in the form of "expert" advice. Embedding practical suggestions on a wide range of domestic issues—punishment, nutrition, clothing, reading, illness, furniture—in a social vision of history and morals, such literature assumed an authority that was as persuasive as it was ostensibly distant. Brokering between personal life and the public whole, the authors sought, by writing about children, to assume both an authority over the family and in the family. Their expertise bound ideological narrative with practical advice in a rhetoric that was ultimately realist in scope and fictional in effect.

Tom's conscience thus comes precisely from the figure who fathered him, the figure who addresses his lesson not to the boy in his story, but to the boys and men who, like Jacob Blivens, like the readers of Rollo, turn to novels for play. Tom's conscience is that of the narrator, careful to construct his boy rightly, to shed "over all the play, infusing into all the glee, a certain sober and thoughtful look of character and principle." Unlike Rollo's father, and unlike mothers at home—who must poke under beds and search closets for their restless boys and who must turn to advice manuals to find help—Tom's father knows best. He is the expert who can comprehend the philosophy of men and the play of boys. And, it is he who most powerfully can construct a "safe amusement."

For, if manhood in the Twainian world of domestic boys is best exemplified by the knowledgeable author, the sign of that mastery lies in how well, how "pleasantly," he entertains. On this count, Twain masters amusement better than does Abbott. Even as the Rollo books were being consumed by millions of readers and trumpeted by educators and parents, others were agreeing with one reviewer who complained, "Most tale-writers are altogether too didactic . . . a tale is not a lecture."[74] Another, surveying the field of children's books in 1866, yearned for the type of boys' books that in the past had been "cautiously transmitted from hand to hand. . . . Nobody knew whence they came, nobody had ever bought them, nobody owned them, everybody borrowed them."[75] Yet these stories, like the wrong language Rollo hears while blueberry picking, posed potential dangers. American youth, complained the experts, was dangerously inundated by a flood of "pernicious" literature that either "pandered directly to lust" or presented "false and unworthy views life."[76] Advice writers for parents and young men regularly included chapters on reading, warning that tales of running away, drinking, and gambling threatened to violate the immaculate seal of child discipline. Complained the critic William Graham Sumner, "In this class of stories, fathers and sons are represented as natural enemies, and the true position of the son is that of suspicion and armed peace."[77]

How better to characterize Tom's own phallic fantasies, his calculated alliance with Huck Finn, and his fascination with Injun Joe? Tom's adventures are those of a naïve reader caught up in the underground world of wrong language and pernicious fiction. Angels and devils, Robin Hood, kings, ghosts, robbers, and pirates: all pose roles to enter into or enemies to be confronted. It is these fictions, as much as Abbott's Rollo tales, that Twain invokes when he asserts he writes "mainly for the entertainment" of children. In eschewing any explicit didactic purpose, Twain at least implicitly calls up the specter of the vast underbody of "sensational" fiction from which children's magazines and genteel authors sought to steer their readers, and which, in weekly story papers, dime novels, and penny libraries, critics feared children were devouring.

Thus, as an author of boys' fiction, Twain writes not only as an authority on boyhood and domesticity, but also as an arbitrator of what was known as "the fiction question." Both his early burlesques of child reading and his novel share the assumption with didactic writers, librarians, educators, and critics that, in their naïveté, children are particularly vulnerable to the impressions of reading and thus ready to build their lives wholly within the architecture of the stories they encounter. To know children was to admit that boys were as vulnerable to, as they were promiscuous readers of, such fiction. To write for children was to negotiate this contradictory terrain; to become an authority in this terrain was to define the qualities of fiction, in particular, and culture, in general, that would best form children's minds.

Michael Denning has argued that distinctions between pernicious and healthy fiction comprised "an exercise of cultural power" within the mass market, dedicated to "drawing and policing . . . a boundary between the *genteel* and the *sensational*. This boundary was a moral as well as aesthetic one, dividing the culture of the 'middle class' from the ways of the 'lower classes.'"[78] Indeed, even those critics such as Howells, who acknowledged himself as "not inclined to despise" literature that tried to "amuse" ("people find pleasure in having their blood curdled for the sake of having it uncurdled again at the end of the book"), characterized such writing in a way that presumed its readers lacked literary taste. Such fiction, he argued, appeals to the "primitive" in all of us: "No sordid details of verity here, . . . but a great, whirling splendor of peril and achievement, a wild scene of heroic adventure and of emotional ground and lofty tumbling, with a stage 'picture' at the fall of the curtain, and all the good characters in a row. . . . [Thus] the poor, foolish, childish old world renews the excitements of its nonage."[79] "[P]rimitive," "poor, foolish, childish": these readers are as naïve as Tom and Jacob Blivens. They revel in the melodrama of adventure and emotion that presumably cultivated, sensible, and mature readers, such as Howells, or Twain's narrator, resist.

Certainly Twain, a writer who liked to identify his audience as "factory hands and . . . farmers," saw the "poor" in the "childish" as quickly as Howells saw the "childish" in the "poor."[80] Not only does Tom give himself up regularly to dime-novel fiction, the novel as a whole, particularly in the plot built around Injun Joe, exhibits elements of dime-novel melodrama. However, in *Tom Sawyer*, Twain does not write for the working masses, but for the middling masses. His is not a dime novel for the simple reason that it cost too much to buy; it aimed at satisfying precisely those buyers who valued at least the image of "mature" reading, used books as signs of their own cultural distinction, and, most important, wanted those books written by known authors.[81]

In promising to "pleasantly remind adults," he ameliorates the threat of the sensational implicit in "entertainment" by situating his audience in precisely that domestic home where the subscription book most often ended up. His target is the feminized domestic reading circle, the sphere of boyhood, a site of literary consumption regulated by what the editor Edmund Clarence Stedman called "the *virginibus* maxim (print nothing to offend a virgin)."[82] Howells put the point more broadly: "Between the editor of a reputable English or American magazine and the families which receive it there is a tacit agreement that he will print nothing which a father may not read to his daughter, or safely leave her to read herself."[83]

In rightly constructing both boy and narrator out of the material of middle-class fantasy, Twain meets just such a contract. Thus the boy and the man, and the author, are born of women and daughters, who themselves labor to build self-made men. But in this story lies a lesson, a philosophy not so much of manhood and work, but of fantasy. The text's essential nostalgia, what Twain will "pleasantly remind" his readers of, is not strictly the "queer enterprises" of youth, but the essential place of fantasy in the "mature" lives of his readers. For Tom's fantasies are not merely those of a boy, but of the culture that made him a boy, a culture that demands amusement as much as, or even more than, safety, and a culture that will, if not stand and applaud, at least reward authors for giving it that fantasy.

III. FRACTURING: INJUN JOE

In his vision of the ideal family for the development of boys, Bushnell describes an environment where "the bond is so intimate" that parents can influence children "unconsciously and undesignedly" in the proper direction. Discipline, not punishment; influence, not coercion: these are the watchwords of family government. His vocabulary is most Foucauldian when he advises his readers to remain ceaselessly vigilant to children's potential for overstepping bounds:

> Observe that great care is needed in the process of detection, or the police of discovery. The child must not be allowed to go on breaking through the orders imposed, or into the ways of vice, not detected. This will make his life a practice of art and hypocrisy; and what is worse, will make him also confident of success in the same. Nothing will corrupt his moral nature more rapidly. There must be a very close and careful watch on the part of fathers and moth-

ers, to let no deviation of childhood pass their discovery. And then, again, the greatest care and address will be needed, to keep their circumspection from taking on the look of deliberate espionage, than which nothing will more certainly alienate the confidence and love needful to their just authority.[84]

The boy, in this view, is enveloped in a house of domestic discipline, an environment bound by, in Foucault's terms, "a meticulously sealed wall, uncrossable in either direction."[85] Protected from the encroachments of outside contamination, the boy emerges as a type of the modern prisoner. Just as Bushnell advocated a "penal discipline" in the family, juvenile asylums established harsh regimes "to create and cultivate a family feeling," and schools sought to extend family influence by organizing the classroom like a factory.[86] Out of these came men and boys who shaped the "man-making" institutions like the YMCA, evangelical youth groups, Boy Scouts, and sport organizations, all of which offered boys contact with their own kind.[87]

In envisioning the child as forever teetering on the edge of depravity, and in formulating the home as a complementary Benthamite apparatus of loving detection, Bushnell links the power of knowledge with an active policing of the normal. The result is a fantasy of absolute power that entreats parents to envelop their children in a gaze so minute that it can detect the least sign of deviance. No amusement is safe here; detection takes its potency by intervening before punishment is needed. Children are fundamentally trained to habits of sincerity and forthrightness, while their play remains innocent because it has never been contaminated by outside influence. Parents are urged to conceal their espionage, in effect to practice the very hypocrisy they will root out of their young ones.[88] This Foucauldian regime, however, has less to say about the state of family life than it does about the rhetoric used to characterize boyhood, a rhetoric that empowered an autonomous authority within the narrative voice itself, and which, even as it magnified the power of the mother to shape the child, subjected mothering to the same proscriptions directed at the boy. Bushnell's representation of parental power augments, because it so perfectly reflects and complements, his authority as an expert.

Surely such draconian vision seems completely at odds with Twain's nostalgic hymn to boyhood. It is Abbott's narrator who keeps such close watch on his charge: even as Rollo stands transfixed by wrong language, the narrator reminds his readers that the boy "ought to have [gone] back to his father." Tom has much freer rein. Neither "bad" nor "good," only "harum-scarum," he evades the strictures of normality imposed on him by adults. When Aunt Polly punishes Tom by forcing on him his whitewashing chore, she fences Tom off from the manifold promises of "delicious expeditions" (12) offered by the beckoning "Delectable Land" (10) of Cardiff Hill. "It's mighty hard to make him work Saturdays," says Aunt Polly, "when all the boys is having holiday, but he hates work more than he hates anything else, and I've *got* to do some of my duty by him, or I'll be the ruination of the child" (3). But Tom knows the philosophy of boyhood, and so he transforms his punishment into an opportunity for a new kind of play. This revision allows him to barter first with Ben Rogers for his apple and, finally, for the pocket wealth of all of his friends. This in turn is reinvested in Sunday-school tickets that allow him to acquire a prize Bible, an emblem of "industry and . . . application" (30) that he rewrites as a vehicle for "glory and eclat."

Tom does not *reject* adult authority so much as plays off of it. His spontaneity subverts because it ignores the invocations of discipline; it substitutes a plenitude of significance for the "meaner" dictates of adulthood. Whitewashing becomes both a sentence and an opportunity; the apple is both a "delicious" substitute for the "Delectable Land" and a counter for exchange; the Bible is a badge of labor and the endpoint of a confidence game. Such plenitude is the product of Tom's own knowledge: he comprehends adults as well as the narrator does boys. "He 'pears to know just how long he can torment me before I get my dander up, and he knows if he can make out to put me off for a minute or make me laugh, it's all down again and I can't hit him a lick" (2–3). He makes "ridiculous" those adults who feel the strictures of authority as much as children; he forces them to applaud his irreverence, his energy.

The narrator assists him in this. By excluding the presence of any father figure, by celebrating Tom's repeated victories over, and subversions of, school, church, and home, and most important, by engaging the narrative voice in a game of comic complicity with the boy, the narrator refuses the didactic injunctions and order-affirming practices that shaped the public rhetoric of boyhood. Encompassed by the pastoral world of eternal summer, the institutions of discipline—church, school, and home—exercise an authority that seems more sadistic than preparatory precisely because there is no future to prepare for. Bushnell's and Abbott's boys must grow up; they must learn the philosophy of manly labor or perish as men. St. Petersburg's boys have no future and are happier for it. In confining the confrontations between child and adult to the comic wars in church and school, Twain at once suspends the question of good and bad and renders problematic the relationship between authority and deviance. He presents the child as a separate subject, confines him in a separate sphere, but defines that space as the whole of the fiction.

In this very suspension of disbelief, however, lies the narrator's own "hypocrisy," his circumspect espionage. Like Tom, he doesn't tear down the fence of discipline, he whitewashes it; the boundaries of youth are so thoroughly concealed that the fiction of boyhood reproduces the meticulous walls of the asylum of childhood. As such, *Tom Sawyer* is a domestic fantasy, the most fantastic premise of which is the degree to which the novel hides its disciplinary authority in a gaze that is as nostalgic, even benevolent, as it is knowing. Inscribed in this nostalgia is "the history of a *man*" who brooks no challenge to his authority.

But challenges are met much more easily from a boy than they are from a man, particularly a man with a history. That man of course is Injun Joe, who at once represents the comic apogee of the narrative's complicit fantasy, and yet who threatens the idyll of boyhood and exposes both the hypocrisy of the narrator's nostalgia and that of adults who indulge in fantasies of safe amusement. So powerful is his presence that he alters the shape of the narrative, shifting its focus from a boyhood idyll to a tale of retribution and revenge, splintering its pastoral asylum into a geography of safety and taboo. Thus, if Twain's novel begins by replicating the Bushnellian rhetoric of authority, it ends by calling that rhetoric—which also creates "The Author"—into question. The result is a text formally unbalanced enough to cause, as it were, a slip in the meticulous seal of boyhood and the borders of the narrative, revealing a thin fissure through which can be glimpsed, and through which Twain himself discovered, new possibilities for the work of fiction.

When Injun Joe's body is found at the mouth of McDougal's cave, where he starved to death behind the newly installed iron door, Tom gazes at the dead man's face, and is "touched, for he knew by his own experience how this wretch had suffered. His pity was moved" (238). Tom, of course, had faced a similar fate with Becky until he had miraculously found his way out, but there is another dimension to this recognition scene. For throughout the narrative the "Injun devil"—conjured into the narrative when Tom and Huck visit the graveyard to work their boyish incantations over a dead cat—haunts the boy as his dark double. When Joe and his companions first appear in the gloom, Huck cries out, "'It's the devils sure enough. . . . Lordy, Tom, we're goners!'"(73). Even when Joe proves corporeal enough to kill Dr. Robinson, he still carries with him an aura of the supernatural. His cool accusation that Muff Potter murdered the doctor leaves the boys certain that "this miscreant had sold himself to Satan" (89). Joe may not be "great Caesar's ghost!" (199), as Tom blurts out when he stumbles across his dead-drunk body in the back room of the Temperance Tavern, but it is he and his accomplice who actually haunt the house at the outskirts of town, and it is he who appears to Tom in the cave only as a bodiless apparition out of the dark.

Injun Joe is the corporeal realization of Tom's dreams. He embodies yet another comic literalization of Tom's boyhood fantasy, his wish to die temporarily. With his apparent imperviousness to the wrath of God and the justice of man, Joe becomes for the boys "the most balefully interesting object they had ever looked upon, and they could not take their fascinated eyes from his face" (89). But Injun Joe is more than a ghost out of boys' imaginations; he is a man—a man more potent, more fascinating, than any other male in the narrative. His furious plots of revenge violently realize Tom's naïve pirate fantasies; he inhabits the regions of boyhood adventure—the night, the haunted house, the cave; and he covets the things boys most covet—buried treasure and power. Most important, as the creature of boys' fantasies, he also suggests what will become of the dreamer; as both the destination of boyish fantasy and a possible destiny for boys, he is the father who speaks with authority.

Thus Tom's "abounding sense of relief and security" that follows his veiled self-recognition in the dead man's face: "he had not fully appreciated before, how vast a weight of dread had been lying upon him since the day he lifted his voice against this bloody-minded outcast" (238). Injun Joe is indeed an outcast; he not only marks the limits of the happy polity of St. Petersburg, he invades the novel's nostalgic asylum, threatening to transform entertainment into didacticism. With Injun Joe loose, how can the narrator let his boys out at night? They must be taught limits: they must learn a philosophy of difference between boys and men, to be sure, but more important, between legitimate and illegitimate.

The Welchman knows such a philosophy. When he hears Huck's breathless description of the villain's plans for Widow Douglas he hesitates, for Huck is only a boy full of a boy's fantasies: "When you talked about notching ears and slitting noses I judged that that was your own embellishment, because white men don't take that sort of revenge. But an Injun! That's a different matter, altogether" (214). Joe is for him an injun of destruction; but his philosophy is only half right, for Joe is a "half-breed," a son of miscegenation. Calling him an Injun is easier; it naturalizes his character, it makes him a savage, and it erases a scandal of the past—thereby eliding the sexual charge to any fascination with "savagery."

But Joe's origins lay not in the timeless fantasies of boys, but in the adult sphere of history and memory. "Five year ago you drove me away from your father's kitchen one night, when I come to ask for something to eat," he reminds Dr. Robinson before he murders him. "[W]hen I swore I'd get even with you if it took a hundred years, your father had me jailed for a vagrant. Did you think I'd forget? The Injun blood ain't in me for nothing" (74–75). Injuns never forget; only white men like Dr. Robinson have to be reminded. Unlike "The Author," however, Joe does not "pleasantly remind." His Injun ways have a point: he will wreak the revenge of the past on the present—first, by killing Dr. Robinson and, second, by doing to the Widow Douglas what her husband did to him:

> her husband was rough on me—many times he was rough on me—and mainly he was the justice of the peace that jugged me for a vagrant. And that ain't all. It ain't the millionth part of it! He had me *horsewhipped!*—horsewhipped in front of the jail, like a nigger!—with all the town looking on! HORSE-WHIPPED!—do you understand? He took advantage of me and died. But I'll take it out on *her*. . . . When you want to get revenge on a woman you don't kill her—bosh! you go for her looks. You slit her nostrils—you notch her ears, like a sow's! (207–8)

The Welchman then is half right: only an injun, an honest injun, will "take that sort of revenge" precisely because it mirrors his own physical humiliation administered jointly by Robinson's father and Judge Douglas. As Joe tells it, his anguish stems not so much from the ordeal of physical punishment, but from the way in which that punishment ritually dehumanized him into a horse, a nigger, a vagrant, and thus banished him from the happy polity. From that point on, "half-breed" means "Injun" means "horse." The outrage of his birth is officially forgotten, but a mutilated widow will remind them of the intolerance of their forgetting.

Thus, the threat of his fury lies not so much in his crimes—he was already "believed to have killed five citizens of the village" (241)—as in his insistence on tying revenge to the past. The persistence of his voice reminds St. Petersburg of its hypocrisy, the duplicity that lies beneath its benevolence. Aunt Polly cannot bring herself to "lash" Tom, but she could watch with all the town—Mrs. Harper, the minister, Mr. Dobbins, and Tom—as the law whipped some sense into Joe. "Spare the rod and spile the child, as the good Book says," and anything worse than a spoiled boy is a spoiled injun.

But Joe, unlike Tom, does not take his punishment as a matter of course; he has learned his lesson, even if it is not the one the scars on his back spell out for everyone else. He is beyond the gaze of discipline, moving along its borders, inhabiting the shadows. Lessons, however, must be learned; discipline and authority must be maintained. So, once again, he becomes the object of a ritual education. The subject of this learning, however, is not the "half-breed"—he is after all ineducable, a deviant—it is Tom who, at the murder trial, is subjected to the "penal discipline" behind the benevolent asylum of boyhood.

Ostensibly, the trial restores the idyllic balance that Dr. Robinson's murder threatened: it reinstates Muff Potter as the "respectable" (white) town drunk, publicly reveals Joe as the murderer, and elevates Tom to yet one more pedestal of celebrity. But the price for such resolution is the exposure of the language of absolute law: "By the oaths of citizens whose simple word is above suspicion," intones the prosecutor, "we have fastened this awful crime beyond all possibility of question, upon the unhappy prisoner at the bar. We rest our case here" (170). The fact that he refers to Muff Potter all the more confirms the ritualistic power of this language. For if, like the minister, the prosecutor—indeed, all the judges and lawyers—claims to speak for the town, he does so in a mean, "simple" language that, unlike that of the sermon, is invulnerable to the misreadings of boyhood and the irony of the narrator. The patriarchal presence, which had to this point appeared only in the impotent "tyrannies" of church and school and the veiled nostalgia of the narrator, here emerges in its full authority.

Because the law speaks with an authority grounded in its supposed discernment of truth and deviance, it is also capable of adjudicating the boundaries of culpable boyhood; for, in convicting Injun Joe, the man, it emphatically displaces Tom, the boy, who merely fantasizes about murder, Indians, and the like. While Injun Joe's social name undergoes yet another transformation—no longer merely a vagrant or even an Injun, he is now a legally defined "criminal"—Tom must answer as witness for the defense to the name "Thomas," "the name they lick me by," as he earlier told Becky Thatcher (55). Tom had answered to this name in school when he was punished for associating with Huck, when he claimed his Sunday-school Bible, and on

Examination Evening when he recited "the unquenchable and indestructible 'Give me liberty or give me death' speech" (155). Each time, however, he failed miserably, "utterly defeated" (156) by his failure to live up to his full name. Tom must have the liberty of his own stage or die a humiliating death. Such places as church and school make no place for boys.

It is equally as difficult to speak in court; Tom suffers from the same stage fright he endures during Examination Evening, even though the lawyer benevolently assures Tom, "Don't be afraid":

> "Thomas Sawyer, where were you on the seventeenth of June, about the hour of midnight?"
>
> Tom glanced at Injun Joe's iron face and his tongue failed him. The audience listened breathless, but the words refused to come. After a few moments, however, the boy got a little of his strength back, and managed to put enough of it into his voice to make part of the house hear:
>
> "In the graveyard!"
> "A little louder, please. Don't be afraid. You were—"
> "In the graveyard." (170–71)

The exact ascertainment of Tom's location in time and place, the insistence that he declare his presence out loud: these are the signatures of Bushnell's "police of discovery," exposing the playful deviance of boys to the gaze of men. Injun Joe may loom as a fearful presence, but Tom's hesitation comes as well from his precarious position as a witness against himself. When he and Huck had witnessed the murder, they fled the scene "speechless with horror" (78). Later they ratified this horror by signing in blood an oath to speechlessness, which they then buried "with some dismal ceremonies and incantations" (81). Their act stands as a fearful recognition of Joe's awful power; as Huck points out, Injun Joe "'wouldn't make any more of drownding us than a couple of cats, if we was to squeak 'bout this'" (79). But it also represents a vow to seal off the fantasy life of boyhood from the adult world of the village; as adventurers into the occult, they have willingly bound themselves to its laws.

Their refusal to talk preserves their sphere, at whatever fearful cost, from the prying attentions of adults. Tom's "harassed conscience," however—the portable parent, the internalized voice of the narrator's propriety—drives him to the attorney and shatters the hidden compact of boyhood (with this, "Huck's confidence in the human race was well nigh obliterated" [173]). In casting his lot with legitimate adult society against the criminal deviance of boys, he must speak the philosophy of distinction, the philosophy of manhood: the voice in the witness stand is not that of a boy, but that of the law—it speaks the same language as the scars on Injun Joe's back. The world of childhood is shorn of its "innocent" association with criminality and forcefully brought into the domain of the "simple word" of jurisprudence: when Tom tells of his bringing a dead cat, he elicits a "ripple of mirth" in the courtroom which is quickly "checked" by the straight and narrow purpose of authoritative truth. The trial thus makes visible the fence of propriety around the culture of boyhood. It may resolve Tom's "secret troubles" (92), but it does so only at the expense of polarizing the delectable idyll into a map of legitimacy and deviance. The comic irony of complicit fantasy is fractured into competing yet complementary elements of sanctioned truth and criminal falsehood. Innocent anarchy no longer so easily coincides with an idyllic world that embraces both the town and the boy.

Taken together, Tom and Joe emerge as subjects of a circumspect process of boundary formation and policing that aspires to incorporate a legitimate sphere of authority, a family-like space of benevolence and authority. Its purpose, however, is not so much the elimination of harmful outsiders as it is the regulation of the internal sphere. After all, Injun Joe's death comes not at the hands of his pursuers, but as the result of a parental concern for the safety of children: the door that transforms the cave into his tomb is erected to seal it off from the dangerous curiosity of inquisitive boys. In a similar gesture, Huck, too, is incarcerated by "the bars and shackles of civilization" when he is adopted by the Widow Douglas (255). Just as he is kept "clean and neat, combed and brushed," so too are the spaces of boys' adventures cleansed. Fueled by the "excitement" inspired by Tom's and Huck's discovery of gold, "Every 'haunted' house in St. Petersburg and the neighboring villages was dissected, plank by plank, and its foundations dug up and ransacked for hidden treasure—and not by boys, but men—pretty grave, unromantic men, too, some of them" (254).

With this, the asylum of childhood is complete. The common haunts of criminals and boys, the "dangerous" spaces of adventure, are cleansed; the play of childhood is interned in the space of discipline, surrounded by a "meticulously sealed wall, uncrossable in either direction." Tom, free from the nightmare of boyhood, secure in the approbation of Judge Thatcher (who now hopes to see Tom as "a great lawyer or a great soldier some day" [255]), understands the meaning of safe amusement. Pirates are out and robbers are in, Tom tells Huck: "A robber is more high-toned than what a pirate is." The only way to join his band of robbers is to remain "respectable" by enduring the tribulations of life at the widow's (258). Tom's is no longer the voice of boyhood, but the rightly constructed voice of the narrator.

This, then, is the lesson of *Tom Sawyer* that lies behind Twain's careful choice of words in explaining his writing to the critic Andrew Lang. "I have seldom deliberately tried to instruct [my audience]," wrote Twain in 1889, "but have done my best to entertain them. To simply amuse them would have satisfied my dearest ambition at anytime, for they could get instruction elsewhere, & I had two chances to help to the teacher's one: for amusement is a good preparation for study & a good healer of fatigue after it."[89] "Simple" amusement is safe amusement, an "entertainment" that may not "deliberately" instruct but nonetheless teaches. It is the only amusement consistent with a philosophy of distinction—not only between cultivation and entertainment, but also between boys and men, men and injuns, and legitimacy and deviance. For a true author does not threaten work, he supports it and makes it easier; he returns the reader refreshed to "the bars and shackles" of legitimate manhood. This is the philosophy that Tom, the narrator, and Twain share in common; it defines the limits of their amusement, and it sets the stage for their entertainment. But the narrator virtually disappears in the novel's final pages, and with him goes the comic complicity that framed even the trial. Tom's bargain with Huck unfolds not in the ironic aura of nostalgia, but as a stark, uneasy accommodation to the patriarchal voice of the law unleashed at the trial. If, for Tom, robbers are nothing more than aristocratic pirates—"dukes and such"—for Twain, they represent an uneasy recognition of how "safe" his amusement really is.

Tom's sobering duplicity in the final chapter suggests that, with the trial, Twain shifted his narrative focus from depicting the nostalgia of boyhood to baring, much like Bushnell and Abbott do in their prescriptive texts, the disciplinary limits of such a vision. With this shift came a concomitant revision of Twain's aspirations for his own authorship. Twain's process of composing his novel suggests as much.[90] Twain wrote *Tom Sawyer* in three widely spaced bursts of effort—during the winter of 1872–73, the spring and summer of 1874, and, finally, during the same months the following year, when he completed it. His first sitting brought him only as far as near the end of chapter 4, when Tom presents himself to receive his Bible. The second period of sustained work carried Twain through chapter 18, in the midst of Tom and Becky's comic courtship. Up to this point, Twain worked by embellishing and stringing together incidents from his own memory often jotted in the margins of his draft. So loose was his plotting that the initial plan of following Tom into manhood had exerted virtually no influence on the material. Twain even considered resolving the murder question by burning Muff Potter to death while in jail, itself a reworking of memory that would have released the threat of Tom's knowledge to the "secret troubles" of boyhood.

When he returned to the manuscript the next summer, he finally united Becky and Tom in love and then apparently planned to follow this chapter with the picnic to Jackson's Island (the present chapter 29). Instead, he began directly with the trial scene.[91] As he initially conceived it, this, too, would have resolved the problem of Injun Joe's revenge. Identified as the murderer, Injun Joe would have been subsequently dealt with by one Ezra Ward, a schoolmate of Aunt Polly, who would somehow lift Tom's "burden" of fear about the half-breed's continued freedom. Instead, Twain once again changed his mind, and not only refused his protagonist relief, but fashioned a narrative in which all roads lead to Injun Joe. Tom hunts for treasure and meets his devil double; he wanders the cave with Becky and encounters him again. In between, the boy spends his time following the outcast.

Twain's ruminations over the plot keynote a more fundamental change in the narrative. No longer does the boyish pursuit of desire disrupt the domesticating spaces of home, school, and church; rather, it carries Tom and Huck outward to the mysterious realms of the haunted house, the woods of Cardiff Hill, and McDougal's Cave.

As such, even as the trial forcefully dissociates Tom and Injun Joe on the scale of legitimacy and deviance, the novel's conceptual geography all the more insistently asserts the link between fantasy and criminality. As Injun Joe hurls himself out of the courtroom window to escape capture, Tom plunges into the taboo spaces of night in pursuit of adventure.

The most fearful space of course is McDougal's Cave, the "intricate tangle of rifts and chasms" where Tom and Becky await their fate: "labyrinth underneath labyrinth, and no end to any of them. No man 'knew' the cave. That was an impossible thing" (204). The cave is a place where fascination outstrips knowledge: its "secret depths," its "bewitching" sights, and "fantastic" architecture leave Tom and Becky "wondering and admiring" (222–23). When Tom, defeated by the cave's labyrinthine passages, shouts for help, his echoes painfully remind him that he has crossed beyond the protective borders of the asylum of childhood, beyond the reach of his would-be rescuers. Despite—indeed, because of—the ordeal that Tom endures with Becky, he returns as soon as he can. For, if the cave's dangerous spaces confound the knowledge of men, they echo and magnify the desires of boys; they protect in their inscrutability the "thing" that boys covet more than jam, cats, bugs, apples, and Bibles.

"There comes a time in every rightly constructed boy's life when he has a raging desire to go somewhere and dig for hidden treasure" (175), and it is this desire, imaged in Tom's fantasy as "a brass pot with a hundred dollars in it, all rusty and gay, or a rotten chest full of di'monds" (177), that leads him back to the cave with Huck. What he finds, like the Sunday-school tokens or Ben Rogers' apple, possesses a double meaning. On the one hand, the money he claims provides a miraculous wealth that installs Tom at the pinnacle of community status; on the other, it is the token of yet another scandalous past. Just as Joe is not strictly an injun, but a half-breed, so too the gold Tom empties on Widow Douglas's parlor table is not just money, but the currency of illicit history, buried by "Murrel's gang," claimed by Injun Joe, and invested for Tom's future.[92]

Gold pieces can be cleansed of their past. Put in a bank, they will, for all intents and purposes, lose their materiality; transformed into currency, the money will generate its own magical interest to finance Tom's, and presumably Huck's, "one horse" futures. But the damage is, in a sense, already done. As yet one more trace of the collectively repressed and forgotten, the coins suggest the most threatening dimension of boyish adventure: the uncanny way it disinters a past that constantly challenges nostalgic memory. Boys must be sealed off not from their own fantasies, but from the "haunts of men" (102) and the sensuous trace of illicit history. In the final nine chapters, Tom and Huck inhabit a world as sensational as Tom's fantasies of revenge and more frightening than the graveyard, precisely because it is a world where the dead remain unburied. "Blame it," sighs Huck, "I don't like ha'nted houses, Tom. Why, they're a dern sight worse'n dead people. Dead people might talk, maybe, but they don't come sliding around in a shroud, when you ain't noticing, and peep over your shoulder all of a sudden and grit their teeth, the way a ghost does" (181). Ghosts know no discipline; they speak out of turn about things that should go unsaid; they sound a "sepulchral note" (180) that means (to be mean). The voices of the night and the fantasies of boyhood are the barely perceptible traces of the past, much like the graffiti in McDougal's Cave, described as a "tangled web-work of names, dates, post-office addresses, and mottoes with which the rocky walls had been frescoed" in candle smoke (222). Amid these ghostly signatures of forgotten times, the nonsensical cravings of boyhood meet the criminality of Injun Joe, who uses these haunted places as refuges from the authority of the law.

Boys enact an Odyssean exploration of those spaces designated deviant and criminal, even as the trial and the subsequent cleansing of St. Petersburg seal legitimate boyhood in its asylum. Such wanderings cannot map such a world—it remains too supernatural, too fantastic, too unknowable. Rather, they map the limits of the legitimate, the power beneath the benevolence that produces these boundaries. The novel links the narrator's philosophy of manhood with the law's philosophy of difference; it links authority and deviance. It expands and fractures the rhetoric of boyhood with which the text was originally conceived.

Out of the representation of these spaces there begins to emerge a new figure of the storyteller and a new understanding on Twain's part of the cultural work of fiction. The tourist and the prospector were born in a world of comic equivalences—Paris is Smyrna is Jerusalem; gold exists only in claims—that provocatively eroded the differences between things and words and, ultimately, between culture and capital. From the beginning, however, the split between Tom and "The Author" signals a fiction grounded in a world of differences—between boy and man, performer and writer, between naïve insider and deviant outsider, between amusement and cultivation. If the frame of nostalgia works to blur these distinctions, if it functions to install "The Author" in his indulging benevolence as the masculine authority of safe, domestic amusement, the problem of Injun Joe violates the meticulous wall of his fiction. As the moniker "half-breed" suggests, Joe embodies the very distinctions that nostalgia would suppress; it suggests that he is as logical a product of the exclusionary vision of nostalgia as is Tom. Insofar as his early appearance makes legitimate Tom's boyish naïveté, Injun Joe links the right constructions of boyhood, and thus the flights of fiction, to the making of deviance.

By the end of the novel, it is precisely this deviance that—like the bad boys who fascinate Rollo—so grips the attention of Twain's novel. Like Tom and Huck, Twain brings back the sheer bulk of "tarnished coins," the stuff of desire, the fruits of criminality, and dumps them on the parlor table. He rummages the spaces of the taboo to discover "novelties to tell the upper world about" (223). That rummaging, however, uncovers not just the stuff of nightmares, but also the boundary-making activity—the policing of social and cultural distinction that designates certain dreams as nightmares. In exploring the boundaries between the legitimate and the taboo, Twain also began to disrupt the boundaries between fiction and authoritative rhetoric.

As such, perhaps the most representative figure of the storyteller in the tale is not Tom, but the man whose purpose set the tale of Injun Joe in motion: Dr. Robinson. It is he who refuses Joe food, thereby drawing the initial line of propriety; and it is he who hires the half-breed and Muff Potter to disinter the body. As a man of science, a man of the gaze, he embodies the text's implicit philosophy of authority: he digs up the buried past in order to know it and to use that knowledge in the present. The author also digs, his nostalgia uncovering the interred past to the gaze of common day. But this amusement cannot remain safe: by representing this buried world as an object of fascination, it carries with it a knowledge that releases the haunting cry of offended history. Thus, if Twain began his first novel in the full grip of his culture's nostalgia for boyhood, if he sought to appropriate the rhetoric of masculine domestic expertise to authorize his own "composite order," he returned to it to fracture the image of play, exposing the dark underside to the profession of utopian faith inherent in the dream of childhood. In doing so, he not only exposed the limits of respectable society, he made legible the process by which these limits were set. In this light, the novel was for Twain not a finished work, but the inscription of a process of discovery. "Entertainment" could no longer, in Twain's mind, constitute "mere amusement": to practice the art of fiction now entailed at some level confronting "the charm of its flow" (252) (as Tom's story about finding the gold is characterized) that would take his narrative through a landscape polarized by his own quest for cultural authority. Thus, if Tom's story is closed before he reaches maturity, Twain, in the course of composition, came of age himself as an author of fiction. His new, and problematic, awareness led him almost immediately to begin yet another revision of his utopian narrative, in what would eventually become *Adventures of Huckleberry Finn.*

FOUR

❧

"By the Book"

Adventures of Huckleberry Finn

I. On the Verge of Authorship

Adventures of Huckleberry Finn (1885) follows *Tom Sawyer* (1876) as both its sequel and its revision. The latter, after all, had not fulfilled Twain's initial plans for following Tom into adult life. "If I went on, now, & took him into manhood," wrote Twain to Howells in his well-known letter on finishing his first novel, "he would just be like all the one-horse men in literature. . . . By & by I shall take a boy of twelve & run him on through life (in the first person) but not Tom Sawyer."[1] Already, in Twain's mind, Huck may well have been that boy; he may well have offered Twain another opportunity to carry out his intention to write some sort of bildungsroman. But, as he appears in the first pages of his book, Huck is a character with more of a past than a future. Huck is, as the title page tells us, "Tom Sawyer's Comrade." From the opening line—"You don't know about me, without you have read a book by the name of 'The Adventures of Tom Sawyer,'"—through the reprise of "the way that the book winds up," to when Huck joins "Tom Sawyer's Gang" of robbers as he was promised when his friend found him in the hogshead, *Tom Sawyer* is everywhere present in the first chapters.[2] Even as late as 1883, after Twain had "pigeonholed" his new novel for several years, he still regarded it as "a kind of companion to Tom Sawyer." In part, Twain was thinking strictly in terms of his books' market potential: his first novel still sold well after seven years, why not hitch his new effort to its coattails and realize even bigger profits? As he wrote to Howells, "Although I mean to publish Huck in a volume by itself, I think I will also jam it & Sawyer into a volume *together* at the same time, since Huck is in some sense a continuation of the former story."[3]

Yet, even as Twain linked his two books together in both generic and narrative terms, he hedged his bet. *Huckleberry Finn* is only "a kind of companion" to, and "in some sense a continuation" of, its predecessor: as sure as he was about the connection between the two books and the two characters, Twain had difficulty defining the exact nature of their relationship. Huck's origins may lie in Twain's romance of childhood, but he never fully inhabits *Tom Sawyer*'s architecture of nostalgia. He never fully fits the restless "pattern" of boyhood, and he has no "raging desire" for either gold or "glory and eclat." Physiologically, Huck may be a boy, but socially he is a "juvenile pariah": he does "not have to go to school or to church, or call any being master or obey anybody." The difference between the two characters emerges most clearly at the end of *Tom Sawyer*. While the demise of Injun Joe and the subsequent cleansing of St. Petersburg frees Tom of his "secret troubles" and liberates him to the safety of a "rightly constructed boy's life," Huck is "dragged" and "hurled" into society. As he tells Tom, his very identity is imperiled: "I've tried it, and it don't work. . . . It ain't for me; I ain't used to it." "The widder's good to me, and friendly," admits Huck, "but I can't stand them ways", precisely because "them ways" threaten to transform him into none other than Tom himself. "I got to go to church and sweat and sweat— I hate them ornery sermons! I can't ketch a fly in there, I can't chaw, I got to wear shoes all Sunday . . . everything's so awful reglar a body can't stand it." Down to the urge to catch a fly, Huck feels the details of his life transformed into those of Tom's. Thus, it is no surprise that when Tom responds simply, "Well, everybody does that way," Huck retorts, "it don't make no difference. I ain't everybody, and I can't *stand* it. It's awful to be tied up so."[4]

Huck is right: it *does* make a difference primarily because Huck is different; he has no interest in entering the domestic asylum of boyhood. What for Tom is a "natural" state of boyhood is for Huck entrapment: to be offered a clean bed and new clothes, to be "rightly constructed," is to be "tied up." When Tom convinces Huck to return nonetheless to the widow's, their compact is uneasy, at best conditional. Twain patches over these troubles with his abrupt ending to *Tom Sawyer*, but it is precisely this fissure of unease in the asylum of childhood that he opens wide in *Huckleberry Finn*. "Well, then, the old thing commenced again" (2), sighs Huck, as he takes up the story in his own narrative, burdened with the nagging injunctions of Miss Watson: "'Don't put your feet up there, Huckleberry;' and 'don't scrunch up like that, Huckleberry— set up straight;' and . . . 'Don't gap and stretch like that, Huckleberry—why don't you try to behave?'" (3). The scope of "the old thing" is suggested by his name: "Huckleberry," like "Thomas," like "Injun," is the name they lick him by. And lick him they do. Huck is locked in the closet, he receives more than one "good going-over" (13), but, most of all, he suffers repeated verbal humiliations. "Why don't you try to behave?" pleads Miss Watson as she tries to beat some sense into her charge, asking, in effect, why don't you try to be a boy? He doesn't try, because he is different. Like the half-breed, his lessons teach him that he is an outsider—that, after all, he is not Tom: "the hiding I got next day done me good and cheered me up" (18).

St. Petersburg compensates Tom for the petty tyrannies he must endure—it is, after all, where he finds his audience, his glory and eclat. For Huck, not even the Widow Douglas's image of heaven, delicious enough "to make a body's mouth water," can tempt him to change his ways. As he did at the end of *Tom Sawyer*, Huck settles the issue conditionally: "seeing I was so ignorant and so kind of low-down and ornery," and seeing as Providence may be the place for everyone who prays, Huck will make do in "the bad place" (13, 14, 3)—after all, he "ain't everybody." Nor does "Tom Sawyer's Gang" offer any relief. When a promised ambush of an arab caravan turns out to be nothing more than the disruption of a Sunday-school picnic, Huck quits in disgust: "I judged that all that stuff was only just one of Tom Sawyer's lies. I reckoned he believed in the A-rabs and the elephants, but as for me I think different. It had all the marks of a Sunday school" (17).

Huck's "thinking different" suggests that if *Huckleberry Finn* serves as "a kind of companion" to *Tom Sawyer*, it does so as a starker drama of legitimacy and deviance, one that recalls more the plot of Injun Joe than the nostalgia of boyhood. In the early chapters, in particular, Huck's resolute marginality exposes as coercion what was, in *Tom Sawyer*, the putatively benevolent process of definition, exclusion, and protection that formed the meticulous asylum of boyhood. Huck, according to the rules of St. Petersburg, must belong—to Tom Sawyer's Gang, to the widow's vision of heaven, to Miss Watson's world of domestic propriety. Even Pap, whose animalistic drunkenness and incoherent ravings place him completely outside the purlieus of domestic culture, is "adopted" by the new judge, who vows "to make a man of him" (26). The judge sees such adoption as a matter of "reform," but Huck sees his own case as a matter of "sivilizing": the power to decide, in Pap's words, "who was Huck Finn's boss" (29). The law may eventually decide against Pap, just as earlier it grants him custody, but "everybody" assumes that Huck can be nothing more than someone's property. Thus Huck's decision to light out, to "get so far away that the old man nor the widow couldn't ever find me any more" (32): "All I wanted was to go somewhere," Huck insists, "all I wanted was a change, I warn't particular" (4).

"Reform," "sivilizing": this is familiar territory for the author of a "rightly constructed boy's life." Yet, if the making of character binds *Huckleberry Finn* to *Tom Sawyer*, it is where the former locates the scene of that making that so thoroughly separates them. In the world of *Tom Sawyer*—where boys are produced by the benevolent machinery of home, church, school, and the courts—running away would be enough. As both Injun Joe and Tom realize, escaping the Bushnellian world of parental knowledge is a spatial matter, a matter of finding some*where* to hide: Jackson's Island, McDougal's Cave, Texas. That most of these spaces do not survive the "unromantic" cleansing of adults suggests that, in Twain's world, such promise is only fleeting; but the text nonetheless stands witness to the possibility of living outside. It is this spatial logic that inspires Huck's romance of escape, but it is a romance that is everywhere undercut by what could only be described as an internal logic of "sivilizing." When Huck escapes St. Petersburg, a few idyllic moments on the raft notwithstanding, he travels more deeply into the dark heart of "sivilizing": the Grangerford feud, the confidence schemes of the duke and the dauphin, Tom's frantic "evasion," and finally the benevolent grasp of Aunt Sally—all entangle Huck in subtle nets of property and propriety. Each of his subsequent flights, in turn, resumes the same search for a "comfortable" existence, "free" from the "close" places of "sivilizing," that he had begun when Tom found him in the hogshead.

But even this formulation misses the point: Huck's problem with escape lies not in civilization's ubiquity. What he most struggles to escape is embodied in the verb "sivilizing," a process that constitutes and incorporates the self, rather than in the noun "civilization," a word that never appears in the text. For Huck, it matters less where he is than who he is. Thus, the noun of choice to describe his ordeal is "conscience," the one Twain used when he described his novel as one "where a sound heart & a deformed conscience come into collision & conscience suffers defeat."[5] Tom has a conscience, but his is so heavily accented by the narrative voice of adult nostalgia as to seem, at the least, extraneous and, at the most, irrelevant. Huck's too speaks its own mind—"a person's conscience ain't got no sense, and just goes for him *anyway*" (290)—but, for him, it sounds from within, a foreign parasite, yet integral to who he is. Its origins, as Henry Nash Smith has shown, lie in Miss Watson's plodding maxims and the domestic proprieties of St. Petersburg, but it has long since left its institutional, much less geographical, place for the more shifting grounds of character.[6] Thus, conscience "sivilizes" wherever one is: Huck must escape from himself.

This need is made all the more urgent and difficult to fulfill by the peculiar way in which Huck's conscience is "deformed." Twain may have summarized what he saw as the book's drama as a whole, but his language also refers to a specific moment of "collision": when Huck uneasily comes to terms with the implications of his companionship with Jim and confronts a "conscience" that insists that Huck return his friend to his "rightful" owner. Insofar as his decision to "go to hell" and rescue Jim recalls his easier, but no less pointed, choice of Miss Watson's "bad place," the scene once again affirms that Huck "ain't everybody." But it also indelibly binds "sivilizing" and slavery, suggesting, as Forrest Robinson has argued, that the "utterly intolerable obstacles of human freedom that Huck associates with civilization, and more than once rejects, are in fact shadows cast by Jim and the monstrous institution that binds him." Just like the Sunday school that teaches Huck about "the bad place," the institution of slavery is virtually invisible in *Huckleberry Finn*; there are no slave auctions, no whippings, no chains. Rather, it is in Huck's mind, or, more accurately, in his language, that the two come together in what Robinson calls a "pathological strand of civilization" that works "time and again to undermine his instinctive sense of human fellowship with Jim."[7]

In one sense, Robinson only reiterates Twain's evaluation of his novel: the collision between "civilization" and "instinctive sense," rather than that between "conscience" and "heart," constitutes the major elements of the text's essentially interior drama of "personal makeup." At the same time, by displacing "conscience" with "civilization," and by darkening the light of the latter with the "shadows" of slavery, Robinson subtly rewrites Twain's psychological formulation in terms more forthrightly ideological. Huck's dilemma is as societal as it is personal; "sivilizing" is as much a matter of incorporation as it is strictly of socialization. Thus, Huck's response to Aunt Sally's concern over his fictional steamboat accident—"'Good gracious! anybody hurt?' 'No'm. Killed a nigger.'" (279)—can be seen as raising a question of character. Does Huck believe what he says despite his previous resolution to follow his heart and free Jim from slavery? Or is his a tactical response to a putatively kind but essentially racist listener? But there is no way to decide this: sincerity—the yardstick of sentimental character evoked by Twain's formulation—is irrelevant precisely because it is Huck who narrates his own "collision." This reticence over character leads to a more searching question. How is Huck put in a position either to reproduce a racist discourse he has rejected or to so segregate his active intentions (to free Jim) from his verbal response that he almost literally does not hear what he says? Or, to put the issue in more general terms: how do beliefs, actions, social institutions, and social discourses work to produce "personal makeup," which in turn both reproduces and embodies "sivilizing?"

On another level, precisely these questions, as Steven Mailloux has argued, have dogged the text itself since the Concord Public Library refused—soon after it was published—to put the book on its shelves, declaring it "of a class that is more profitable for the slums than it is for respectable people, and . . . trash of the veriest sort."[8] At stake were the very links between cultural distinction and literature that Twain had engaged since *The Innocents Abroad* and had most recently explored in his speech at the Whittier Birthday banquet.[9] The library, as the Boston *Globe* put it, had drawn "the line on literature," separating "coarse" productions like Twain's from "the classic tomes that educate and edify the public."[10] Yet, as both quotations make clear, the canvas upon which Concord drew this line stretched over, in Mailloux's words, the framing "assumption that fiction ha[d] real, tangible effects on [in particular] juvenile behavior."[11] As he and Russell Reising suggest, it is precisely the text's propensity for provoking debates over the "effects" of literature on readers and the place of literature in society that best accounts for the history of both its popular and critical reception. Van Wyck Brooks's disappointment over Twain's feminization and his pursuit of the market, Lionel Trilling's and Leo Marx's use of the novel as a stage for their diverging inquiries into the links between aesthetic form and cultural politics, contemporary debates over the novel's racial politics and its presence in the schools— all stem from, in Reising's terms, how uncomfortably the novel fits "liberalism's basic premises about individuality" and the educational efficacy of literature.[12]

The persistence of such irresolution over the text suggests that Twain drew through the novel itself "the line on literature." As Mailloux has argued, the text enacts an "ideological performance" that has challenged its readers to confront the tensions between two diverging uses of the literary: "social critique and entertaining humor."[13] From Miss Watson's biblical literalism, to Huck's lectures to Jim on the indulgences of royalty, to the frantic comedy of Tom Sawyer's use of adventure fiction as conduct guides, *Huckleberry Finn* raises questions about the place of fiction and the literary in ideological discourse. Thus, Twain's uncertainty over the relationship between *Tom*

Sawyer and *Huckleberry Finn* may well have stemmed from his awareness of how profoundly the latter extended and complicated, even as it built upon, the former. In splitting boy protagonist and adult narrator in *The Adventures of Tom Sawyer*, Twain was able to figure his authorial performance as the function of a discourse of cultural distinctions between boyhood and manhood, deviance and authority, entertainment and uplift. Casting Huck as the author of his own tale, however, allowed Twain to craft a drama of ideology and identity that make problematic the divisions of the previous fiction. The result is a text that bears not just an uncertain connection to *Tom Sawyer*, but to the literary in general. To read *Huckleberry Finn* in these terms is to take seriously the "Notice" that prefaces the narrative, warning "persons" against finding "motive," "moral," or "plot." The threat of violent reprisal by the "Chief of Ordinance" recalls not so much the glint of Emerson's bowie knife as it does the purposeful contradictions of the writer who put it in his hand.

❦

The collision between conscience and heart is not the only dimension of "sivilizing" in the novel, nor is "personal makeup" the only product of this collision. Nor, for that matter, is the line of literature the only one drawn in the narrative. For, at the heart of the novel, lies the fictional transformation of the outcast boy first encountered in *Tom Sawyer*—a boy who, at the outset of his own tale, is "so ignorant and so kind of low-down and ornery" that he can only sign an "X" to join Tom's gang of robbers—into the writer of his own text. Huck's assumption of authorship and, finally, of the narrative itself stands as the most compelling product of "sivilizing" and its most divided form of resistance.

This drama emerges early in the narrative, when, after concluding his reprise of *Tom Sawyer*, Huck turns to describing the ordeals of his new life:

> After supper [the Widow Douglas] got out her book and learned me about Moses and the Bulrushers; and I was in a sweat to find out all about him; but by and by she let it out that Moses had been dead a considerable long time; so then I didn't care no more about him; because I don't take no stock in dead people.
>
> Pretty soon I wanted to smoke, and asked the widow to let me. But she wouldn't. She said it was mean practice and wasn't clean, and I must try to not do it any more. That is just the way with some people. They get down on a thing when they don't know nothing about it. Here she was a bothering about Moses, which was no kin to her, and no use to anybody, being gone, you see, yet finding a power of fault with me for doing a thing that had some good in it. And she took snuff too; of course that was all right, because she done it herself. (2–3)

As numerous critics have noted, it is not just the line of literature, but the line of literacy, that runs directly through passages such as these.[14] Huck's language here is resolutely linear, with phrases linked by "and" and "but"; it seems to be a discourse that has not been reworked, but spoken as thoughts occur, effortlessly turning from the narration of past events to conversational asides in the present tense. The marred grammar and Huck's easy, colloquial digressions inscribe in his voice a politics of what Henry Nash Smith has called the "vernacular perspective"—a localized, essentially oral language, consciously positioned against the prescriptive norms that dominate the habits and language of St. Petersburg.[15] Yet Huck's language is not speech captured by writing, but writing verging on speech. His voice is not marked by the phonetic misspellings and apostrophes that conventionally (and elsewhere in the text) register the idiomatic speech of comic vernacular characters.[16] Rather, his linguistic struggle emerges in a series of divergent metonymies: "learned" replaces "taught," "Moses and the Bulrushers" replaces "Moses in the bulrushes," "no more" substitutes for "any more." Far from registering orality, the grammatical mistakes, the often halting vocabulary, all register what Neil Schmitz has called "the continuous ordeal of Huck's writing," his ongoing struggle to put words on the page.[17]

Moreover, Huck's struggle *with* his narrative is also implicated in his struggle *in* his narrative. When he writes, "She said it was mean practice and wasn't clean, and I must try to not do it any more," the imperfect parallel phrasing does more than evoke his labor with the pen; it also enacts the collision of two voices. By the very awkwardness with which they are integrated into the sentence, words like "mean practice," "clean," and "not do it any more," stand out as the widow's words. As they were uttered, they conveyed the power to prevent Huck from smoking. As they stand in the narrative, however, they have lost that authority. Huck's is the direct language here, not hers; he is the one who positions the reader in relation to what happens. In telling his story, he works to argue a case, to recruit the reader to affirm his skepticism of adult authority and thus confirm his self-proclaimed difference. This incident sets the strategy for his entire narrative: Huck proposes to negate his subjection to the incorporating fictions of others by making himself the subject of his own writing. At the end of the book, he claims the last word in his dialogue with authority, by signing his name: "Yours Truly Huck Finn." Huck's ordeal of writing allows him to assume the authority denied him in the story.

Yet, even as Huck's writing works to establish his difference, it also implicates him in the very process of incorporation he resists. Immediately following the passage above, Huck tells how Miss Watson "took a set at me now, with a spelling-book. She worked me middling hard for about an hour, and the widow made her ease up. I couldn't stood it much longer" (3). Yet one more incident in Huck's comic struggle, it also marks the contradictory origins of his narrative act. For, as his language betrays, despite all of Huck's resistance, he learned his lesson well: Huck can spell quite proficiently. This is only the first instance of Huck's education, a process about which he tells little. After several months, during which "I had been to school most all the time," Huck admits that he "could spell, and read, and write just a little" (18). Despite all of his resistance to the attentions of his adoptive guardians, Huck soon adjusts to life as a civilized boy: "At first I hated the school, but by and by I got so I could stand it. . . . So the longer I went to school the easier it got to be. I was getting sort of used to the widow's ways, too, and they weren't so raspy on me. . . . I liked the old ways best, but I was getting so I liked the new ones, too, a little bit" (18). While this may seem a kind of tactical adaptation to his new life, it is clear that his ability to find some sense of comfort in domestic culture continues even after he makes his escape from St. Petersburg. The Grangerford clan is certified as "a mighty nice family" with a house "that was so nice and had so much style" (136). While there, Huck is inspired enough by his newfound comforts to don clothes, read John Bunyan's *Pilgrim's Progress*, and even try his hand at fashioning a few verses for the departed daughter Emmeline.

But it is Huck's final paragraph that suggests how integral the cultural politics of authorship are to the struggle between "sivilizing" and freedom thematized in the novel:

> Tom's most well, now, and got his bullet around his neck on a watch-guard for a watch, and is always seeing what time it is, and so there ain't nothing more to write about, and I am rotten glad of it, because if I'd a knowed what a trouble it was to make a book I wouldn't a tackled it and ain't agoing to no more. But I reckon I got to light out for the Territory ahead of the rest, because aunt Sally she's going to adopt me and sivilize me and I can't stand it. I been there before. (362)

As the shift from past to present tense signals, Huck "makes" his book as Tom recovers from the wound he suffered during the evasion. As such, Huck's writing is the penultimate point of his story; his narrative is, in some way, the product of the very tale he tells. At the same time, however, the narrative is not enough: confronted once again with the prospect of being "sivilized," as he was when he and Tom found the gold, Huck casts aside the "trouble" of composition. In an act that registers his desperation, as he does every time he finds himself in a "close place," he plans to "light out." This time, however, his resolution is accompanied by a definitive gesture: silence. Writing, for Huck, functions both as a necessary prelude to his planned escape from "sivilizing" and as yet one more "close place" to flee.

Thus, in situating Huck as the narrator of his own tale of "sivilizing," Twain locates the most profound dimension of the text's drama of difference in the composition of, as the book's working title put it, "Huck Finn's Autobiography."[18] Huck resists the incorporating fictions of others by empowering himself as the subject of his own discourse, yet his autobiographical strategy is itself the product of his submission to an education that reforms him into a literate subject. The result, as Twain implies, is a subject divided between conscience and heart: in attempting to write himself *out* of the clutches of "sivilizing" even as his medium draws him *in*, Huck becomes different from himself.

Moreover, this ideological drama of literacy reaches, as it were, outside of the narrative. For St. Petersburg is not the only seat of propriety in the novel. Huck opens his narrative in contention with neither Miss Watson nor his conscience, but with "Mr. Mark Twain," the "maker," "The Author," of *Tom Sawyer*: "You don't know about me, without you have read a book by the name of "The Adventures of Tom Sawyer," but that ain't no matter. That book was made by Mr. Mark Twain, and he told the truth, mainly. There was things which he stretched, but mainly he told the truth." In the text's opening lines, Huck may not "compose" like the children at Examination Evening, nor does he evince the mild irony and erudition of the narrator of *Tom Sawyer*. Nonetheless, he assumes the role of "Mr. Mark Twain" even as he distances himself from it with his offhand criticism of his veracity. At one level, this merely anticipates the game of "sivilizing." At another, however, the opening suggests the extent to which Huck's struggle with literacy served as the site for Twain's complex attempt to explore the convergence of comic authorship and cultural authority. It suggests that the narrative provided Twain with the means not just to continue his own autobiography of authorship, but to confront critically the strategies of authority that shaped—and were, in turn, shaped by—the making of the literate and authorial self.

The first edition of the book initiated this authorial posturing even before Huck began his narrative. For on the opening pages of the volume appeared two starkly contrasting illustrations. In one, Huck smiles at the viewer, holding in one hand a dead rabbit and in the other a rifle. The other features a photograph of an austerely lit bust of Twain in profile "From the Bust by Karl Gerhardt," captioned with his signature. The inclusion of the latter image had incurred extra expense and time; the production run was well along when Twain ordered the image tipped in by hand to every volume. Very likely, Twain, who was pleased with the sculpture, saw it as a way to increase his sales.[19] Yet there is more at stake, for the image is not only of Twain as "a standard author," it also signifies a cultural arbiter—Twain had acted as Gerhardt's patron, financing a year of study in Europe and helping gain him commissions.[20] As such, the severe bust is "Mr. Mark Twain" not as the humorist, but as the famous author of *Tom Sawyer*, a literary authority as fully dignified and formal as those Twain burlesqued at the Whittier Birthday dinner. It represents the writer shaped in the image of the author, both the model for Huck's own authorship and his dialectical opposite.

The two prefatorial notes following the frontispieces continue this authorial posturing. Both the "Notice" placed "BY ORDER OF THE AUTHOR Per G.G., CHIEF OF ORDNANCE" ("G. G." may have been a private joke on the "iron man" General Grant) and the "Explanatory," in which "THE AUTHOR" pedantically identifies seven different dialects used in the text, continue the authorial jockeying for position initiated by the two images and continued between "Mr. Mark Twain" and Huck. If Huck's narrative is the work of a "low-down and ornery" boy, *Huckleberry Finn* is the "composite" creation of "Mr. Mark Twain," who is present in his text as a celebrity humorist, as a novelist and cultural icon, and, most powerfully, as the "ignorant" voice of Huck. Thus, the simple tactic of centering Huck as the teller gets caught up in a writerly game of trumps: who authorizes whom, and on what grounds? Such games enmesh Huck's struggles with literacy, conscience, and slavery in the production of the literary even as they suggest the degree to which literary authorship makes legitimate the literacy Huck embodies. With Huck as the fictional author of his narrative, *Huckleberry Finn* performs the scene of Twain's writing, defining a cultural space in which the act of writing itself is produced by a writer who, in turn, makes himself into an author. Inscribed in Huck's struggles to "make" his book are those of a writer to come to terms with the authority of his own authorship. Precisely these struggles shaped the local politics of Twain's most profound narrative engagement with the cultural significance of his own authorship.

II. Autobiography and the Making of the Literate Author

During the nine years that Twain wrestled with *Huckleberry Finn*, there is much to suggest a growing impatience with the authorial role he had built in the marketplace and thematized textually. On the one hand, Twain's astonishing activity between the summer of 1876 and August of 1885, the span of time during which he worked on his novel, suggests a writer hitting his stride; on the other, it betrays a fitful discomfort with his direction. No longer content to divide what were impressive profits, Twain broke with Bliss's American Publishing Company and began to finance his books with his own money, using first James Osgood to publish *The Prince and the Pauper* (1882) and *Life on the Mississippi* (1883), and then, having grown impatient with Osgood's inexperience in subscription marketing, founding in 1883 his own company, managed by and named for his nephew Charles Webster. He also invested heavily in a kaolotype printing process, and, during the same period, began a disastrous investment as a silent backer of the Paige typesetting machine. Like the comically dreaming prospector in *Roughing It* (1872), Twain was ready as a literary capitalist to turn words into money. This plunge into the marketing of words was accompanied both by his emergence as a literary celebrity of prodigious proportions and by a critical recognition as a "serious" author marked by, in the words of Howells's important 1882 article in *Century Magazine*, his "indignant sense of right and wrong, a scorn of all affectation and pretense, an ardent hate of meanness and injustice."[21]

Yet, even as Twain exploited and reveled in this renown, he suffered from the burden of his celebrity. Flooded with requests for interviews, articles, books, and speeches, as well as requests to read manuscripts, sign autographs, and even endorse products and stock schemes, he regularly complained that his very success left him little time for the writing that had made him successful. As he put it in a letter, "Only Bunyan, Sir Walter Raleigh, the author of Don Quixotte [*sic*], & a few other people have had the *best* of opportunities for working, in this world. Solitary imprisonment, by compulsion, is the one perfect condition for perfect performance. No letters, no telegrams, no boxes, no responsibilities, no gaddings about, no seductive pleasures beckoning one away & dividing his mind."[22]

To be sure, Twain's restless search for a productive space represented an effort to shrug off the cares of business and celebrity: "The bane of Americans is overwork," he wrote to his brother Orion, "and the ruin of *any* work is a divided interest. Concentrate—*concentrate*. One thing at a time."[23] But it was also a sign of how much at a loss he was to establish just what kind of writer he would be. Even as his income, his growing critical reputation, and the tide of correspondence affirmed his fame as an author, the fitful diversity of his work points to how confused he was about what that fame implied.

Despite his complaints about lack of time, Twain undertook a wide range of literary projects, a remarkable number of which remained unfinished, attracting the fury of a week's or a month's interest only to be dropped again. Those he did finish betray a fitful grasping at various literary poses.[24] As a literary entrepreneur, he pursued fortune by investing much of his time in a series of dramatic efforts, including a play based on *Tom Sawyer*, a mystery burlesque entitled *Cap'n Simon Wheeler, The Amateur Detective* (1877) (in which he had hopes of acting), and collaborative efforts with Bret Harte and Howells. As a humorist, he published a number of short stories and worked on editing his *Library of Humor* (1888). He also privately circulated *1601*, a bawdy sketch of the private conversation of Queen Elizabeth's court. In 1878, Twain contracted with Bliss to write *A Tramp Abroad* (1880) during his planned visit to Europe, only to find he could no longer approach Europe as an "innocent," as he did in his first book. Four years later, Twain returned to quite different origins when, in 1882, he visited the Mississippi to collect material for what would become *Life on the Mississippi*, a subscription book expanding on his "Old Times on the Mississippi." A year earlier, he had published *The Prince and the Pauper*, a book conceived, executed, and published as a venture into literary propriety. Subtitled "A Tale for Young People of All Ages," it was self-consciously tasteful enough for Howells to review it as "a manual of republicanism which might fitly be introduced into the schools."[25] Twain himself claimed, "I like this tale better than *Tom Sawyer*—because I haven't put any fun in it."[26]

Taken together, the broad range of Twain's literary and financial efforts suggests a writer as confused about his place in the literary market as he was eager to corner it. Was he a humorist, a novelist, an editor, a publisher, a dramatist, a genteel author? To be sure, insisting on too clear a distinction between each of these roles is to miss how useful all of them were to a committed literary entrepreneur. Nonetheless, the range of failures and successes, and the frustrations and anxieties that accompanied them, points to a writer driven by the same question that ignited the Whittier Birthday and the "Plymouth Rock" speeches (both of which he delivered during this same period) and that fueled *Huckleberry Finn*: what is an author?

It may well have been this question that led Twain to decide that it would be "fatal" to continue *Tom Sawyer* or to begin any other project "in any shape but autobiographically."[27] But *Huckleberry Finn* was not the only example of Twain's thinking "autobiographically" during the period. To be sure, he had grown adept after six years at telling at least some version of his own story; just months before his evaluation of *Tom Sawyer*, he had finished his satisfying, and what would prove to be successful, reminiscence, "Old Times on the Mississippi." Within the next year, he had begun to speak of a more ambitious autobiographical project, arguing that "Every man feels that his experience is unlike that of anybody else, and therefore he should write it down."[28] A year later, he would add the second installment, entitled "Early Years in Florida, Missouri," to just such a project begun tentatively in 1870, which would later become his sprawling autobiography.

It was during 1877 as well (seven months after completing the first installment of *Huckleberry Finn*) that Twain plunged into yet another of his uncompleted enthusiasms: a savage burlesque autobiography in the voice of his older brother, Orion.[29] In part "Autobiography of a Damned Fool," as it was called, vented Twain's long-building frustrations over what he saw as his brother's failures. At the same time, its few frenetic chapters suggest that the form allowed Twain to return to some old concerns in a new way. On the surface, the manuscript's protagonist recalls the unfortunate Jacob Blivens. Like the earlier character, the damned fool labors mightily and sincerely to improve his character, falling prey to a series of misplaced and righteous enthusiasms for evangelical reform, "the religion of Mahomet," and temperance. But it is with his discovery of Benjamin Franklin's *Autobiography* ("a man after my own heart") that he most closely recalls Jacob and most clearly diverges from him. "[D]elighted and heartened to perceive . . . the resemblance" between himself and his hero, the fool initiates a program of rigorous self-training, with the *Autobiography* as his "model."[30] His absurdly literal efforts "to become everything that [Franklin] had been" end when he is brought "near to death's door" by following his hero's prescription for cold baths. Yet, even as he is cured of this regimen and turns elsewhere for inspiration, the damned fool remains comic victim to the letter of Franklin's text by literarily emulating his model with his own autobiography. Jacob Blivens wanted to be put in a Sunday-school book; the damned fool puts himself in his own story. The fool to reading reemerges in the fragment as a fool to writing.

The details of the fool's enthusiasms give evidence of Twain's fresh knowledge of Franklin's text.[31] (He did purchase, in 1875, the new edition of the *Autobiography*, based on its author's own manuscript.) More significant is Twain's response, voiced soon after he had put aside "Damned Fool," to Howells's query about appropriate texts for a series of "Choice Autobiographies": "Autobiog's? I didn't know there *were* any but old Franklin's & Benvenuto Cellini's."[32] This high opinion, coming as it did during a period when Twain turned more consciously to a number of autobiographical projects, suggests an important role for Franklin in Twain's search for "the sole form." More particularly, a fresh reading of "old Franklin's" memoir may well have led Twain to correct the "mistake" of *Tom Sawyer* with "Huck Finn's Autobiography." Thus, if anyone was fool to Franklin, it was Twain himself; and the product of that foolishness is both the drama of Huck's adoption of, and his struggle with, "sivilizing" literacy and Twain's own appropriation of that struggle for his own uses. Insofar as

Huck's effort "to make a book" reenacts Franklin's effort "to recollect a living of . . . life in Prose," *Huckleberry Finn* embeds the making of Mark Twain in one of his culture's most profound processes of legitimation: the literate construction of character.

❧

Twain's 1875 reading of Franklin was by no means his first encounter with him. As a young printer working in his brother's office, he had regularly set in type Franklin's maxims to fill the columns of Orion's paper. In 1853, while traveling the East, Twain made a point of visiting Franklin's grave in Philadelphia, and he participated in a banquet to raise money to build a monument to the patron figure of American printers.[33] In 1856, and again thirty years later, Twain delivered talks at the meeting of the Typothetae, a printer's organization that celebrated Franklin's birthday. Nor was Twain blind to the resemblance of his career to that of Franklin: "I had made of myself a tolerable printer," he wrote in *Roughing It*, "under the impression that I would be another Franklin some day, but somehow had missed the connection thus far."[34] Franklin's presence may have at times been so palpable that missing the connection may have been at least as important to Twain as making it. In a short piece entitled "The Late Benjamin Franklin" (1870), Twain comically presented Franklin as the representative father who had "early prostituted his talents to the invention of maxims and aphorisms calculated to inflict suffering upon the rising generation of all subsequent ages. His simplest acts, also, were contrived with a view to their being held up for the emulation of boys forever—boys who might otherwise have been happy. . . . Nowadays a boy cannot follow out a single natural instinct without tumbling over some of those everlasting aphorisms" seemingly invented to make "a Franklin of every father's fool." For the son who would escape the influence of such a "vicious disposition," Twain suggested that "the simple idea is to snub those maxims." This is exactly what he did throughout his career, regularly turning them into material for burlesque ("Never put off till to-morrow what you can do day after to-morrow just as well"; "Masturbation is the mother of invention").[35] However, snubbing, it seems, was not enough for Twain. His burlesques suggest a writer struggling under an anxiety of influence in a manner represented by Twain's lampoon of Orion (who, in fact, and often to Twain's impatience, wholeheartedly adopted Franklin as his hero).

Yet perhaps this is to put too Bloomian a cast on Twain's relationship to Franklin. For the target of his humor in both the essay and the fool's autobiography is not so much Franklin himself as it is the Franklin resurrected by fathers and fools who search his text for models of themselves. Franklin may well have represented for Twain a rival writer, but his autobiography also typified the power of public narrative to produce both authors and model readers. Orion's journalistic practice represents but a small instance of the remarkably wide currency of his maxims and aphorisms, but it was the *Autobiography* itself, first sold at the beginning of the century by Parson

Weems, reprinted countless times throughout the century, and adapted and retold in school texts and didactic literature, that made Franklin an exemplar of the self-educated rational man and his *Autobiography* what Sacvan Bercovitch has called one of the best-known "canonized do-it-yourself guides" for the molding of the self into a public citizen.[36] As Noah Porter, the president of Yale, put it in 1888, "The life of Franklin is attractive for many reasons; but pre-eminently because it was written by himself, and because he tells a story which of itself is fitted to interest every poor boy who is beginning life, with a simplicity and directness which enlists the sympathies and holds the attention of every reader. No book has been more popular in our country than this. None has exerted a more powerful influence."[37]

The ideal audience for this influence, as both Porter's praise and Twain's early burlesque acknowledge, was boys.[38] "Perhaps no character of the present age could be exhibited," intoned one of the century's numerous children's biographies, "which would be likely to promote a greater spirit of industry and early attention to business, frugality and temperance in the American youth, as that of FRANKLIN'S."[39] Young readers were called to "compare Franklin's situation and prospects with [their] own," and were promised that through the "study" of his character, they could discover those "certain qualities that are indispensable to eminence in one's vocation."[40] Virtually all of these didactic hagiographies dwelled on Franklin's efforts at "self-improvement" through the assiduous application of "honesty, industry, frugality, and study."[41] But what made Franklin's autobiography so compelling was how it supplied both model and method for the right construction of character. Much of the rhetoric celebrating Franklin manifested a certain slippage, exemplified best by Porter's language ("The life of Franklin is attractive . . . pre-eminently because it was written by himself"), between the historical "life" of Franklin and the textual "life" of the autobiography. While this may represent a conventional shorthand equating author and text, in the case of Franklin, at least, it suggests clearly the degree to which both model and subsequent modelers sought to equate writing one's life with living one's life and to equate the quality of the final product with the producer's character. Thus, while one hagiographic biography commended Franklin's writing—"at once a model of good English, and a fountain of clearly arranged thought"—as worthy of imitation through "study and practice," Jacob Abbott saw the influence of the *Autobiography* reaching far beyond prose style when he advised "any intelligent boy" ("Girls can do this too," he adds as an afterthought) to write a Franklinian personal history in order to discover "the power of writing" to shape the self.[42] As such, the autobiographical act itself, the process of setting one's life in writing, stood both as a sign of character and as a vehicle whereby that character was rightly constructed. As it was rewritten and read in the nineteenth century, the *Autobiography* embodied the literacy it celebrated; it ratified the link between good grammar and good character and linked the emergence of the social self with the formation of the literate self. Out of this dialectic emerged, for Twain and his contemporaries, the parameters shaping the more specialized cultural authority of authorship.

Pedagogical appropriations of Franklin's text were nothing if not true to his seem-ingly modest intention of presenting his account as a model for his "Posterity . . . fit to be imitated."[43] Yet this modeling was accompanied by a profoundly radical recon-ception of social authority that anticipated—indeed, helped make possible—the manly art of authorship pursued by Twain and his contemporaries. On one level, the narra-tive of part 1 in particular (that section most often retold) unfolds as a simple break with patriarchal bonds, as Franklin abandons the "harsh and tyrannical" (69) demands of filial obligation in Boston for the "wide World" (107) of Philadelphia, where he can make himself into a man in a fraternal world "remote from the Eye and Advice of my Father" (115).[44] This plot, however, runs alongside another set in motion most clearly by Franklin's well-known primal account of his learning the "Manner" of written argumentation by carefully imitating that of Joseph Addison's and Richard Steele's *The Spectator*. As he tells it, his lesson in "improving my Language" (64) rep-resents an apprenticeship to a certain kind of literacy—marked by rules of grammar, pointing, and expression—every bit as binding as that to which his father signed him over by placing him in his brother's print shop.[45] To "master" the language of prose, Franklin must, in Christopher Looby's words, "*submit* himself to language—to be-come, as it were, an *instance* of a discourse that he encountered ready-made."[46] As such, *The Spectator* stands as an "Original" authority, one that serves both as a stan-dard by which Franklin can measure his writing and as a generative locus for a "Prose Writing" that will turn out to be the "principal Means of [his] Advancement" (60). More particularly, it displaces his biological parent with a textual "parent" for the Franklin represented in the *Autobiography*.

In this sense, his text dramatizes in prose what Michael Warner has argued Franklin pursued in life. Both protagonist and author "may be said to have embodied the written subject, to have lived within the structures of career and personality in a way that was profoundly shaped by the printed discourse of the public sphere, articulating a career for the subject of that discourse."[47] The shape of this career in the *Autobiography* emerges most clearly in the differences between *The Spectator*'s au-thority and paternal will. Addison and Steele may offer the most important "Origi-nal" for Franklin's development as a prose writer, but, in the end, their writing proves to be only one source among many. In the process of "improving my Language" (64), Franklin feels free to adopt such authorities as John Locke, Socrates, and James Greenwood's *Practical English Grammar*. This, in turn, reiterates his recruitment in Philadelphia of a series of surrogate fathers—Sir William Keith, Andrew Bradford, Thomas Dunham, even Samuel Keimer—from whom he can solicit aid and, most important, from whom he can sever his relationship when convenient. Because they can be abandoned or superseded when no longer useful, such fathers, whether tex-tual or real, serve well the cause of fraternity: just as Keimer brings him in contact with "useful" associates, so too does Franklin's literacy allow him to circulate among fellow "Lovers of Reading" (79). If he loosens the chains of patriarchy, Franklin refig-ures its authority in terms similar to those governing his book: like his memoir, the surrogate fathers serve as models "suitable to [his] own Situation and, therefore, fit to be imitated" (43) or discarded as meets his purpose.

At the core of Franklin's rhetorical strategy, then, is a vision of social reproduction maintained not by the enforcement of patrilineal will, but by the cultural construction of literate authority—an authority that, in Warner's words, inhabits a public sphere of print, which "holds validity not in persons, but despite them."[48] After all, it is not Franklin himself who serves as the model—as he puts it, it "is not to be expected" that he should repeat his life either literally or by proxy through his heirs. Rather, it is his revisionary "*Recollection* of that Life" made "as durable as possible, [by] putting it down in Writing" (44). As Franklin shaped it, and the nineteenth century legitimated it, autobiography assumed the place of biological patriarchy. Like the childrearing books discussed in chapter 3—indeed, like the advice literature of all kinds that flooded the market—the *Autobiography* intervenes in the familial continuity of father and son, reconstructing it as an expanding circle of influence that includes, at the end of part 1, the "Tradesmen and Farmers" of America (131).[49]

Accompanying this reconception of cultural authority is a concomitant figuring of a literate self based more on the "Manner" of expression than on its substance, a self that fits perfectly into a fraternal world structured on the mutual dependency of and, finally, the blurred lines between "Character and Credit" (119). In Franklin's Philadelphia, economic success depends on the presentation of a public self rational and stable enough to merit investment. One claims authority not just by imitating models of deportment and expression, but also by making these models vessels into which the self is poured. Whatever is outside of that self-signifying style—in short, whatever is not written into the public record—is, at the very least, irrelevant and, at the worst, a "Fault" to be corrected by revision and finally erased, as Franklin did in his moral tables in part 2.[50] Thus, in place of the son subjected to the will of the father, Franklin offers a self made in and by "Prose"—a self that is the subject of literate language—as a model for imitation. As *The Spectator* did for him, his memoir shows his readers—his "Posterity"—how to write themselves into public life.

The autobiographical act thus emerges as a trope of identity: it both represents the culmination of the life in literate culture it helps make legitimate—the final gesture toward public "mutual Improvement"—and suggests the means whereby that culture can be perpetuated in time. Not only did Twain grasp this congruence of identity and social reproduction in his two Franklinian burlesques, he refined it in his searching critique of his nom de guerre in the Whittier Birthday Speech. If, for Franklin, to use Warner's words, "the life most consistent with [his] model of writing would be the public life" of republican virtue, for Twain, it would be the commodified life of literary authorship.[51]

❦

Twain's most explicit adaptation of the Franklinian paradigm of self-education appeared as "A Biographical Sketch" in the final volume of his authorized collected works, published by Bliss in 1899. Ostensibly authored by his nephew Samuel Moffett, the sketch was, in fact, based on Twain's own autobiographical account, which Moffett revised in the third person and returned to Twain for final approval. On one level, the sketch's echoes of the *Autobiography* reiterate how powerfully Franklin's paradigm of self-making shaped Twain's public presentation of his career. On another, the ways in which the essay outlines that career against a background of conventional ideologies of literacy and education suggest the depth of Twain's agon with his model. Thus, at the heart of Twain's exploration of literary authority lay a contradictory engagement with the trope of literacy. The sketch, then, not only returns us to much the same ground covered by chapter 1, via the route of education, but also leads us to Twain's most explicit engagement with literacy and authorship: his account of his apprenticeship to steamboating in *Life on the Mississippi*. Written while *Huckleberry Finn* was "pigeonholed," the book stands both as Twain's most searching retelling of Franklin's encounter with *The Spectator* and as a kind of hidden chapter on both Twain's and Huck's education into authorship.[52]

The sketch opens on "the extreme fringe" of the "Western empire of America," where, in one of its "eddies and back currents," Twain was born. Burdened by "the phantom vision of wealth" conferred by his father's acquisition of 80,000 acres of worthless land in Tennessee ("They could have bought the entire city of Chicago for a pair of boots"), Twain "missed a fortune [but] inherited good blood," which is traced in Franklinian fashion through Virginia to twelfth-century England.[53] Twain's "high school" was his brother's printing office, but, by 1853, "the Hannibal tether had become too short for him." He wanders the East, becomes a steamboat pilot, joins the Confederate army, travels the West and Europe as a newspaper correspondent, and returns East to write *The Innocents Abroad*. With this, his account focuses on his "steady literary development" as "the humorist began to evolve into the philosopher" embodied by his collected works. *Huckleberry Finn* is "a most moving study of the workings of the untutored human soul, in boy and man"; *Joan of Arc* elevates Twain to "a prophet of humanity." All of his writing evidences both a "spiritual growth [and] a growth in knowledge and in culture." In the end, Twain becomes a literary "master," "a classic, not only at home but in all lands whose people read and think about the common joys and sorrows of humanity." His authorship and his exemplary character merge as the product of the very self-made education that his writings make legitimate.[54]

Twain's account of his career follows the paradigm of self-improvement advocated by hagiographic renditions of Franklin's life. At the same time, however, it deliberately distances itself from the very institution that most expressly took Franklin's lesson to heart: the common school. In summing up Franklin's apprenticeship to Addison and Steele, one biography noted, "In improving his English, it will be noticed, . . . that he adopted the plan which is recommended in many, if not all school treatises upon rhetoric."[55] Nineteenth-century educators rewrote Franklin's individualism into a paradigm for institutional "training," as schooling was often referred to. As a young boy, William Torrey Harris, the nation's preeminent educator during the

1880s, had turned to Locke's *Human Understanding*, "having read somewhere that Franklin prided himself on reading that work at my age." But it was Hegel who most powerfully shaped his vision that the "great object of all education is to fit the individual to combine with his fellow-men."[56] Since man "makes his advent upon this planet as a mere animal, and without the evolution of his second and higher nature, it is clear that he must obtain it by a *process* of growth and culture; this we call education."[57] Thus, schools should give the pupil "the conventional view of the world. Each individual must be taught how his fellow-citizens look at things and events, or else he cannot understand their actions nor direct his own to any good purpose."[58] This education involved both a "practical initiation" in the form of learning a trade and a "theoretical initiation into the consciousness of the directive principles and solvent ideas through which directive power is achieved."[59] The student was trained to be Tom Sawyer's "everybody."

Against this universal training Twain defines his biography. If his life begins on the Western margins of the conventional, his career begins in Franklinian manner with the death of his father, when his "formal education came to an end, and his education in life began." His father, a judge, had always wanted his children to be "well educated," but Twain fulfilled those wishes "not in the way he had expected. It is a fortunate thing for literature that Mark Twain was never ground into smooth uniformity under the scholastic emery wheel." For Twain, like Franklin, is a self-made man. "He has made the world his university, and in men, and books, and strange places, and all the phases of an infinitely varied life, has built an education broad and deep, on the foundations of an undisturbed individuality."[60]

The sketch's anti-intellectualism expressly presents Twain in familiar terms, as the popular writer whose purpose, as he put it in his letter to Lang, was to entertain the masses ("common . . . humanity") rather than cultivate the classes. He is an author despite himself, a "master" of culture, whose grounding in experience recasts the innocent abroad's studied ignorance into a practical skepticism. Just as the printing office was his high school, his pilot's license "was the diploma of the river university": compared to "the incredible labor necessary to attain it . . . the efforts needed to acquire the degree of Doctor of Philosophy at a University are as light as a summer course of modern novels."[61] The importance of this diploma is emphasized by a lengthy excerpt from *Life on the Mississippi* praising the power of the pilot's memory (although the text refers to virtually all of his books—it is, after all, puffing the collected edition—it quotes from only this one). As such, the excerpt stands in the place of Franklin's lesson from *The Spectator*: "To know the Old and New Testaments by heart, and be able to recite them glibly, forward or backward, . . . is no extravagant mass of knowledge, and no marvelous facility, compared to a pilot's massed knowledge of the Mississippi, and his marvelous facility in handling it."[62] Set alongside both Franklin's text and the remarks about formal education, the passage's implication here is clear: if Franklin authored himself from other writers, if rightly constructed schoolboys developed character from books, Twain authored himself from life. Like Leonardo

Da Vinci, he is a true original; his writing is grounded in the "common" experience of all "humanity," not the rarified products of culture.

The sketch's use of the trope of formal education to describe, and finally legitimate, Twain's more authoritative "education in life" reiterates much the same pattern that numerous critics have discerned in "Old Times on the Mississippi."[63] There, however, Twain narrates the transformation of an ignorant boy into a knowledgeable steamboat pilot in terms more explicitly grounded in actual literacy. As an uninitiated passenger, Twain "had often seen pilots gazing at the water and pretending to read it as if it were a book; . . . a book that told me nothing" (63).[64] After his apprenticeship to piloting, however, Twain finds himself able to read "[t]he face of the water . . . [as] a wonderful book—a book that was a dead language to the uneducated passenger, but which told its mind to me without reserve, delivering its most cherished secrets as clearly as if it uttered them with a voice" (66–67). As the mercurial instructor Bixby tells his cub apprentice, "There's only one way to be a pilot, and that is to get this entire river by heart. You have to know it just like A B C" (49).

This more explicit language of learning clarifies the figural work of "A Biographical Sketch." On the one hand, Twain grounds his authority, his office of "master" and "philosopher," in his experience. On the other, if "the world" is Twain's "university," then his "education in life" resembles nothing more than the "formal education" it belittles. Indeed, the language of education certifies Twain's status as an author at least as much as the experience it ratifies. The result is the same split, and the same uncertainty over the connection between experience and fiction, voiced in the letter with which this study begins (written in 1891, eight years before the sketch). Thus, the sketch leaves unanswered the very question its developmental narrative strives to answer: how did the rough-and-tumble student of life become "master" of the culture he so disdained in his "education"? "Old Times," particularly when read in context of *Life on the Mississippi*, addresses this question more usefully simply because it takes seriously Franklinian literacy as a trope of mastery and, finally, of literary authority. What the cub learns on the river is not just the science of steamboating, but the power of language; what he attains with this education is not just his pilot's license, but also his name, "Mark Twain." Thus, the trope of literacy bridges the gap between boyhood and manhood, naïve performer and author, that Twain was unwilling to negotiate in *Tom Sawyer* and which implicitly structures *Huckleberry Finn*.

Ostensibly, the transformation from youth to maturity is measured by the degree to which the cub's rigorous schooling of memorization and humiliation dispels his "romantic" fantasies with a more "worklike" literacy. The pilot not only must know the "letters of the [river's] alphabet," he also must know its vocabulary, its grammar, and its vernacular before he can claim to have "mastered the language of this water" (67). Having undergone the trial of literacy, the adult pilot is no longer "bewitched" by "the glories and the charms" of twilight; no longer is he a naïve fool to reading. Now he comprehends only the "scientific" language of piloting: "this sun means that we are going to have wind to-morrow; that floating log means that the river is rising." His mastery of his vessel is predicated on the assurance that what he reads is interpretable in "scientific" terms: the one certifiable meaning of each mark on the river is maintained only by rejecting the suggestive "poetry" of "images" that render navigation impossible. As he puts it, "the romance and the beauty were all gone from the river. All the value any feature of it had for me now was the amount of usefulness it could furnish toward compassing the safe piloting of a steamboat" (68).

This loss of romance to the demands of science dramatizes Twain's Franklinian submission to models of language in order to master them. In doing so, however, he furthers a more fundamental romance. For "Old Times" opens by recreating much the same nostalgia for small-town boyhood as does *Tom Sawyer*. "When I was a boy," begins the narrator, "there was but one permanent ambition among my comrades. . . . That was, to be a steamboatman." Other ambitions arise—like Tom, Hannibal's boys yearn to join the circus, to join the minstrel show, to become pirates—but these "faded out" (37) with the persistent call of the steamboat whistle. Caught in the boredom of small-town life and lured by the romantic stories of a steamboat watchman who is both a victim and purveyor of "wildcat literature and . . . its marvels" (44), Twain falls under the "potent" spell of the "fascination of river life" (45) and runs away filled with "an exultant sense of being bound for mysterious lands and distant climes" (41). His anticipation frames the disillusioning hardship of the education that transforms him, if not into the "one horse man" Twain feared Tom would become, then at least into one of the "pretty grave, unromantic" men who overrun the mysterious boyish places of St. Petersburg.

This yearning for the mysterious and distant fades as well when the pilot realizes the child's dream of ruling as the absolute master of his world, "the only unfettered and entirely independent human being that lived in the earth. . . . The moment that the boat was under way in the river, she was under the sole and unquestioned control of the pilot. He could do with her exactly as he pleased, run her when and whither he chose, and tie her up to the bank whenever his judgment said that that course was best" (93–94). To be sure, as Twain demonstrates, this mastery—the skill with which the pilot navigates the twists and turns of the river, harnessing its indirection into a journey from one point to another—attests not to individual heroism, but to how completely the cub has submitted himself to, and finally internalized, his lessons. Nonetheless, piloting may subject the student to a knowledge ultimately as partial as that of the romantic ignorance of the passenger, but it fulfills the romance of ambition.

Like Huck, Twain the pilot learns his lessons well—"I loved the profession far better than any I have followed since" (93). However, in this admission lies the tale of another profession. For "the pilot's boundless authority" (94) vanished in "the twinkling of an eye" with the coming of the railroad, tugboats and barges, and the Civil War, all of which has left "the noble science of piloting . . . [among] things of the dead and pathetic past!" (109). So, Twain argues, he has turned his ambition to obtaining a far more impeachable, but nonetheless similar, authority: authorship. Like kings who must answer to parliaments, like parliaments who must answer to their constituents, like the newspaper editor who "must work with one hand tied behind him by party and patrons, and be content to utter only half or two thirds of his mind; . . . writers of all kinds are manacled servants of the public. We write frankly and fearlessly, but then we 'modify' before we print" (93–94). If the pilot was "a king without a keeper, an absolute monarch who was absolute in sober truth and not by a fiction of words," the writer must make do with just those fictions.

Yet, as Twain tells it, it is the words and fictions of piloting that initially most attracted him to steamboating. It was, after all, "wildcat literature" that first fired the imaginations of Hannibal boys. The first boy to escape to the river returns as an object of envy, in part because "he used all sorts of steamboat technicalities in his talk, as if he were so used to them that he forgot common people could not understand them" (39). When Twain, as a passenger, hears a steamboat mate "roar out" a string of commands, he sighs, "I wished I could talk like that" (43). As a cub, he sits as spellbound by the shoptalk of pilots as he was by the "wildcat" stories of the "humbug" watchman. What becomes clear is that, rather than using literacy as the trope for his tale of piloting, Twain's narrative of his days on the river serves as a trope for his mastery of language. The transformation of cub to pilot dramatizes the emergence of "Mark Twain," the fool to writing, out of a Jacob Blivens-like fool to romance.

The analogy between pilot and author emerges most clearly in how each manages language. "[A]ll pilots are tireless talkers" (52), but the best pilots are the most accomplished talkers. For when a pilot's prodigious memory is "built," revised, and repeatedly edited for extraneous information, he also attains the skill of telling a good story. This is precisely, for instance, what the pilot Mr. Brown cannot do. Despite his impressive natural memory, he "could *not* forget any thing." While this lack of discrimination scars his storytelling more than it does his piloting, it is still the mark of a man unable to stay on course: "His was not simply a pilot's memory; its grasp was universal." Constantly losing "the true line of his talk," he was "bound to clog his narrative with tiresome details and make himself an insufferable bore" (89). In the end, then, Mr. Brown's ineptitude recalls the comic storyteller who Twain dismissed in "How to Tell a Story." The well-tuned pilot, like the humorous storyteller, must learn both the alphabet and the "judgment" to use it "*unconsciously*"; only then can he negotiate language with the same skill it takes to navigate the river. Piloting enacts plotting; navigation is a form of narration.

Twain ends the "Old Times" section of *Life on the Mississippi* by closing the book, as it were, on what is now for him the lost days of steamboating. Now he is "a scribbler of books, and an immovable fixture among the other rocks of New England" (139). But it is precisely as a scribbler that Twain can cull his final lesson from his education: "in that brief, sharp schooling, I got personally and familiarly acquainted with about all the different types of human nature that are to be found in fiction, biography, or history. . . . When I find a well-drawn character in fiction or biography, I generally take a warm personal interest in him, for the reason that I have known him before—met him on the river" (125). Yet, even this does not tell all the story, for the most important character he met on the river is "Mark Twain." Heard first by the cub in the leadsman's cry measuring the depth of the water, the figure is brought to life precisely when steamboating dies, and he is fleshed out in subsequent chapters when the bearer of that name returns to the river.

The rest of the text relates the ambiguous return of an author to the scene of his earlier education. What he finds in place of the busy highway he had once piloted is a river so changed that he barely recognizes its contours. Most "impressive—and depressing" (165) is the lack of boat traffic of any kind. "Formerly . . . we should have passed acres of lumber rafts, and dozens of big coal barges; also occasional little trading-scows. . . . But these were all absent" (170). When he spies a single steam-boat that bears his name, it signifies both his fame and the wholesale demise of his former profession. The river itself, once a formidably perilous way of snags, sand-bars, fogs, and dark nights, now resembles "a sort of two-thousand-mile torchlight procession": beacons burn at every point and crossing, and government boats patrol the river for snags. Those boats that still run the river can do so "with a confidence unknown in the old days," but such markers have "knocked the romance out of piloting"—it "is now nearly as safe and simple as driving stage." In this day of efficient travel, pilots—"once the aristocrats of the river"—now stand second in wages and authority to the captain (171–72).

Twain's return to the river, however, does yield one more story of his cub days. Captain Isaiah Sellers, "that real and only genuine Son of Antiquity," was a pilot whose knowledge of the river dated from the appearance of the first steamboat. So com-manding was his mastery of the constantly shifting river that he could remember when "the State of Mississippi was where Arkansas now is." His appearance in a pilothouse could silence the strutting boasts of his fellow pilots; his command of facts "spread disaster and humiliation" as he spoke of islands that disappeared before many of his listeners had been born (282). Most important, Sellers was a writer as well. Although not "of literary turn or capacity," he published articles in the New Orleans *Picayune* giving data, and more important, writing the history of the river under the pen name "Mark Twain."

While Sellers's "antique interjections lay poison and bitterness for the other old pilots" by publicly challenging their knowledge and their authority ("they used to chaff the 'Mark Twain' paragraphs with unsparing mockery"), his writings also provided the cub with an opportunity to assert his own authority by burlesquing Sellers in his "first newspaper article." While "[t]here was no malice in my rubbish; . . . it laughed at the captain. It laughed at a man to whom such a thing was new and strange and dreadful. I did not know then, though I do now, that there is no suffering compa-rable with that which a private person feels when he is for the first time pilloried in print" (283). The burlesque has its effect: Sellers "never printed another paragraph while he lived, and he never again signed 'Mark Twain' to anything." But the cub would. Years later, as "a fresh new journalist" on the Pacific coast, Twain hears of

Sellers's death and, "need[ing] a *nom de guerre*; . . . confiscated the ancient mariner's discarded one, and have done my best to make it remain what it was in his hands—a sign and symbol and warrant that whatever is found in its company may be gambled on as being the petrified truth; how I have succeeded, it would not be modest in me to say" (284).

As Twain tells it, the story is not strictly accurate: he had adopted his pen name before he traveled to San Francisco. But its pattern was already a familiar one by the time he wrote it here. For, as his use of "nom de guerre" suggests, in his "enthusiasm" Twain has "exaggerated the details a little" and "deflected from perpendicular fact," just as he did in his Whittier Birthday Speech. ("Old Times" appeared before the banquet; the Sellers passage was written after it.) The Sellers episode retells the story of literary origins as a confrontation of speech and silence. Just as he imagined in his later account of the dinner, Twain here humiliates a prior authority to silence, appropriating, not his boots as does Longfellow, but his name—the "sign, symbol, and warrant" of truth. With this tale of literary vandalism, Twain seizes the grand authority of the patriarch of pilots as his own: pilots may have been "absolute in sober truth" but they are nonetheless vulnerable to the "fiction of words." Moreover, with this literary trumping of the pilot, Twain also revises his earlier fantasy of authority. For the author may answer to his readers, but he is powerful enough to silence, indeed speak for, other writers. With his burlesque, Twain pillories the "private person" in the war of names and claims Sellers's nom de guerre as his trophy. Thus, if the pilot serves as the image of Twain's yearned-for absolute authority, he also stands as its insufficient embodiment. In a "fiction of words"—which because they are words are always vulnerable to confiscation, stealing, and burlesque—authority must constantly be fought for.

With this violent wresting of literary identity, Twain not only brings to culmination his narrative of literate education, he also in uncanny ways echoes that of Franklin's story. For Franklin's turn to *The Spectator* was motivated not so much by an enlightened commitment to self-improvement as by his rivalry with "another Bookish Lad in the Town, John Collins by Name" (60). Both of them were "very fond" of "a very bad Habit" of "confuting one another" ("productive of Disgusts and perhaps Enmities where you may have occasion for Friendship"). Collins, Franklin writes, "was naturally more eloquent, had a Plenty of Words, and sometimes as I thought bore me down more by his Fluency than by the Strength of his Reasons" (60–61). So, like any good disputant, Franklin turns to Addison and Steele to arm himself with both "A Stock of Words" and a "Method in the Arrangement of Thoughts" (62) to carry the battle forward. The argument, however, does not end there, despite the fact that Franklin never returns to the original circumstances that sparked his education. Instead, the rivalry between the two Bookish Lads takes a more personal turn when Franklin once again meets his "Friend Collins" after the latter had helped him escape Boston. Here, argument becomes more a test of character: despite Collins's having "had the Advantage of more time for reading, and Studying" he has tarnished his reputation with drinking and gaming. They quarrel about his drinking ("for when a little intoxicated he was very fractious" [85]). Finally, on a boat journey on the Delaware River, Collins refuses to row his turn, and Franklin pitches his rival in the water, refusing to allow him back in until Collins is exhausted from swimming. "We hardly exchang'd a civil Word afterwards," writes Franklin.

Thus, like Twain's nom de guerre, Franklin's literate authority, his signature "Manner," is not only the product of education and physical confrontation; it is also ratified by the silence of a rival. Just as this rivalrous literacy transforms Franklin from a "lad" into a man, so, too, does river literacy transform the cub into the pilot, the "bewitched" reader into the author, Jacob Blivens into Mark Twain. For Franklin, this contentiousness is harnessed by a rigorous program of self-government that produces the stable economy of "Credit" and "Manner" of fraternal Philadelphia; Twain, however, envisions a world in which authority is gained and exercised on an always shifting battleground best negotiated with a nom de guerre. It is on this geography of violence and threat that he maps the course of literacy in *Huckleberry Finn*.

III. Fighting Words

When Pap confronts Huck alone in his room at the widow's, the young boy receives a "jolt." "I used to be scared of him all the time, he tanned me so much"—scared enough, in fact, to sign away his money to Judge Thatcher and anxiously to seek counsel from Jim's hairball. Yet, when he meets his father face to face, things have changed. "I reckoned I was scared now, too; but in a minute I see I was mistaken. . . . I see I warn't scared of him worth bothering about" (23). Pap also senses a change as he looks around the room furnished with bed, mirror, and carpet. For two days, he "hain't heard nothing but about you bein' rich" (25), and now he has come to collect his due as Huck's father. But Huck no longer acts as his son. "You're educated, too, they say; can read and write. You think you're better'n your father, now, don't you, because he can't?" Huck's literacy is more than an affront to the patriarchal rights Pap insists on, it is a defamation of the family name. Huck is no longer a true Finn: "Your mother couldn't read, and she couldn't write, nuther, before she died. None of the family couldn't, before *they* died. *I* can't; and here you're a-swelling yourself up like this. . . . I'll lay for you, my smarty; and if I catch you about that school I'll tan you good" (24).

Pap's anger is further inflamed by Huck's cool, even insolent responses to his father's threats. "Looky here—mind how you talk to me," he warns, but, in fact, Huck minds how Pap talks to him, carefully transcribing his father's colloquial inflections while still maintaining his correct spelling. For, as Pap well understands, his son's literacy represents more than the acquisition of language tools; it is, like the other "frills" of Huck's life, the visible sign of civilizing. Huck is no longer a fool to his father. Huck is aware of this too: "I didn't want to go to school much, before, but I reckoned I'd go now to spite pap" (29). The sheer fact of Huck's mastery of reading gives him the potential to be his own "boss."

Just as it had Franklin, literacy endows Huck with a "plenty of words," a certain power of fluency and manner that leaves Pap uneasy and uncertain. However, before Huck can escape the "tyranny" of his father, as Franklin would put it, he must learn another lesson in eloquence. For, if Huck wins the argument, if he successfully challenges his father's authority, Pap wins the contest of wills by locking Huck away in an isolated cabin. "Fluency" may grant Huck a degree of independence, but its authority is vulnerable to—indeed, is best enforced by—physical violence. The judge learned this when he realized that he could reform Pap only with a shotgun, which is exactly what Colonel Sherburn uses when mocking the mob intent on lynching him: "The idea of you thinking you had pluck enough to lynch a *man*!" (190). Real men may be eloquent, but they back their words with guns, daring others to look them in the eye. The austere, "well-born" Colonel Grangerford understands this as well: "I don't like that shooting from behind a bush" (145), he chastises Buck, when the latter tells of his encounter with a Sheperdson. Buck needs to learn to give and to take it like a man.

Whereas Franklin's escape to Philadelphia thrusts him alone into a "wide world . . . remote from the Eye and Advice of my Father," Huck escapes with his lesson well taught. For judicious violence is the mark of a gentleman: he would rather kill or be killed than be humiliated. This is why Buck so virulently defends the courage of the Sheperdsons: their dedication to a code of violence affirms the bloodline and character of both clans. Mere mortals, as the mob realizes when it disperses under Sherburn's withering challenge, must learn to live with disgrace. It is a question of honor, a symptom of what Twain calls in *Life on the Mississippi* the "Sir Walter disease." The South as a region, he argues, is populated by fools to reading. It was the chivalric romances of Sir Walter Scott that made dueling and feuding so attractive, that perhaps even caused the Civil War. It was Scott who "made every gentleman in the South a Major or a Colonel, or a General or a Judge . . . it was he that created rank and caste down there, and also reverence for rank and caste, and pride and pleasure in them."[65] Such pride lies at the core of Pap's kidnapping of Huck. It is not the pleasure of the money that drives him so much as it is the humiliation of having been denied what caste tells him is rightly his: "The law takes a man worth six thousand dollars and upards, and jams him into an old trap of a cabin like this, and lets him go round in clothes that ain't fitten for a hog. They call that govment!" (33).

Pap is illiterate, but he has learned his lesson from his betters. Violence is the end of eloquence in both senses of the phrase. As the final gambit in an argument, it stops a man's mouth and overcomes an opponent's "ready plenty of words." But violence is also the goal of an eloquence that can humiliate a man, leave him speechless, unable to defend himself from ridicule. The cub pilot of "Old Times" came to understand this double meaning. When Bixby places his apprentice under the charge of Mr. Brown, Twain finds, beneath a garrulous memory, a "stingy, malicious, snarling, fault-hunting, mote-magnifying tyrant." After enduring a series of pointedly harsh embarrassments at the hands of his new instructor, the cub loses control when Brown accuses Twain's younger brother, Henry, who also serves on the boat, of lying. In his fury, the pilot attacks Henry with a ten-pound lump of coal, only to be knocked down by Twain with "a good honest blow" with a stool. Twain's intervention is against all river law—"I was booked for the penitentiary sure"—but the violence is not the end of the confrontation. Brown wields a spyglass like a club and orders the cub out of the pilothouse, "[b]ut I was not afraid of him now; so, instead of going, I tarried, and criticized his grammar; I reformed his ferocious speeches for him, and put them into good English, calling his attention to the advantage of pure English over [his] bastard dialect." Like Captain Sellers, the original "Mark Twain," Brown "was not equipped for this species of controversy," and so is reduced to "muttering and shaking his head" before he, not the cub, is dismissed from the boat.[66]

Franklin, too, understands the ends of eloquence, but he also understands the limits of violence: citing Socrates, he urges that a "dogmatical Manner in advancing your Sentiments, may provoke Contradiction and prevent a candid Attention."[67] Not so on the Mississippi—there, in the mouths of men, eloquence is a weapon of provocation that as often as not leads to violence. It is a dangerous game, as Boggs, gunned down in the street by Colonel Sherburn, finds out at the cost of his life. Huck, however, understands the point of Franklin's lesson: the trick of eloquence is to wield it, to assert one's difference, to argue, without provoking violence. The duke and the dauphin, he knows, are "just low-down humbugs and frauds. But I never said nothing, never let on; kept it to myself; it's the best way; then you don't have no quarrels, and don't get into no trouble" (165). Huck is also vulnerable to violence; he is, after all, just a boy, with no interest in entering the feuding debates of men. If his nausea over the Grangerford massacre did not convince him, the tarring and feathering of the two rogues does: "Human beings *can* be awful cruel to one another" (290).

But it is just this cruelty, this violence of Huck's "wide world," that makes eloquence so necessary. For at stake in fluency's arguments is the assertion of one's name, one's identity. It is in defense of the family name that the cub springs at Captain Brown in order to protect his younger brother; Twain claims Sellers's pen name as his trophy; it is the Finn family name that Huck threatens to usurp from his father with his literacy. Colonel Sherburn defends his honor, his name, by killing Boggs and by humbling an unfortunate "Buck Harkness" by calling him "only *half* a man" (190). Eloquence cannot kill, but it can unman by renaming.

Or, it can make a man anew. The two rogues without any names of their own survive under a bewildering array of "borrowed" aliases: the Duke of Bridgewater, "Looy the Seventeen," "Dr. Armand de Montalban of Paris," "Garrick the Younger, of Drury Lane, London," "Edmund Kean, the elder," Harvey and William Wilks. Huck, too, has his own names: "Sarah Williams," "George Peters," "George Jaxon," the "valet" "Adolphus" and, finally, of course, "Tom Sawyer." Each name is in essence an autobiography; it implies a story, a past; its authority depends on how well the story can be maintained. It is also a confidence game: one's identity depends on how much confidence others have in your stories about yourself.[68] When Judith Loftus loses confidence in Huck's identity as a girl, he patiently allows her to construct her own story that he is a runaway apprentice. Similarly, the bounty hunters who want to visit his raft transform his hesitation over revealing Jim into a story about smallpox.

Names are the currency of the Mississippi; their credit lies in the "Appearance" and "Manner" of their bearer, his ability to manipulate the social codes of identity. For Franklin, these codes are part of an ordered circulation of fraternal credit; one may have to judge a man by his appearance, but, in the public world of Philadelphia, he is as good as his word. In Huck's world, however, names circulate in an economy with no standard of value: as Dr. Robinson realizes when he tries to establish the identity of the Wilks brothers, it is easier to prove all appearance a sham than it is to find the truth. No name, no identity, is safe in a world of strangers; it must be argued for, constantly reaffirmed, if it is to withstand the attacks of eloquence.

Given this violent indeterminacy, how is Huck to assert a difference, to maintain an identity, when everybody is potentially different even from themselves? It was relatively easy in the closed hegemony of St. Petersburg, but in the wide world, apart from the eye and threats of his father and guardians, where can he stand? How can he pursue his romance of escape from "sivilizing," a romance that goes hand in hand with his decision to write his autobiography? One way is to adopt the very fictions of proprietary reform that he would escape from, to draw a boundary of legitimacy that excludes those who deal in confidence without credit. This is what begins to emerge in Huck's account of his journey downriver. For the scope of Huck's commitment to writing—his struggle to write an autobiography, an account of the self—emerges, in part, in the increasingly forthright and critical voice that struggles to stand *outside* the verbal and physical dueling it describes. The text suggests Huck's maturation from a sense of difference to a stance of criticism, one as authoritative as Colonel Sherburn's withering denunciation of the cowardice of lynching, but also eloquent enough to stand without the shotgun. Eloquence, for Huck, becomes a tool for social criticism without the violence.

There are early traces of such a stance in Huck's resistance to Miss Watson and the widow. There are also traces that emerge while Huck is at the Grangerford home: his cautious encounters with the cultural riches of the parlor, his tentative relationship with the specter of Emmeline Grangerford, his attempt to write his own poem for her—all prepare him for the nausea of death that he expresses after the last day's incidents. His critical stance emerges full-blown in describing the duke's and the dauphin's confidence game with the Wilks daughters. He may maintain a kind of speculative neutrality while he is with them, but, in the safety of his authorship, his narrative voice grows increasingly impatient with their scheming. But what if the object of criticism is one's self? Writing offers no space of comfort to a boy locked in a struggle with his conscience. That, at least, is the crisis Huck must negotiate in his relationship with Jim. When Jim anticipates his imminent freedom as they approach Cairo, Huck realizes he is implicated in helping a slave to freedom. "Conscience says to me, 'What had poor Miss Watson done to you, that you could see her nigger go off right under your eyes and never say one single word?'" (124). No matter that "it don't make no difference whether you do right or wrong," the fluency, the plenty of words of "a person's conscience," bears down on him anyway, threatening to silence him, to re-form him into "everybody" (290).

It is, for Huck, a question of protecting his name, his identity: "It would get all around, that Huck Finn helped a nigger to get his freedom; and if I was to ever see anybody from that town again, I'd be ready to get down and lick his boots for shame" (268). Huck fails his first test of honor when, with Cairo's appearance seemingly imminent, he meets two bounty hunters looking for runaway slaves. When they ask him the color of his companion on the raft, however, he "warn't man enough" to reply directly, to speak his conscience and tell the truth (125). However, alone on the raft, with Jim in the hands of the Phelps family, he shows more courage by writing a letter to Miss Watson telling her where she can find "your runaway nigger Jim" (269). With his letter, Huck signs his name as a literate subject of a culture of conscience, the basis for which is the sanctity of property. Property represents wealth, but, more pervasively, property is the legal "fiction of words" that claims the Murrell gang's gold as Huck's, Huck as Pap's, Jim as Miss Watson's, the Wilks's money as the brothers'. But these words are slippery, they won't stay in one place, they can be turned around, remade. The Widow Douglas adopts Huck, but the new judge in town reads the law differently—the courts should not break up the family. When Huck and Jim "borrow" produce and chickens from the farms they drift past—"Pap always said it warn't no harm to borrow things, if you was meaning to pay them back, sometime; but the widow said it warn't anything but a soft name for stealing" (80)—they give their tithe to conscience (Jim reckons that both were "partly right") by refraining from taking crabapples and persimmons.

But Pap is completely right about one form of property. What kind of a country is it, he wants to know, that allows a nigger to remain free in a free state: "why ain't this nigger put up at auction and sold? . . . they said he couldn't be sold till he'd been in the State six months, and he hadn't been there that long yet. There, now—that's a specimen" (34). It is a specimen of the arbitrary power of law to render people property, to make them a form of currency, to change "Jim," as Huck does in his letter to Miss Watson, into "your runaway nigger Jim." As Jim well knows, the law sees identity as a matter of property. Freedom for him means self-possession: "I's rich now, come to look at it. I owns mysef, en I's wuth eight hund'd dollars" (57). Or at least he is worth that much to the widow. As a runaway slave, he is worth less to Judith Loftus: "Does three hundred dollars lay round every day for people to pick up?" (70). Those masters of the manner of fluency, the duke and the dauphin, value him at two hundred dollars in the "notice" they print up to cover their story, but the dauphin sells out his chance on him for only forty dollars, the same amount that Tom pays Jim "for being prisoner for us so patient" (360).

Conscience, then, has no sense of value; it does not matter what Jim is worth so long as he remains a slave. Rather, it speaks only in the voice of brute property, its voice a fiction of words the very arbitrariness of which measures its power. It is the voice that Jim violates when, thinking Cairo is imminent, he vows to free his family even if he must steal them. "It most froze me to hear such talk," admits Huck. "He wouldn't ever dared to talk such talk in his life before. Just see what a difference it made in him the minute he judged he was about free . . . I was sorry to hear Jim say that, it was such a lowering of him" (124–25). But Huck, too, is "low-down and ornery": not "man enough" to speak, much less write, his conscience, he tears up his note to Miss Watson and decides to "go to hell":

> It was awful thoughts, and awful words, but they was said. And I let them
> stay said, and never thought no more about reforming. . . . I would take up
> wickedness again, which was in my line, being brung up to it, and the other
> warn't. And for a starter, I would go to work and steal Jim out of slavery again;
> and if I could think up anything worse, I would do that, too; because as long
> as I was in, and in for good, I might as well go the whole hog.   (271)

Huck's resolution represents the most articulate pronouncement of his sense of differ- ence: by inverting the polarized language of St. Petersburg morality, he finds a space for himself that ratifies the critical distance toward which his account has tended. He turns the fluency of manly conscience against itself and finds his own eloquence, his own identity, one that he will eventually inscribe in a longer letter—his autobiogra- phy, a text he can sign "Yours truly."

Twain thus reproduces the Franklinian paradigm of self-authorizing literacy by inverting it in just the same way as does Huck the language of conscience. To be sure, Huck comes to writing outside, rather than within, the "stable" social world of slavery; but his very pledge of difference works to reincorporate him into the stable moral universe of Twain's readers. However radical Huck's decision "to go to hell" may be in the context of the antebellum South, in the context of the Northeast in the 1880s it dares very little. As a resolution to free Jim, Huck's declaration of difference paradoxically confirms the orthodoxy of his heart. He merely affirms the inevitability of a history that has revised the Civil War as a glorious victory over slavery. Far from penning a "true" account of difference, Twain's autobiography of Huck affirms that even an ignorant racist white boy can write himself into a correct moral stance. It draws the edifying line of literature: Huck's autobiography allows him to discover the same "power of writing" to make character as that offered boys by hagiographies of Franklin. It affirms, as well, the politics of moral uplift that critics like T. S. Eliot and Lionel Trilling could find in the novel, even if the Con- cord public library could not.

Or at least this would be the case if the narrative ended before Huck finds himself "born again" as Tom Sawyer and subjected, along with Jim, to the absurd machina- tions of his friend. For the major affront of the final chapters comes not so much from the coincidence of Tom's reappearance, or even from his obsessive pursuit of "adventure"—he is, after all, in the final chapters sublimely in character—but from the ease with which Huck cedes his hard-won initiative. To be sure, Huck repeatedly voices his frustration over Tom's endless scheming, and he even refuses to carry out some of Tom's more outrageous abuses of Jim. This awareness, however, points all the more to his culpability: if Huck senses the violence beneath Tom's "fun," why doesn't he act on it?

The text suggests several answers to this question, all of which unsettle the readerly expectations raised by Huck's moral awakening. Huck's decision to "go to hell" is merely one of a number of resolutions to act that he makes during his journey. He is as determined to arrange for the rescue of the men trapped aboard the Sir Walter Scott, to act as lookout for Buck Grangerford in his battle with the Sheperdsons, to protect the Wilks daughters from the duke and the dauphin, as he is to paddle ashore and turn in Jim as an escaped slave. But Huck is incapable of following through on any of these resolutions. The thieves presumably drown in the river, Buck is surprised and killed while Huck watches, the true heirs appear to thwart the confidence men, and Huck impulsively protects Jim from the bounty hunters. Even Huck's dramatic overthrow of his conscience is made redundant by Miss Watson's deathbed manumission.

Tom's reappearance and subsequent assumption of authority is but one more instance of Huck's ineffectiveness, an ineffectiveness that radically qualifies the narrative of moral growth that the text posits. When Huck, on discovering that Jim has been sold back into slavery, mourns that "After all this long journey, . . . here was it all come to nothing, everything all busted up and ruined" (268), his words not only refer to his life with Jim, but also anticipate the travesty of the final chapters. However, it is not the evasion sequence alone that "ruins" Huck's romance of escape and moral growth; it only makes explicit the extent of Tom's power over his friend throughout the entire narrative. For while Huck seems finally unable to establish a critical distance, Tom emerges as the most powerful authority in the text. It is he, not Huck, who is the narrative's most Franklinian figure; it is he who has best learned his reading lesson and who most powerfully explores and exploits its authority. Finally, it is Tom's frantic machinations that serve as the model for Huck's autobiographical and Twain's literary act.

❦

The Tom Sawyer of *Huckleberry Finn* is the quintessential fool to reading, a fevered victim of the "Sir Walter disease." Still reveling in dime-novel fantasies, he has put behind him the coarser pleasures of piracy for the more "high-toned" respectability of robbers. To this, he has added a virtually encyclopedic knowledge of the classics of adventure literature, from Miguel de Cervantes and Benvenuto Cellini to Sir Walter Scott, Alexandre Dumas, and even Thomas Carlyle. But his reading is now more than a staple for his boyish imagination. When he calls together his St. Petersburg "Gang" to administer its oath and explain its "line of business" (10), it grows immediately clear that he is as much an administrator of literate authority as he is its comic victim. When each boy signs his name to the oath, they pledge themselves not only to revenge ruthlessly anyone who would reveal its secrets, but also to endure what becomes a lesson in literacy every bit as rigorous as the cub pilot's in water reading.

Tom, in effect, becomes the gang's Horace Bixby, browbeating his cubs to submit to their ABCs. Unlike piloting, however, the alphabet resides strictly in Tom's head. When Tom insists that, as robbers, they must ransom their captives, Ben Rogers asks, "Ransomed? What's that?" Tom does not know, but he's "seen it in books; and so of course that's what we've got to do." When Ben persists in wanting a definition—"how can we do it if we don't know what it is?"—Tom loses his patience: "Why blame it all, we've *got* to do it. Don't I tell you it's in the books? Do you want to go to doing different from what's in the books, and get things all muddled up?" (10–11). Even if it is contrary to reason, he insists, they must play by the book: "Now, Ben Rogers, do you want to do things regular, or don't you?—that's the idea. Don't you reckon that the people that made the books knows what's the correct thing to do? Do you reckon *you* can learn 'em anything? Not by a good deal" (11). Tom's authority is final; he knows the books, and his gang will be "regular" and "correct" according to his reading of them.

Tom thus rescues Huck from the "dismal regular" life at the widow's only to incorporate him into an authoritative fiction all the more "cramped up and sivilized." In this case, Huck dismisses Tom's Sunday-school lies, but when he meets Tom again on the Phelps's farm, he once again falls for a devil's bargain. Tom promises to free Jim, whom he knows is already free, in exchange for enlisting Huck in his fantasies. And again, as it did at the beginning of Huck's tale, "the old thing commenced," as Tom abuses his companion for his ignorance: "Well, if that ain't just like you, Huck Finn. You *can* get up the infant-schooliest ways of going at a thing. Why, hain't you ever read any books at all?—Baron Trenck, nor Casanova, nor Benvunuto Chelleeny, nor Henry IV, nor none of them heroes?" (299). As Huck and even Jim react with increasing skepticism to his elaborate scheming—the final chapters at times unfold as nothing more than endless bickering over the "sense" of the evasion plans—Tom shrilly insists all the more on the necessity of playing by the book. When Huck points out the absurdity of digging Jim out of his cabin with case knives instead of picks and shovels, Tom retorts: "It don't make no difference how foolish it is, it's the *right* way— and it's the regular way. And there ain't no *other* way, that ever *I* heard of; and I've read all the books that gives any information about these things" (304).

In one sense, then, Huck is right when he translates Tom's "regular" as "regulations" (301). Tom enslaves Jim and captures Huck in order to make them characters in his own fiction. He is, as it were, Huck's Collins: because Huck lacks "a ready Plenty of Words," Tom bears him "down more by his Fluency than by the strength of his Reasons." But, in another sense, Huck's translation misses the point. For all of his insistence on "regulations," Tom repeatedly cites authorities only to deviate from them, adapting them to immediate circumstances. Thus, when he finds himself "dog-tired" (306) from digging his tunnel with case knives, he conveniently decides, "we got to dig him out with the picks, and *let on* its case-knives" (307). This is but one of a number of comic accommodations that Tom makes to the difficulties of "representing prisoners" on the Phelps's farm rather than in a gothic castle. For Tom not only wants to make himself the hero of the romances he has read, he wants to be the author of his own heroism. His fun lies as much in having to "invent *all* the difficulties" (298) as it does in following prescriptions for escaping them.

In his willful quest for authority, Tom is the parodic version of the self-making Franklinian man of literacy. His frantic machinations transmute the rational discipline of the fraternal member of a society of credit into the self-aggrandizement of the unleashed ego in a culture of violence. Jim, in his ignorance, may not know enough to take advantage of "more gaudier chances than a prisoner ever had in the world to make a name for himself" (328), but Tom is ready to use the man's plight to "spread" his own name, a name spelled not only as "Tom Sawyer," but also as all the figures of his fantasy—"Huck Finn," "Jim," "Benvunuto Chelleeny," "Casanova," and the other hero-authors of his romance. As such, he is, in his own words, a comic "prisoner of style" (333): he makes himself an instance in the discourse of literate power, a damned fool to reading who knows better than to read literally. Using a pickaxe to dig a tunnel may be all right for someone like Huck, "because you don't know no better; but it wouldn't for me, because I do know better" (307). As a prisoner of style, he cannot escape his literacy; he can only merge so completely into "pirate books, and robber books" that he is able to hide behind literacy, using it as a mask even as the "Manner" of his use proclaims his identity. Thus, as Tom explains to Huck, "When a prisoner of style escapes, it's called an evasion" (333). Tom does not plan to escape to anywhere, but only to evade into other roles, other "adventures plumb to the mouth of the river" (360). He hopes to "spread" himself by endlessly adopting other fictions, to continue the proliferation of his signature "style," by putting on yet more masks.

It is exactly this learned style of evasion, Tom's very confidence, his capacity for self-aggrandizement, that so confuses and intimidates Huck. "[I]f I was as ignorant as you," he tells Huck, "I'd keep still" (301). But if Tom is his Collins, he is also his Bixby, who after a particularly egregious blunder by his cub dismisses him as "more different kinds of an ass than any creature I ever saw before."[69] Huck accepts Tom's withering barrage of abuse because he is willing to learn his lesson in fluency from him. When Tom dismisses Huck's plan for rescuing Jim, the cub Huck remains silent "because I warn't expecting nothing different," satisfied that Tom's plan is "worth fifteen of mine, for style" (292). From the beginning, Tom is the yardstick against which Huck measures himself, his muse for his romance of escape, the model whom he follows in outwitting the violence of "sivilizing." When Huck and Jim come upon the *Walter Scott*, Huck "can't rest . . . till we give her a rummaging. Do you reckon Tom Sawyer would ever go by this thing? Not for pie, he wouldn't. He'd call it an adventure—that's what he'd call it; and he'd land on that wreck if it was his last act. And wouldn't he throw style into it?—wouldn't he spread himself, nor nothing?" (81). Even when he arranges things "pretty neat," as he does when he plots to return the

Wilks's money, Huck acknowledges his friend's greater mastery: "I reckoned Tom Sawyer couldn't a done it no neater, himself. Of course he would a throwed more style into it, but I can't do that very handy, not being brung up to it" (248). Tom's style is the capacity to "throw in the fancy touches" (41), to "spread himself" in and with his fictions. For Huck, his play magically sustains an extended signature of the self powerful enough to silence others, a self that emerges solely in the "Manner" of the play's elaboration.

Moreover, it is Huck's fascination with—indeed, his willingness to believe in— this magic that makes Tom into both his most enduring model and his most powerful antagonist. When Huck discovers that what Tom had promised would be a caravan of "Spanish merchants and rich A-rabs" is nothing but a Sunday-school picnic, Tom confidently insists that the caravan had been there:

> He said if I warn't so ignorant, but had read a book called "Don Quixote," I would know without asking. He said it was all done by enchantment. He said there was hundreds of soldiers there, and elephants and treasure, and so on, but we had enemies which he called magicians, and they had turned the whole thing into an infant Sunday school, just out of spite. I said, all right, then the thing for us to do was to go for the magicians. Tom Sawyer said I was a numskull. (15–16)

Ostensibly, the magicians Huck goes for are the genies in the lamp, but the real power of enchantment, he soon discovers, lies in books—whether it be the Bible or *Don Quixote*. Books offer access to a magical power that can reach into worlds of death and enchantment, empowering their readers.

Huck's introduction to "Moses and the Bulrushers" had marked his first confrontation with this power; yet, if the Bible was a book about death, a prescriptive guide for preparation for "Providence," Huck rejected it because "I don't take no stock in dead people." However, when he encounters it again in the Grangerford parlor, on the table with *Friendship's Offering*, *Henry Clay's Speeches*, Bunyan's *Pilgrim's Progress*, and "Dr. Gunn's Family Medicine, which told you all about what to do if a body was sick or dead" (137), his attitude has changed. The books, like the parlor's corpse-like crockery reproductions of animals and fruit, are preserved as fetishes in a mausoleum of pious culture by a family caught in an obsessive and senseless feud. To Huck, however, they are mysterious objects that certify the family's "style" (136). He discovers most powerfully the spell of style in the maudlin sketches and poems of the departed Emmeline. Not only does he leaf through her scrapbook and gaze at her pictures, he tries to "sweat out a verse or two," in tribute to her: "I liked all that family, dead ones and all, and warn't going to let anything come between us. Poor Emmeline made poetry about all the dead people when she was alive, and it didn't seem right that there warn't nobody to make some about her, now she was gone" (141). The Grangerford parlor marks the site of a dead, yet powerful, authority: books speak of death, they rest in a house permeated with the odor of death, and their meaning remains for Huck as shrouded as death. *Pilgrim's Progress*—"about a man that left his family it didn't say why"—yields as little to Huck as the crockery dog and cat, which squeak when handled yet don't "open their mouths nor looks different nor interested" (136–37).

Huck's darkly comic obeisance at the shrine of books not only confirms that he has indeed come to take stock in dead people, but also represents books as autonomous, contumacious authorities that *make* sense even if they make no *sense*. They help to manufacture identity by supplying fictions as the raw material for style. When the duke pieces together Hamlet's soliloquy, he invokes the "Manner" of Shakespeare and thus the cultural authority of his name; like the graffiti in the floating house that Jim and Huck explore, "the ignorantest kinds of words" (61) embody the most powerful forms of authority. Thus, literacy impresses on Miss Watson, on the duke and the dauphin, and most powerfully on Tom, not any sense of rational truth, but the authority of written language. They lead literate lives not by imitating texts in any Franklinian manner, but by recreating in the social realm their own victimizations to the "dead" authority of writing. The result is a narrative world in which cultural reproduction unfolds not in a Franklinian pattern of rational imitation—for if books make no sense they cannot serve as rational models—but rather as a sustained cacophony of parody and travesty.

❦

Tom's reappearance and Aunt Sally's threat of adoption merely make explicit what has been clear all along: for all of Huck's efforts, he cannot escape the burden of "sivilizing," simply because he too is "a prisoner of style." For "sivilizing" demands that the self be made the subject of a sentence the preterit of which is a culture of "moral" literacy. In adopting Huck, Widow Douglas sentences him to her own fictions of domestic reform, which validate her membership in a community of conscience. In order to resist this adoption, Huck, in turn, is forced to objectify that identity and make it the subject of his own version of the self, a version which, no matter how uncertain it may be, must still account for, and be accountable to, the incursions of culture. Huck's incorporation thus takes place most fundamentally in the recognition that he has an identity at all: he is "sivilized" the moment he "lights out" from the widow's home to the hogshead and declares his difference.

Thus, Huck's and Jim's journey downriver, far from enacting a romance of escape, dramatizes and extends the process of "sivilizing" by entangling them in a perilous world of violence and argument that demands that they repeatedly face and deflect the most insistent and threatening question in the narrative: who are you? From the haunting "who-whoing" of an owl (4) and Jim's startled "Who dah?" (6) to the more imperative demands of the Grangerfords' "Who's there?" (132) and the insidious questioning of the bounty hunters and the duke and the dauphin, Huck must repeatedly give account of himself and Jim. To remain silent in this world of strangers is to risk subjection to the questioner's fictions, to risk finding oneself unknowingly identified as a Sheperdson, an abolitionist, a "low-down and ornery" boy, or a slave. To speak the truth risks being once again "sivilized," either by being returned to St. Petersburg as a truant, a slave, or—as Huck finds out with Aunt Sally—by being adopted once more.

In the immediate sense, Huck meets these demands by building his own stories, which both account for his being alone and make it clear that, as a boy, he "belongs" to someone else—an absent uncle or aunt, an ill father. These sentimental stories of broken families provide him with a role that is both close enough to his actual circumstances to allow him to act it with ease and far enough from the truth to mask his real identity. His stories are, in effect, evasions. For despite Jim's sense that a proper escape "doan' *make* no track" (53), Huck realizes that to escape without a trace only incites a concerted search. Thus, one of his most successful evasions comes when he escapes from Pap's cabin by fashioning a false track with pig's blood and a sack of rocks: "I says to myself, they'll follow the track of that sackful of rocks to the shore and then drag the river for me. And they'll follow that meal track to the lake and go browsing down the creek that leads out of it to find the robbers that killed me and took the things. They won't ever hunt the river for anything but my dead carcass. They'll soon get tired of that, and won't bother no more about me" (41). By scattering dust on the traces of his own work, Huck constructs a story without an author, a "nonnamous letter" of his own murder like those Tom sends to make his own evasion more exciting. But it is not excitement Huck wants; it is death and rebirth—his ruse frees him to die in St. Petersburg and forge his own identities. Yet, with his death, he is born into an endless cycle of evasions and a frantic effort to cover his tracks. He and Jim are forced to abandon Jackson's Island because their campfires attract the notice of Judith Loftus, so Huck builds a fire at one end of the island as he and Jim escape from the other. He flees the Grangerfords by leaving "something up there that'll help them to think" he is dead (154). Troubled by the duke and the dauphin's scheme to cheat Mary Jane Wilks out of her inheritance, he plans to steal the money back "some way that they won't suspicion that I done it," in order not to "get mixed up in the business" (226).

Yet Huck is already "mixed up in the business." He cannot simply expose the two rogues without risk of meeting the violence behind their fluency, and he cannot allow Mary Jane to get help without running the risk of exposing himself as a slave stealer. His solution is to hide the money, escape, and then "by and by, when I'm away down the river, . . . write a letter and tell Mary Jane where it's hid." Once again, he plans to write a letter of conscience; like the one he contemplates sending to Miss Watson, it will return stolen property to the rightful owner (his exposure would presumably also return their slaves). This letter, however, is safer to write precisely because no one knows his name. It would allow him to act without having to account for himself; indeed, it would allow him to cover his tracks, to make off with Jim—the more valuable contraband in his eyes—while leaving a trace of his good conscience. It is a close place to be sure, but if Huck realizes later "You can't pray a lie" (269), he can, by neglecting to sign his name to his letter to Mary Jane, write half a lie. He can write an evasion.

And it is precisely as an extended evasion that he writes his "autobiography." In signing himself in writing, he reveals himself in order to absent himself; he transforms himself into a literate subject in order to preserve the full dimension of his difference. As he does when he builds the false fire on Jackson's Island, he "play[s] it as low-down . . . as I could" (77). Just as the fire misleads Mr. Loftus, so, too, does Huck's self-styled "low-down and ornery" language mislead, revealing not a "true" self, but a literate self, a self with a conscience, creating an autobiography that is less an account of his adventures than an accounting of a self in the language of "sivilizing." As such, Huck's autobiographical act is Franklinian precisely insofar as it takes Franklin's memoir at its word. While the latter willfully locates his origins in a regression of writings and authors, Huck gives birth to himself out of a book by "Mr. Mark Twain." If Franklin creates himself in the manner and appearance of a world of credit, Huck "makes" his book about himself in the style of a world of confidence. Thus, when he ends his account still perched on the margins of literacy, vowing to "light out for the Territory," where presumably he will borrow still more versions of himself, he evades into a silence, a reticence, that has accompanied his narrative all along. His plans for his immediate future may represent yet one more false track, his last evasive maneuver. In making his book, he adopts the parodist's skepticism of the world's stories about itself; he disfigures them to expose their senselessness, and then he cloaks his own sense in their language. Huck responds to the threatening question of identity with a "yours truly". Like Tom, he makes a name for himself that is itself the composite of others' names, a name that is "*yours* truly," one that reflects the assumptions of his audience without necessarily betraying his own.

Thus, to borrow the phrase Twain earlier used to describe *Tom Sawyer*, if evasion represents the composite order of Huck's authorship, he builds, or "makes," his book as a scavenger. Just as he "borrows" watermelons and chickens on his journey downriver, he borrows the authority of writing to effect what Jim calls "de smartes' dodge" (128). For Twain, however, Huck's autobiography represents what the dauphin calls "the boss dodge" (215). On the one hand, Twain appropriates Huck's semi-literate strategies of disguise to evade—indeed, to burlesque—the cultural authority invested in his authorship, represented by the bust that opens the text. As he did at the Whittier Birthday banquet, he mocks the literary reverence that would ascribe to "Mr. Mark Twain" a generative power, a sincerity, a character that authors were thought to embody. On the other hand, just as he did in his tale about the miner and his ruffian guests, he uses that very burlesque, his pointed evasion, to construct his nom de plume as the fictional embodiment of a more powerful, a more eloquent, authority. He reanimates his dead bust as the composite of Huck, Tom, Jim, "Mr. Mark Twain," and all the other characters enmeshed in the eloquence of his text. For, if Tom is a prisoner of style, so is Twain; indeed, Tom's reading is his reading, his style.

Coda

"Speaking from the Grave"

WRITERS are, as Twain put it in *Life on the Mississippi* (1883), "manacled servants of the public. We write frankly and fearlessly, but then we 'modify' before we print." When Twain turned in earnest, during the last decade of his life, to compose, or assemble, or "make," his autobiography (it is difficult to characterize what he did with the inchoate mass of material he left behind), it was with the intention of escaping the manacles of his reading audience. In this sense, his autobiography represents his last effort to put down the pen (after "forty years of slavery to the pen I have earned my freedom"[1]), to escape the print shop, and to return to the speaking voice. "You will never know how much enjoyment you have lost," he wrote exultantly to Howells, "until you get to dictating your autobiography." As he "yarned it off," to use Howells's advice to him about writing for the *Atlantic*, Twain discovered "the nameless . . . subtle something which makes good talk so much better than the best imitation of it that can be done with a pen."[2]

The result, as he described it, was a text designed to give its maker complete freedom in composition. "I shall talk about the matter which for the moment interests me, and cast it aside and talk about something else the moment its interest for me is exhausted. . . . It is a system which is a complete and purposed jumble—a course which begins nowhere, follows no specified route, and can never reach an end while I am alive." By following this "apparently systemless system," perched on the borders of the writerly, Twain generated a sprawling mass of manuscript over half a million words in length, stuffed with stories, diatribes, nostalgic reminiscences, articles clipped from the newspaper, and passages from his daughter's memoir of her father.[3] Such freedom, he insisted in another letter to Howells, yielded an honesty scandalous enough to "get my heirs & assigns burnt alive if they venture to print it this side of 2006 AD."[4] As he put it in the preface, his memoirs are "as frank and free and unembarrassed as a love letter" because he will not meet his audience: a writer "never would have unbosomed himself to that large and honest degree if he had known that he was writing for the public."[5]

Twain planned to preserve his freedom and guarantee his honesty by allowing his autobiography to be published only after his death. Thus, he urged his reader in the preface to "keep in mind the fact that I am speaking from the grave." But Twain, like Huck, could not so easily escape the burdens of authorship; he was as much the product of the medium of writing as he was its "master." For speaking from the grave represents not the freedom of speech, but that of the writer released into an absence that comes from signing oneself to the dead letter of print. This, then, was why he could insist to Howells that autobiography is "the truest of all books": not because "death" emboldens the writer to speak directly, but because the writer subjects himself so completely to the writerly. Autobiography's truth, he continues, comes in the evasions and inconsistencies that only an author can indulge in, for it "inevitably consists mainly of extinctions of the truth, shirkings of the truth, partial revealments of the truth." Thus, the living, breathing, speaker lies somewhere "between the lines, where the author-cat is raking dust upon it which hides from the disinterested spectator neither it nor its smell . . . —the result being that the reader knows the author in spite of his wily diligences."[6] In short, an autobiography tells only of its evasions, of the author's efforts to shirk the very matter he claims to reveal. It is a duel with the reader, a rhetorical game that, as Twain figures it, the writer always wins. For, if the reader is a wily opponent, someone dedicated to finding the man "behind" the author, what the reader eventually "knows" is not the man, but the "author." Like Huck, then, Twain writes not a "private history," but a "personal narrative"—a narrative of an individual constructed in and by a public that will "know" him, that will make him their own.

Twain may have been at his most authorly when he agreed to break his plans and publish twenty-five "Chapters from My Autobiography" in the *North American Review* in 1906. After all, they were at least partially selected and edited by the *Review*'s editor, Colonel George Harvey, who a year earlier had sponsored the seventieth birthday party for Twain that so neatly mirrored the one held for Whittier nearly thirty years earlier. With an editorial headnote that obliquely invoked the dinner, the chapters seemed but the natural outgrowth of an honored man obligated to conclude "that a considerable portion" of his life story "might now be suitable to be given to the public."[7] When, in the course of the articles, Twain offers a loose narrative of the same "personal experience" that served as the "capital or culture or education" that supplied his "novels"—reminiscences of his family, quotations from his daughter's memoir, identifications of the models for Huck Finn—he emerges partly as a famous author and partly as yet one more character by that author.

Thus, it is no surprise that he begins his final installment with his account of the Whittier Birthday banquet. Coming as it does at the conclusion of two dozen "author-cat" performances, the speech seems to stand as Twain's most recognizable autobiographical moment, as both the origin and the endpoint of Twain's yarning narrative. Read as part of that narrative, the speech works less to evoke a showdown of authorial prowess—the contestants, like so many of the people Twain reminisces about, are gone, "ghosts now to me, and nameless forever more"—than to uncannily echo the autobiographical project itself. "This is an occasion peculiarly meet for the digging up of pleasant reminiscences concerning literary folk," begins the forty-two-year-old rising star in 1877, "therefore I will drop lightly into history myself."[8] As a younger writer, Twain discovered at the Parker House what Dr. Robinson discovered in *Tom Sawyer*: digging up anything has its risks. Exhuming literary folk, looking for them beneath their writing, is particularly dangerous, for their disinterment reveals nothing more than "pallid, stiff, and repulsive cadavers" (as he called the unfortunate victims of the power of print), or, as he put it that evening in Boston, "imposters." In 1877, Twain had refused to "pursue the subject" of imposture when challenged by the miner; in his autobiography, after carrying his "nom de guerre" to the public for nearly thirty years, he will not let the subject go.

Beneath the masks of humorist, of novelist, of the literary rock of New England embodied in the stony sobriety of his *Huckleberry Finn* bust, lay a writer who himself suffered from "Sir Walter's disease," who was ready to duel in the courts, in the marketplace, and even in his texts for the honor, the privacy, of his name. "Mark Twain" was a pen name, a name of war, built, like "Huck Finn" in the very texts he wrote. It was a name that was "borrowed," literarily as well as literally—and not just from Captain Sellers, but also from all the writers Twain, like Tom, pillaged for his own narratives—and then "self-made" in the "style" of its telling, a style set by the nineteenth-century culture of the literary. For, of course, "style" was not Tom's word, just as the romance literature of escape was not his reading. It was Twain's, learned as a printer's apprentice and wielded in his eloquence as an author perched, if not on the verge of literacy, then on the verge of the literary. It was he who was the master of evasion. For Twain, then, the great lesson of autobiography—indeed, of the literary, in general—lay not in the power of truth but in the authority of writing. "Now, then, that is the tale," he wrote, as the closing words of his *North American Review* installments. "Some of it is true."[9]

Notes

Introduction

1. Letter to unidentified person, 1891, *Mark Twain's Letters*, ed. Albert Bigelow Paine, vol. 2 (New York: Harper & Bros., 1917) 541–43.

2. Mark Twain, *Life on the Mississippi* (New York: New American Library, 1961) 139; *Pudd'nhead Wilson and Those Extraordinary Twins*, ed. Malcolm Bradbury (New York: Penguin, 1969) 229.

3. William Dean Howells, "The Man of Letters as a Man of Business," *Literature and Life: Studies* (New York: Harper & Bros., 1902) 30, 31.

4. On Arnold and American uses of "culture," see Alan Trachtenberg, "American Studies as a Cultural Program," *Ideology and Classic American Literature*, ed. Sacvan Bercovitch and Myra Jehlen (New York: Cambridge UP, 1986) 172–87; see also his *The Incorporation of America: Culture and Society in the Gilded Age* (New York: Hill & Wang, 1982).

5. Thomas Wentworth Higginson, "A Plea for Culture," *Atlantic Monthly* 19 (Jan. 1867): 30, 31, 33.

6. Howells, "Man of Letters," 35.

7. Letter to Henry Houghton, 12 Feb. 1875, *Mark Twain's Letters to His Publishers 1867–1894*, ed. Hamlin Hill (Berkeley: U of California P, 1967) 83.

8. Philip Fisher, "Appearing and Disappearing in Public: Social Space in Late-Nineteenth-Century Literature and Culture," *Reconstructing American Literary History*, ed. Sacvan Bercovitch (Cambridge: Harvard UP, 1986) 165.

9. Van Wyck Brooks, *The Ordeal of Mark Twain* (New York: Dutton, 1920).

10. *The Profession of Authorship in America, 1800–1870: The Papers of William Charvat*, ed. Matthew Bruccoli (Columbus: Ohio State UP, 1968); Lewis P. Simpson, *The Man of Letters in New England and the South: Essays on the History of the Literary Vocation in America* (Baton Rouge: Louisiana State UP, 1973); Raymond Williams, *Marxism and Literature* (New York: Oxford UP, 1977); and Williams, *The Sociology of Culture* (New York: Schocken, 1982).

11. Amy Kaplan, *The Social Construction of American Realism* (Chicago: U of Chicago P, 1988); Richard H. Brodhead, *The School of Hawthorne* (New York: Oxford UP, 1986); and *Cultures of Letters: Scenes of Reading and Writing in Nineteenth-Century America* (Chicago: U of Chicago P, 1993); Daniel H. Borus, *Writing Realism: Howells, James, and Norris in the Mass Market* (Chapel Hill: U of North Carolina P, 1989); Christopher Wilson, *The Labor of Words: Literary Professionalism in the Progressive Era* (Athens: U of Georgia P, 1985); Michael Denning, *Mechanic Accents: Dime Novels and Working-Class Culture in America* (London: Verso, 1987).

12. Borus, *Writing Realism*, 24.

13. Borus, *Writing Realism*, 28. See also David D. Hall, "Introduction: The Uses of Literacy in New England, 1600–1850," *Printing and Society in Early America*, ed. William L. Joyce, David D. Hall, Richard D. Brown, and John B. Hench (Worcester, Mass.: American Antiquarian Society, 1983) 1–47; and Cathy Davidson's "Introduction" to *Reading in America: Literature and Social History*, ed. Cathy N. Davidson (Baltimore: Johns Hopkins UP, 1989) 1–26.

14. Lawrence Levine, *Highbrow/Lowbrow: The Emergence of Cultural Hierarchy in America* (Cambridge: Harvard UP, 1988); Denning, *Mechanic Accents*, 47–61; Alan Trachtenberg, *The Incorporation of America: Culture and Society in the Gilded Age* (New York: Hill & Wang, 1982). See also John Tomsich, *A Genteel Endeavor: American Culture and Politics in the Gilded Age* (Stanford: Stanford UP, 1971).

15. Denning, *Mechanic Accents*, 208.

16. Brodhead, *School of Hawthorne*, 228 n. 56; Amy Kaplan and Borus make only passing reference to Twain.

17. Pierre Bourdieu, "The Field of Cultural Production, or: the Economic World Reversed," *Poetics* 12 (1983): 313. See also his *Language and Symbolic Power*, ed. John B. Thompson (Cambridge: Harvard UP, 1991) 66, where he argues that "linguistic exchange," of which he sees the literary as a subset, "is also an economic exchange which is established within a particular symbolic relation of power between a producer, endowed with a certain linguistic capital, and a consumer (or a market), and which is capable of procuring a certain material or symbolic profit. In other words, utterances are not only (save in exceptional circumstances) signs to be understood and deciphered; they are also *signs of wealth*, intended to be evaluated and appreciated, and *signs of authority*, intended to be believed and obeyed."

18. Bourdieu, "The Field of Cultural Production," 324, 342.

19. Justin Kaplan, *Mr. Clemens and Mark Twain* (New York: Simon & Schuster, 1966).

20. Susan Gillman, *Dark Twins: Imposture and Identity in Mark Twain's America* (Chicago: U of Chicago P, 1989) 14–52.

21. "Mark Twain Tells the Secrets of Novelists," *New York American* (May 1907) 26, in *Mark Twain: Life As I Find It*, ed. Charles Neider (Garden City, N.Y.: Hanover House, 1961) 388.

22. Amy Kaplan offers an intriguing discussion of this moment, *Social Construction*, 66–67.

23. Henry Nash Smith, *Mark Twain: The Development of a Writer* (Cambridge: Harvard UP, 1962); Everett Emerson, *The Authentic Mark Twain: A Literary Biography of Samuel L. Clemens* (Philadelphia: U of Pennsylvania P, 1984); Louis Budd, *Our Mark Twain: The Making of His Public Personality* (Philadelphia: U of Pennsylvania P, 1983).

24. Michel Foucault, "What Is an Author?" *Language, Counter-Memory, Practice: Selected Essays and Interviews*, ed. Donald F. Bouchard (Ithaca: Cornell UP, 1977) 113–38.

25. Miles Orvell, *The Real Thing: Imitation and Authenticity in American Culture, 1880–1940* (Chapel Hill: U of North Carolina P, 1989).

26. Joan Scott, "The Evidence of Experience," *Critical Inquiry* 17 (Summer 1991): 793.

27. Like Michael Herr, who encountered the argot of the Vietnam combat soldier, I, too, "understood what he said, I just wanted to find where he got his language." See Michael Herr, *Dispatches* (New York: Avon, 1980) 28. In effect, Herr senses historically what Mikhail Bakhtin makes explicit theoretically, that linguistic understanding depends on ascertaining "[w]ho speaks and under what conditions he speaks." See Bakhtin's "Discourse in the Novel," *The Dialogic Imagination: Four Essays*, ed. Michael Holquist (Austin: U of Texas P, 1981) 401.

28. James M. Cox's *Mark Twain: The Fate of Humor* (Princeton: Princeton UP, 1966) remains the most far-reaching study of the significance of Twain's humor.

29. Franklin R. Rogers, *Mark Twain's Burlesque Patterns: As Seen in the Novels and Narratives, 1855–1885* (Dallas: Southern Methodist U, 1960).

30. Shelley Fisher Fishkin, *Was Huck Black? Mark Twain and African-American Voices* (New York: Oxford UP, 1993).

31. Rogers, *Burlesque Patterns*, 3–25.

32. Cox, *Fate of Humor*, 44.

33. Harold Bloom, *The Anxiety of Influence: A Theory of Poetry* (New York: Oxford UP, 1973).

34. Cox, *Fate of Humor*, 24.

35. The relevant texts by Bakhtin include *Problems in Dostoevsky's Poetics*, trans. R. W. Rotsel (Ann Arbor: Ardis, 1973) and the essays in *The Dialogic Imagination*. Both David R. Sewell, *Mark Twain's Languages: Discourse, Dialogue, and Linguistic Variety* (Berkeley: U of California P, 1987) and Forrest G. Robinson, *In Bad Faith: The Dynamics of Deception in Mark Twain's America* (Cambridge: Harvard UP, 1986) make explicit use of Bakhtin. Roland Ballorain was the first to read Twain through Bakhtin, in "Mark Twain's Capers: A Chameleon in King Carnival's Court," *American Novelists Revisited: Essays in Feminist Criticism*, ed. Fritz Fleischmann (Boston: G. K. Hall, 1982).

36. Smith, *Development of a Writer*, 20. Smith lays out his critical perspective 4–20.

37. Smith, *Development of a Writer*, 7.

38. Fishkin offers a similar argument when she poses the oral tradition of the black vernacular against the canonized discourse of literature.

39. Bakhtin, "Prehistory," 47, and "Discourse in the Novel," 289, both in *Dialogic Imagination*. Emphasis is in the original.

40. The word "documents" appears in Dominick LaCapra, "Rethinking Intellectual History and Reading Texts," in his *Rethinking Intellectual History: Texts Contexts Language* (Ithaca: Cornell UP, 1983) 30.

41. Williams, *Marxism and Literature*, 128–35.

Chapter One. *"Littery Man"*

1. Letter to William Dean Howells, 3 Sept. 1881, *The Mark Twain–Howells Letters: The Correspondence of Samuel L. Clemens and William D. Howells, 1872–1910*, ed. Henry Nash Smith and William M. Gibson, vol. 1 (Cambridge: Harvard UP, 1960) 369. Hereafter cited as *MTHL*.

2. Letter to Howells, 26 May 1878, *MTHL*, vol. 1, 231. Twain here refers to his composition of *Tom Sawyer*. Typically, the "call" came, as he describes it in the same letter, "loud & decided, at last. So tomorrow I shall begin regular, steady work, & stick to it till middle of July or 1st August."

3. Justin Kaplan, *Mr. Clemens and Mark Twain* (New York: Simon & Schuster, 1966) 179–80.

4. Autobiographical dictation, 30 Aug. 1906, *Mark Twain in Eruption: Hitherto Unpublished Pages about Men and Events*, ed. Bernard DeVoto (New York: Capricorn Books, 1968) 197.

5. Letter to Howells, 16 Aug. 1898, *MTHL*, vol. 2, 674–75.

6. Autobiographical dictation, 30 Aug. 1906, *Mark Twain in Eruption*, ed. DeVoto, 196.

7. Susan Gillman, *Dark Twins: Imposture and Identity in Mark Twain's America* (Chicago: U of Chicago P, 1989) 38.

8. Letter to Howells, 8 Dec. 1874, *MTHL*, vol. 1, 49.

9. Gillman, *Dark Twins*, 34.

10. Mark Twain, "How to Tell a Story," in *"How to Tell a Story" and Other Essays*, vol. 22 of *The Writings of Mark Twain*, Hillcrest Edition (New York: Harper & Bros., 1906) 7–15.

11. Letter to Livy Clemens, quoted in Justin Kaplan, *Mr. Clemens and Mark Twain*, 71.

12. *The Autobiography of Mark Twain*, ed. Charles Neider (New York: HarperCollins, 1990) 14.

13. *Autobiography*, ed. Neider, 6.

14. Letter to Edward Bok, n.d. [1888], *Mark Twain's Letters*, ed. Albert Bigelow Paine, vol. 2 (New York: Harper & Bros., 1917) 504. Hereafter cited as *Letters*. Twain refused Bok permission to publish an interview, but he did allow him to print the letter.

15. Letter to Howells, 17 Nov. 1879, *MTHL*, vol. 1, 279. The martial metaphors are prompted by the fact that Twain refers to a reunion for the Army of the Tennessee.

Twain himself vowed at one point to give up banquet speaking because his talks looked so "miserably pale and vapid and lifeless in the cold print of a damp newspaper next morning." Quoted in Louis Budd, *Our Mark Twain: The Making of His Public Personality* (Philadelphia: U of Pennsylvania P, 1983) 57.

16. Walter Ong, "The Writer's Audience Is Always a Fiction," *PMLA* 90. 1 (1975): 10.

17. William Dean Howells, "The Man of Letters as a Man of Business," *Literature and Life: Studies* (New York: Harper & Bros., 1902) 32.

18. Letter to Andrew Lang, 1889, *Letters*, vol. 2, 528.

19. Howells, letter to Twain, 3 Dec. 1874, *MTHL*, vol. 1, 46.

20. Ong, "Writer's Audience," 11.

21. Letter to Howells, 8 Dec. 1874, *MTHL*, vol. 1, 49.

22. Letter to Henry Rogers, Nov. 1896, *Mark Twain's Letters to His Publishers, 1867–1894*, ed. Hamlin Hill (Berkeley: U of California P, 1967) 7.

23. Letter to Howells, 12 May to 13 May 1899, *MTHL*, vol. 2, 698. A year before he died, Twain found even this scheme too restrictive and wanted to dispense with *all* audiences. Even a stenographer, he wrote, "is a lecture-audience; . . . he is a restraint, because there is only one of him, & one alien auditor can seldom be an inspiration." Thus, he wanted to experiment with writing "letters to friends & *not to send them*." Letter to Howells, 17 Apr. 1909, *MTHL*, vol. 2, 844.

24. On such changes see *The Profession of Authorship in America, 1800–1870: The Papers of William Charvat*, ed. Matthew Bruccoli (Columbus: Ohio State UP, 1968); Daniel H. Borus, *Writing Realism: Howells, James, Norris and the Mass Market* (Chapel Hill: U of North Carolina P, 1989); Ann Douglas, *The Feminization of American Culture* (New York: Avon, 1977); Mary Kelley, *Private Woman, Public Stage: Literary Domesticity in Nineteenth-Century America* (New York: Oxford UP, 1984) 3–27; and Christopher Wilson, *The Labor of Words: Literary Professionalism in the Progressive Era* (Athens: U of Georgia P, 1985).

25. John Tomsich, *A Genteel Endeavor: American Culture and Politics in the Gilded Age* (Stanford: Stanford UP, 1971).

26. William Dean Howells, *My Mark Twain: Reminiscences and Criticisms* (New York: Harper & Bros., 1910) 101.

27. Letter to Andrew Lang, 1889, *Letters*, vol. 2, 526, 527, 528.

28. R. Jackson Wilson, *Figures of Speech: American Writers and the Literary Marketplace from Benjamin Franklin to Emily Dickinson* (New York: Knopf, 1989) 8.

29. Nina Baym, *Novel, Readers, and Reviewers: Responses to Fiction in Antebellum America* (Ithaca: Cornell UP, 1984). See also Borus, *Writing Realism* 118–30.

30. William Dean Howells, *Years of My Youth and Three Essays*, ed. David J. Nordloh, vol. 29, *A Selected Edition of W. D. Howells* (Bloomington: Indiana UP, 1975) 110.

31. The quotations are taken from, in order, the prefaces to *Roughing It*, *Adventures of Huckleberry Finn*, *The Adventures of Tom Sawyer*, and *The Innocents Abroad*.

32. Alan Gribben, "Autobiography as Property: Mark Twain and His Legend," *The Mythologizing of Mark Twain*, ed. Sara DeSaussure Davis and Philip D. Beidler (University, Ala.: U of Alabama P, 1984) 48.

33. T. M. Parrott, "Mark Twain: Made in America," *Booklover's Magazine* 3 (Feb. 1904), reprinted in *Mark Twain: The Critical Heritage*, ed. Frederick Anderson (London: Routledge & Kegan Paul, 1971) 244.

34. George Ade, "Mark Twain as Our Emissary," *Century Magazine* 81 (Dec. 1910), reprinted in *Critical Essays on Mark Twain, 1867–1910*, ed. Louis J. Budd (Boston: G. K. Hall, 1982) 241. For an analysis of Twain's public personality, see Budd's *Our Mark Twain*.

35. Twain wrote to his brother Orion Clemens in 1887: "I have never yet allowed an interviewer or biography-sketcher to get out of me any circumstance of my history which I thought might be worth putting some day into my *auto*biography." Quoted in Gribben, "Autobiography as Property," 46.

36. Gribben quotes Twain as writing: "I hate all public mention of my private history, anyway. It is none of the public's business"; in "Autobiography as Property," 46.

37. Mark Twain, *Mark Twain's Own Autobiography: The Chapters from the "North American Review,"* ed. Michael J. Kiskis (Madison: U of Wisconsin P, 1990) 230. Twain dates the entry 11 Jan. 1906.

38. Gillman, *Dark Twins*, 21.

39. The text of the speech is taken from *Mark Twain Speaking*, ed. Paul Fatout (Iowa City: U of Iowa P, 1976) 110–15.

40. Letter to Howells, 27 Mar. 1882, *MTHL*, vol. 1, 398.

41. Letter to Mary Fairbanks, 5 Feb. 1878, *Mark Twain to Mrs. Fairbanks*, ed. Dixon Wecter (San Marino, Calif.: Huntington Library, 1949) 217.

42. Twain, *Own Autobiography*, 237.

43. Later still, he recovered "my former admiration of it." Quoted in Henry Nash Smith, "That Hideous Mistake of Poor Clemens's," *Harvard Library Bulletin* 9 (Spring 1955): 175.

44. Twain, *Own Autobiography*, 234–35.

45. Twain, *Own Autobiography*, 236.

46. Howells's introduction of Twain is quoted in Kenneth S. Lynn, *William Dean Howells: An American Life* (New York: Harcourt Brace Jovanovich, 1971) 170. Howells's later remarks are in *My Mark Twain*, 60. Howells may have, in fact, been writing with Twain's autobiographical account in mind.

47. For accounts of the dinner, see Smith, "Hideous Mistake," Lynn, *An American Life*, and Justin Kaplan, *Mr. Clemens and Mark Twain*, all cited earlier; Smith's *Mark Twain: The Development of a Writer* (Cambridge: Harvard UP, 1962) 92–112; J. C. Derby, *Fifty Years among Authors, Books and Publishers* (New York: G. W. Carleton, 1884) 280–85; Arthur Gilman, "Atlantic Dinners and Diners," *Atlantic Monthly* 100.5 (1907): 646–57; and Ellen B. Ballou, *The Building of the House: Houghton Mifflin's Formative Years* (Boston: Houghton Mifflin, 1970) 217–23.

48. Quoted in Albert Bigelow Paine, *Mark Twain: A Biography*, vol. 4 (New York: Harper & Bros., 1912) 1269.

49. Twain, *Own Autobiography*, 287.

50. As Smith points out in "Hideous Mistake," newspaper debates fell generally into a

pattern of at least mild support by the Boston papers and varying levels of outrage by more Western papers like the conservative Springfield *Republican* and the Worcester *Gazette*. Lawrence Buell's study of New England literary culture suggests that this split may have reflected the varying expectations of urban and non-urban reading communities. See his *New England Literary Culture: From Revolution through Renaissance* (New York: Cambridge UP, 1986).

51. Justin Kaplan, in particular, makes this point in *Mr. Clemens and Mark Twain*, as does Smith in *Development of a Writer*.

52. Letter to Mary Fairbanks, *Mark Twain to Mrs. Fairbanks*, 217. Twain expressed admiration for the work of all three of the writers he burlesqued. "Nobody writes a finer & purer English than [the historian John Lothrop] Motley[,] Howells, Hawthorne & Holmes," he wrote in his notebooks. He regularly made gifts of Longfellow's books to his family and liberally quoted him in his correspondence. He had a quotation from Emerson's essay "Domestic Life" engraved on his mantle in Hartford. On all three writers, see Alan Gribben, *Mark Twain's Library: A Reconstruction*, vol. 1 (Boston: G. K. Hall, 1980) 220–22, 317–20, 419–22. The remark on Holmes is quoted on 318.

53. On Shakespeare's place in American culture, see Lawrence Levine, *Highbrow/Lowbrow: The Emergence of Cultural Hierarchy in America* (Cambridge: Harvard UP, 1988). On Twain's engagements with Shakespeare, see Thomas J. Richardson, "Is Shakespeare Dead? Mark Twain's Irreverent Question," *Shakespeare and Southern Writers: A Study in Influence*, ed. Philip C. Kolin (Jackson, Mississippi: UP of Mississippi, 1985) 63–82. Twain's burlesque, *1601, Conversation As It Was by the Social Fireside in the Time of the Tudors*, was privately distributed (Twain considered it too coarse for publication) the year before the banquet.

54. Letter to Howells, 3 Sept. 1881, *MTHL*, vol. 1, 369.

55. Quoted in Levine, *Highbrow/Lowbrow*, 72.

56. Boston *Daily Advertiser*, 18 Dec. 1877, 1.

57. Boston *Evening Transcript*, 18 Dec. 1877, 3.

58. Twain, *Own Autobiography*, 234.

59. Cincinnati *Commercial*, 26 Dec. 1877, 3, in Smith "Hideous Mistake," 158.

60. Holmes to Twain, 29 Dec. 1877, in Smith, "Hideous Mistake," 165.

61. *Daily Advertiser*, 18 Dec. 1877, 1.

62. Howells, *My Mark Twain*, 59.

63. Howells, *My Mark Twain*, 63.

64. Lionel Trilling, *Sincerity and Authenticity* (Cambridge: Harvard UP, 1971).

65. *Daily Advertiser*, 18 Dec. 1877, 1.

66. The text is from an advertisement on page 2 of the *Daily Advertiser*, 17 Dec. 1877. The portrait is offered for $1 to any new subscriber to the *Atlantic*. The next day the portrait was endorsed by Holmes ("This fine presentment of a noble face"), Longfellow, Charles Dudley Warner, John Townsend Trowbridge, and Edmund Clarence Stedman, all of whom attended the banquet; *Daily Advertiser*, 18 Dec. 1877, 2.

67. *Daily Advertiser*, 18 Dec. 1877, 1; 20 Dec. 1877, 1.

68. *Daily Advertiser*, 18 Dec. 1877, 1.

69. Ballou, *Houghton Mifflin's Formative Years*, 339–41, 389. The series also included a biography of James Russell Lowell, who, as the *Atlantic*'s first editor, was invited to, but could not attend, the dinner.

70. On Scudder, see Nina Baym, "Early Histories of American Literature: A Chapter in the Institution of New England," *American Literary History* 1.3 (Fall 1989): 462. See also Richard H. Brodhead, *The School of Hawthorne* (New York: Oxford UP, 1986) 59–62. Brodhead argues that, in general, the close-knit relationships between writers, reviewers, and editors formed a Hawthornian canon.

71. Brodhead, *School of Hawthorne*,55; see also Buell, *New England Literary Culture*, 44–55.

72. George Parsons Lathrop, "Literary and Social Boston," *Harper's Monthly* 62 (February 1881): 381–98; Edward Waldo Emerson, *The Early Years of the Saturday Club, 1855–1870* (Boston: Houghton Mifflin, 1918); and William Dean Howells, "Literary Boston as I Knew It," *Literary Friends and Acquaintance: A Personal Retrospect of American Authorship*, ed. David F. Hiatt and Edwin H. Cady, vol. 32, *A Selected Edition of William Dean Howells*, Edwin H. Cady, gen. ed. (Bloomington: Indiana UP, 1968) 98–124.

73. I borrow "distinction" from the title of Pierre Bourdieu's *Distinction: A Social Critique of the Judgement of Taste*, trans. Richard Nice (Cambridge: Harvard UP, 1984).

74. On Longfellow and Bonner, see *Profession of Authorship*, ed. Bruccoli, 155–67.

75. Quoted in James Playsted Wood, *Magazines in the United States* (New York: Ronald, 1956) 32.

76. Quoted in Brodhead, *School of Hawthorne*, 54.

77. Horace E. Scudder, "Nursery Classics in School," *Atlantic* 59 (June 1887): 802.

78. A young Theodore Dreiser interviewed Howells in 1898 for the first issue of *Success* magazine, which subsequently featured Carnegie and Edison, along with a whole range of other figures. On the implications of this for Dreiser's own sense of authorship, see Amy Kaplan, *The Social Construction of American Realism*, (Chicago: U of Chicago P, 1988) 104–39.

79. Wilson, *Figures of Speech*, and Tomsich, *A Genteel Endeavor*, both develop at length this tension between ideologies of genteel and mass cultural literary production.

80. Mark Twain, *Adventures of Huckleberry Finn*, ed. Walter Blair and Victor Fischer, *The Works of Mark Twain*, ed. Robert H. Hirst, vol. 8 (Berkeley, U of California P, 1988) 179.

81. Mark Twain, *Satires & Burlesques*, ed. Franklin R. Rogers (Berkeley: U of California P, 1967) 69.

82. Francis Underwood wrote in his official biography of Whittier: "The manner in which the poets were supposed to have pelted each other with quotations was wholly irresistible." *John Greenleaf Whittier* (Boston, 1884) 310, quoted in Smith, "Hideous Mistake," 153.

83. Chicago *Tribune*, 23 Dec. 1877, 16, quoted in Smith, "Hideous Mistake," 154.

84. Letter to Howells, 23 Dec. 1877, *MTHL*, vol. 1, 212.

85. I refer, in order, to Smith, *Development of a Writer*; Justin Kaplan, *Mr. Clemens and Mark Twain*, and Bernard DeVoto, *Mark Twain's America* (Cambridge: Houghton Mifflin, 1932).

86. "[Houghton] had always believed that Mark Twain was literature, and it was his zeal and courage which justified me in asking for more and more contributions from him." William Dean Howells, "Recollections of an Atlantic Editorship," *Atlantic* C. 601 (November 1907), quoted in *MTHL*, vol. 1, 26.

87. Ballou, *Houghton Mifflin's Formative Years*, 209.

88. Twain, *Own Autobiography*, 235.

89. Letter to Howells, 5 July 1875, in *MTHL*, vol. 1, 92.

90. Letter to Henry Houghton, 12 Feb. 1875, *Letters to Publishers*, ed. Hill, 83.

91. Howells, "Man of Letters," 1.

92. *Daily Advertiser*, 18 Dec. 1877, 1.

93. *New York Times*, 6 Dec. 1905, 1. For a compelling comparison of Whittier's and Twain's seventieth birthday celebrations, see Henry Nash Smith, "Mark Twain, 'Funniest Man in the World,'" *Mythologizing of Mark Twain*, ed. Davis and Beidler, 56–76.

94. See Smith on Twain's revisions, "Hideous Mistake," 176–77.

95. *Daily Advertiser*, 20 Dec. 1877, 1. Brief accounts of the controversy can be found in Smith, "Hideous Mistake," 150, and Derby, *Fifty Years*, 283–84.

96. *Daily Advertiser*, 20 Dec. 1877, 1.

97. Reprinted in the *Daily Advertiser*, 28 Dec. 1877, 2.

98. Quoted in Gilman, "Atlantic Dinners," 655. The seriousness of the gaffe is reflected in Gilman's account, written in 1907, which makes much of the exclusion. Similarly Derby, writing in 1884, quotes an article from "a Western paper" entitled "Mr. Houghton's Mistake," 283–85.

99. *New York Times*, 6 Dec. 1905, 1.

100 For an account of the banquet, see Gilman, "Atlantic Dinners," 650–51.

101. *Daily Advertiser*, 20 Dec. 1877, 1.

102. On Fink and Lovingood, see Kenneth Lynn, *Mark Twain and Southwestern Humor* (Boston: Little, Brown, 1959). On Crockett, see Caroll Smith-Rosenberg's very suggestive article, "Davy Crockett as Trickster: Pornography, Liminality, and Symbolic Inversion in Victorian America," *Disorderly Conduct: Visions of Gender in Victorian America* (New York: Knopf, 1985) 90–108.

103. Jane Tompkins, *Sensational Designs: The Cultural Work of American Fiction, 1790–1860* (New York: Oxford UP, 1985).

104. Walter Benjamin, "The Author as Producer," *Reflections: Essays, Aphorisms, Autobiographical Writings*, ed. Peter Demetz (New York: Schocken, 1978) 222.

105. Text is taken from *Mark Twain Speaking*, ed. Fatout, 162–65.

106. Fredric Jameson, *The Political Unconscious: Narrative as a Socially Symbolic Act* (Ithaca: Cornell UP, 1981) 81; see also "Symbolic Inference; or Kenneth Burke and Ideological Analysis," in Jameson's *Situations of Theory* (Minneapolis: U of Minnesota P, 1988) 137–52, vol. 1, *The Ideologies of Theory: Essays 1971–1986*.

Chapter Two. *Consuming Desire*

1. William Dean Howells, *My Mark Twain: Reminiscences and Criticisms*, (New York: Harper & Bros., 1910) 58.

2. William Dean Howells, "America's Literary Centres," *Literature and Life: Studies* (New York: Harper & Bros., 1902) 179. Howells is contrasting literary Boston of the past with New York.

3. *Publishers Weekly*, 21 June 1880, quoted in Donald Sheehan, *This Was Publishing: A Chronicle of the Book Trade in the Gilded Age* (Bloomington: Indiana UP, 1952) 35.

4. William Dean Howells, "The Man of Letters as a Man of Business," *Literature and Life: Studies* (New York: Harper & Bros., 1902) 29, 11, 4, 6, 30.

5. Richard H. Brodhead, *The School of Hawthorne*, (New York: Oxford UP, 1986) 101.

6. William Dean Howells, "Criticism and Fiction," *Criticism and Fiction and Other Essays*, ed. Clara Marburg Kirk and Rudolf Kirk (New York: New York UP, 1959) 46–47.

7. Howells, "Criticism and Fiction," 46.

8. Adams Sherman Hill, "English in Newspapers and Novels," *Scribner's*, vol. 2 (1887): 374.

9. Howells, "Criticism and Fiction," 45.

10. Howells, "Man of Letters," 34.

11. Amy Kaplan, *The Social Construction of American Realism* (Chicago: U of Chicago P, 1988) 16, 17, 13.

12. See, in particular, Howells's essay, "Mark Twain," which appeared in *Century* magazine in 1882, reprinted in *Mark Twain: The Critical Heritage*, ed. Frederick Anderson (London: Routledge & Kegan Paul, 1971) 98–103.

13. On Twain's pursuit of inventions, see Justin Kaplan, *Mr. Clemens and Mark Twain*

(New York: Simon & Schuster, 1966) 150–51, 251–53. On his attitudes toward money, see Kaplan, 95–97, 322–23.

14. Letter to Charles Webster, 16 May 1881, in Samuel C. Webster, *Mark Twain, Business Man* (Boston: Little, Brown, 1946) 156.

15. *The Autobiography of Mark Twain*, ed. Charles Neider (New York: HarperCollins, 1990) 152.

16. On the Riley scheme, see Justin Kaplan, *Mr. Clemens and Mark Twain*, 124–29.

17. On the meanings of, and historical tensions between, market and market*place*, see Peter Stallybrass and Allon White, *The Politics and Poetics of Transgression* (Ithaca: Cornell UP, 1986) 27–79 and Jean-Christophe Agnew, *Worlds Apart: The Market and the Theater in Anglo-American Thought, 1550–1750* (New York: Cambridge UP, 1986) 17–56.

18. Kenneth R. Andrews, *Nook Farm: Mark Twain's Hartford Circle* (Cambridge: Harvard UP, 1950) 120.

19. John Tebbel, *A History of Book Publishing in the United States*, vol. 1 (New York: R. R. Bowker, 1972) 238.

20. Tebbel, *History of Book Publishing*, vol. 2, 104.

21. In August 1869, Twain took a further step in this direction by taking over one-third ownership of the newspaper, the Buffalo *Express*, with the $25,000 capital loaned to him by his new father-in-law, the coal baron Jervis Langdon.

22. On the success of the book, see Justin Kaplan, *Mr. Clemens and Mark Twain*, 104–8.

23. Letter to Elisha Bliss, 28 Jan. 1870, *Mark Twain's Letters*, ed. Albert Bigelow Paine, vol. 1 (New York: Harper & Bros., 1917) 169. Hereafter cited as *Letters*.

24. Letter to Dan DeQuille [William Wright], 1875, in Oscar Lewis's introduction, *The Big Bonanza*, by Dan DeQuille (New York: Knopf, 1947) xviii–xix.

25. For a thorough discussion of Twain's revisions, see Leon T. Dickinson, "Mark Twain's Revisions in Writing *The Innocents Abroad*," *American Literature* 19 (May 1947): 139–57. Daniel Morley McKeithan collects and edits all of Twain's travel letters in *Traveling with the Innocents Abroad: Mark Twain's Original Reports from Europe and the Holy Land* (Norman: U of Oklahoma P, 1958).

26. Quoted in Louis Budd, *Our Mark Twain: The Making of His Public Personality* (Philadelphia: U of Pennsylvania P, 1983) 34.

27. Mark Twain, *The Innocents Abroad* (New York: New American Library, 1966) 136. Subsequent citations will appear in the text.

28. Harriet Beecher Stowe, *Sunny Memories of Foreign Lands*, vol. 2 (Boston: Phillips, Sampson, 1854) 159, 160.

29. Henry Ward Beecher, *Star Papers; or, Experiences of Art and Nature* (New York: J. C. Derby, 1855) 59, 57.

30. James Jackson Jarves, *The Art Idea*, ed. Benjamin Rowland (1864; Cambridge: Harvard UP, 1960) 44.

31. For an important discussion of antebellum travel accounts of encounters with European art, see Neil Harris, *The Artist in American Society: The Formative Years, 1790–1860* (Chicago: U of Chicago P, 1966) 124–69. See also William L. Vance, *America's Rome*, 2 vols. (New Haven: Yale UP, 1989).

32. John Overton Choules, *The Cruise of the Steam Yacht North Star; a Narrative of the Excursion of Mr. Vanderbilt's Party* (Boston: Gould and Lincoln, 1854) 221.

33. [W. M. Gillespie], *Rome: As Seen by a New-Yorker in 1843–4* (New York, 1845) 82; quoted in Harris, *Artist in American Society*, 128.

34. In his popular treatise *The Art Idea*, Jarves put the case in language that prefigured Henry James's better-known lament, mourning that America had "no abbeys in picturesque

ruins; no stately cathedrals, . . . no mediaeval architecture, . . . venerable with age; no aristocratic mansions, in which art enshrines itself in a selfish and unappreciating era, to come forth to the people in more auspicious times; no state collections to guide a growing taste; no caste of persons of whom fashion demands encouragement to art-growth; no ancestral homes, . . . ; no legendary lore . . . ; and, the greatest loss of all, no lofty and sublime poetry, . . . " (151).

35. Cushing Strout, *The American Image of the Old World* (New York: Harper, 1963) 64.

36. For an account of the Athenaeum's founding, see Lewis P. Simpson, "Joseph Stevens Buckminster: The Rise of the New England Clerisy," in his *The Man of Letters in New England and the South: Essays on the History of the Literary Vocation in America* (Baton Rouge: Louisiana State UP, 1973).

37. Strout, *American Image*, 70, 72. On Jarves's travel writing, see Willard Thorp, "Pilgrims' Return," *The Literary History of the United States*, ed. Robert E. Spiller et. al., 3rd ed., vol. 1 (London: Collier Macmillan, 1963) 826, 836–37.

38. Bayard Taylor, *By-Ways of Europe* (1869; New York: G. P. Putnam, 1889) 8.

39. Bayard Taylor, *Views Afoot, or Europe Seen with Knapsack and Staff*, household ed., rev. (1855; New York: G. P. Putnam, 1890) 407.

40. As John Sears has pointed out, the roots of the motivations behind modern travel and tourism lie in the eighteenth-century appropriation of landscape for aesthetic fulfillment. Having thus turned nature into a veritable art museum, it would be but logical for travelers to discover the quintessence of travel in the actual museums. See Sears, *Sacred Places: American Tourist Attractions in the Nineteenth Century* (New York: Oxford UP, 1989).

41. Rev. John E. Edwards, A. M., *Random Sketches and Notes of European Travel in 1856* (New York: Harper & Bros., 1857) 268.

42. Johann Wolfgang von Goethe, "Observations on Leonardo da Vinci's Celebrated Picture of The Last Supper," *Goethe on Art*, trans. G. H. Noehden, ed. John Gage (Berkeley: U of California P, 1980) 166. This translation originally appeared as a separate pamphlet in 1821.

43. Mrs. [Anna] Jameson, *Sacred and Legendary Art*, 8th ed., vol. 1 (1848; London: Longmans, Green, 1879) 268.

44. Charles Eliot Norton, *Notes of Travel and Study in Italy* (Boston: Houghton Mifflin, 1859) 317.

45. Mark Twain, "The American Vandal Abroad," *Mark Twain Speaking*, ed. Paul Fatout (Iowa City: U of Iowa P, 1976) 27, 29. The lecture was delivered during the winter lyceum season of 1868–69.

46. Unsigned review, *Saturday Review* (8 Oct. 1870), reprinted in *Critical Heritage*, ed. Anderson, 43.

47. Bret Harte, unsigned review, *Overland Monthly* (Jan. 1870), in *Critical Heritage*, ed. Anderson, 33.

48. Edwards, *Random Sketches*, 268.

49. Taylor, *Views Afoot*, 352.

50. Stowe, *Sunny Memories*, 23.

51. Goethe, "Leonardo Da Vinci," 166.

52. Jameson, *Sacred and Legendary Art*, 269; Grace Greenwood [Sara Jane Lippincott], *Haps and Mishaps or A Tour in Europe* (Boston: Ticknor, Reed, and Fields, 1854) 397.

53. "Aura," of course, comes from Walter Benjamin, "The Work of Art in the Age of Mechanical Reproduction," *Illuminations*, trans. Harry Zohn, ed. Hannah Arendt (New York: Schocken, 1969).

54. The distinction comes from Dean MacCannell, *The Tourist: A New Theory of the Leisure Class* (New York: Schocken, 1976). See also James Clifford, *The Predicament of Culture: Twentieth-Century Ethnography, Literature, and Art* (Cambridge: Harvard UP, 1988) 215–51.

55. Henry James, "Preface to 'The Reverberator,'" *The Art of the Novel*, ed. R. P. Blackmur (New York: Scribner's, 1962) 189.

56. Strout, *American Images,* remains the standard text on this subject. See also the more narrowly focused Van Wyck Brooks, *The Dream of Arcadia: American Writers and Artists in Italy, 1760–1915* (New York: Dutton, 1958).

57. Cited in Dewey Ganzel, *Mark Twain Abroad: The Cruise of the "Quaker City"* (Chicago: U of Chicago P, 1968) 3.

58. Foster Rhea Dulles, *Americans Abroad: Two Centuries of European Travel* (Ann Arbor: U of Michigan P, 1964) 44. Dulles argues that the 100,000 mark was not reached until the end of the century.

59. On chromolithography, see Peter C. Marzio, *The Democratic Art: Pictures for a 19th-Century America* (Boston: David Godine, 1979). On the popularity of stereopticon viewing and vicarious travel, see Richard Masteller, "Western Views in Eastern Parlors: The Contribution of the Stereograph Photographer to the Conquest of the West," *Prospects* 6 (1981): 55–71; and my "Iron Frames: Reconstructing the Landscape Views of A. J. Russell's Photography," *Nineteenth-Century Contexts*, 13.1 (Spring 1989): 41–66. On the general issue of mass representation and authenticity, see Miles Orvell, *The Real Thing: Imitation and Authenticity in American Culture, 1880–1940* (Chapel Hill: U of North Carolina P, 1989).

60. Sears, *Sacred Places*, 123.

61. Taylor, *By-Ways*, 12.

62. Beecher, *Star Papers*, 86; Julia Ward Howe, *From the Oak to the Olive. A Plain Record of a Pleasant Journey* (Boston: Lee and Shepard, 1868) 61.

63. Choules, *Cruise*, 225. Emphasis in the original.

64. The quotation is from Jarves, *Art Idea*, 152. In their efforts to assay a distinct value for culture in what they saw as a utilitarian society, writers regularly defined it in terms of capital. "Some preparation must be made beforehand," advised one writer in urging his readers to study history before leaving home, just as "some capital is necessary to start business." [Charles Bullard Fairbanks], *Aguecheek,* (Boston: Shepard, Clark, and Brown, 1859) 155.

65. Jarves, *Art Idea*, 39, 44, 45.

66. Beecher, *Star Papers*, 80; Greenwood, *Haps and Mishaps*, 141, 354.

67. On disposition, see Pierre Bourdieu, *Distinction: A Social Critique of the Judgment of Taste,* trans. Richard Nice (Cambridge: Harvard UP, 1984) 29 *passim*; and Bourdieu, "The Field of Cultural Production, or the Economic World Reversed," *Poetics* 12 (1983).

68. *Aguecheek,* 127, 128, 129. This is but the most vivid example of what was a common theme; see, for instance, Jarves for a number of extended discussions on the same issues. On travelers' theories of art's possibilities as an instrument of social control, see Harris, *Artist in American Society*, 146–68. On the formation of American hierarchies of cultural taste and their implications for social order, see Lawrence Levine, *Highbrow/Lowbrow: The Emergence of Cultural Hierarchy in America* (Cambridge: Harvard UP, 1988).

69. The phrase "mercenary eye" appears in a letter to Henry Houghton, 12 Feb. 1875, *Mark Twain's Letters to Publishers, 1867–1894*, ed. Hamlin Hill (Berkeley: U of California P, 1967) 83.

70. On the circumstances of the trip, see Ganzel, *Mark Twain Abroad.*

71. *Publishers Weekly*, 21 June 1880, 8; G. Mercer Adams, *Publishers Weekly*, 2 Feb. 1884, 149–50.

72. *Publishers Weekly*, 14 May 1887, 640, quoted in Tebbel, *History of Book Publishing*, vol. 2, 518.

73. "The Subscription Book Trade," *Publishers Weekly* II (23 July 1872) 94.

74. Lyman Abbott, "Suggestions For Household Libraries," *Hints For Home Reading: A*

Series of Chapters on Books and Their Use, ed. Lyman Abbott (New York: G. P. Putnam, 1880) 112.

75. Charles F. Richardson, *The Choice of Books* (New York: American Book Exchange, 1881) 74–75.

76. In their domestic advice guide, *The American Woman's Home, or, Principles of Domestic Science*, Catherine Beecher and Harriet Beecher Stowe urge their readers to use chromolithographs to decorate their home: "[S]urrounded by such suggestions of the beautiful, and such reminders of history and art, children are constantly trained to correctness of taste and refinement of thought, and stimulated—sometimes to efforts at artistic imitation, always to the eager and intelligent inquiry about the scenes, the places, the incidents represented." (1869; Hartford, Conn.: Stowe-Day Foundation, 1975) 94.

77. The bookselling guide is reprinted in *Mark Twain and Elisha Bliss*, ed. Hamlin Hill, (Columbia, Mo.: U of Missouri P, 1964) 170–82.

78. Twain's name, as well, was used to attract passengers; he was, in the end, the only celebrity to actually make the journey.

79. Jean-Christophe Agnew, "A House of Fiction: Domestic Interiors and the Commodity Aesthetic," *Consuming Visions: Accumulation and Display of Goods in America, 1880–1920*, ed. Simon J. Bronner (New York: Norton, 1989) 135.

80. *Autobiography*, ed. Neider, 150–51.

81. See Susan Gillman, *Dark Twins: Imposture and Identity in Mark Twain's America* (Chicago: U of Chicago P, 1989) 14–52.

82. Interview in Portland *Oregonian*, 11 Aug. 1895, reprinted in Walter Blair, *Mark Twain and Huck Finn* (Berkeley: U of California P, 1960) 270.

83. *Critical Heritage*, ed. Anderson, 34.

84. Everett Emerson, *The Authentic Mark Twain: A Literary Biography of Samuel L. Clemens* (Philadelphia: U of Pennsylvania P, 1984) 48.

85. Ganzel, *Mark Twain Abroad*, 219–20, 110. Henry Nash Smith notes how Twain modeled his celebrated description of the Sphinx on those of other writers; see his *Mark Twain: The Development of a Writer* (Cambridge: Harvard UP, 1962) 46–50.

86. Hamlin Hill, "Mark Twain: Audience and Artistry," *American Quarterly* 15.1 (Spring 1963): 25–40; Alan Gribben, "'Stolen from Books, Tho' Credit Given': Mark Twain's Use of Literary Sources," *Mosaic* 12.4 (1979): 149–55.

87. New York *Evening Post*, 20 Jan. 1883, 3; "How 'Innocents Abroad' Was Written," *Letters*, vol. 2, 194.

88. On the aesthetics of collecting, see Susan Stewart, *On Longing: Narrative of the Miniature, the Gigantic, the Souvenir, the Collection* (Baltimore: Johns Hopkins UP, 1984); and Clifford, *Predicament of Culture*, 215–51.

89. Jean Baudrillard, *For a Critique of the Political Economy of the Sign*, trans. Charles Levin (St. Louis: Telos Press, 1981).

90. On sign systems of domestic interiors, see Orvell, *Real Thing*, 40–72.

91. *Autobiography*, ed. Neider, 151.

92. Thomas Starr King, *A Vacation among the Sierras* (1860) 36, quoted in Sears, *Sacred Places*, 145.

93. Mark Twain, *Roughing It* (New York: New American Library, 1980) 29. Subsequent citations will appear in the text.

94. Smith, *Development of a Writer*, 52–70; Stephen Fender, *Plotting the Golden West: American Literature and the Rhetoric of the California Trail* (New York: Cambridge UP, 1981) 129–60.

95. Lee Clark Mitchell, "Verbally *Roughing It*: The West of Words," *Nineteenth-Century Literature* 44 (1989): 86, 70, 77.

96. Smith entitles his chapter on *Roughing It* in *Development of a Writer*, "Transformation of a Tenderfoot," 52–70.

97. Everett Emerson makes a similar point in *Authentic Mark Twain*, 65. See also James M. Cox, *Mark Twain: The Fate of Humor* (Princeton: Princeton UP, 1966) 87–95.

98. Smith notes the narrator's growing passivity toward his material throughout much of the last half of the book. It is as if prospectors and speculators have no place in the world of labor and production, much less in the Sandwich Islands. See *Development of a Writer*, 61–69.

99. Georg Lukács, "Reification and the Consciousness of the Proletariat," *History and Class Consciousness*, trans. Rodney Livingstone (Cambridge: MIT Press, 1971) 83–110.

CHAPTER THREE. *A "Rightly Constructed Boy's Life"*

1. Letter to Howells, 3 Apr. 1876, *The Mark Twain–Howells Letters: The Correspondence of Samuel L. Clemens and William D. Howells, 1872–1910*, ed. Henry Nash Smith and William M. Gibson, vol. 1 (Cambridge: Harvard UP, 1960) 128. Hereafter cited as *MTHL*. Whether "American" meant "national" (Twain was also concerned with the book's release in England at the time) or referred to Bliss's American Publishing Company is unclear.

2. Mark Twain, *The Adventures of Tom Sawyer* (Berkeley: U of California P, 1980) 100, 79. Subsequent citations will appear in the text.

3. See for instance, James M. Cox, *Mark Twain: The Fate of Humor* (Princeton: Princeton UP, 1966) 136–40, and Judith Fetterley, "Mark Twain and the Anxiety of Entertainment," *Georgia Review* 33 (1979): 382–91.

4. Henry Nash Smith, *Mark Twain: The Development of a Writer* (Cambridge: Harvard UP, 1962).

5. As Twain insisted to Howells, to whom he sent the manuscript for revisions: "[It] is *not* a boy's book, at all. It will only be read by adults. It is only written for adults." Howells, however, did not agree—nor did the manuscript's other reader, Twain's wife, Livy—and argued that Twain could increase his market by targeting children. Only when revising the novel had Twain "ceased to regard the volume as being for adults." Letters to Howells, 5 July 1875, *MTHL*, vol. 1, 91; 18 Jan. 1876, *MTHL*, vol. 1, 122. See also Howells's letter to Twain, 21 Nov. 1875, *MTHL*, vol. 1, 110–11.

6. Letter to Orion Clemens, 15 Mar. 1871, quoted in Albert E. Stone, Jr., *The Innocent Eye: Childhood in Mark Twain's Imagination* (New Haven: Yale UP, 1961) 51.

7. Mark Twain, "The Story of the Bad Little Boy," and "The Story of the Good Little Boy," *The Complete Short Stories of Mark Twain*, ed. Charles Neider (New York: Bantam, 1981) 7, 70.

8. Twain, "Good Little Boy," 76.

9. On gender and literary authorship, see Mary Kelley, *Private Woman, Public Stage: Literary Domesticity in Nineteenth-Century America* (New York: Oxford UP, 1984); Lawrence Buell, *New England Literary Culture: From Revolution Through Renaissance* (New York: Cambridge UP, 1986); Christopher Wilson, *The Labor of Words: Literary Professionalism in the Progressive Era* (Athens: U of Georgia P, 1985); and Ann Douglas, *The Feminization of American Culture* (New York: Avon, 1977).

10. Kelley, *Private Woman, Public Stage*.

11. The phrase is taken from Louis Budd, *Our Mark Twain: The Making of His Public Personality* (Philadelphia: U of Pennsylvania P, 1983).

12. The obvious exceptions to this may be figures like Harriet Beecher Stowe and, later in the century, Frances Watkins Harper, both of whom carried a public "presence" or character that allowed them to speak on a range of issues. Yet Stowe, who was excluded from the

Whittier Birthday dinner, suffered criticism for what was seen as her violation of gender. (For a particularly pithy critique of the gender ideologies framing the reception of *Uncle Tom's Cabin*, see Fanny Fern's mock review of the book in *Ruth Hall and Other Writings*, ed. Joyce Warren [New Brunswick: Rutgers UP, 1986] 255–56.) And Harper's *Iola Leroy* was reviewed in the context of her already extensive career as a political speaker; see Hazel Carby, *Reconstructing Womanhood: The Emergence of the Afro-American Woman Novelist* (New York: Oxford UP, 1987) 62–94. For a discussion of how public discourse legitimates masculinity, see Michael Warner, "The Mass Public and the Mass Subject," *Habermas and the Public Sphere*, ed. Craig Calhoun (Cambridge: MIT P, 1992) 377–401.

13. Michael Davitt Bell, "The Sin of Art and the Problem of American Realism: William Dean Howells," *Prospects* 9 (1984): 125. See also Alfred Habegger, *Gender, Fantasy, and Realism in American Literature* (New York: Columbia UP, 1982).

14. William Dean Howells, "The Man of Letters as a Man of Business," *Literature and Life: Studies* (New York: Harper & Bros., 1902) 3.

15. William Dean Howells, "Criticism and Fiction," *Criticism and Fiction and Other Essays*, ed. Clara Marburg Kirk and Rudolf Kirk (New York: New York UP, 1959) 26.

16. On professional language, see JoAnne Brown, "Professional Language: Words That Succeed," *Radical History Review* 34.1 (1986): 33–51. On professional authority, see Burton J. Bledstein, *The Culture of Professionalism: The Middle Class and the Development of Higher Education in America* (New York: Norton, 1978) 88–102.

17. George Bainton, *The Art of Authorship* (New York, 1890) 87–88.

18. Leslie Fiedler offers a provocative discussion of the two neighbours' rivalry in his *What Was Literataure? Class Culture and Mass Society* (New York: Simon & Schuster, 1982) 242–44.

19. Justin Kaplan, in *Mr. Clemens and Mark Twain* (New York: Simon & Schuster, 1966), posits that Twain's "ideal audience" for *The Prince and the Pauper* is suggested by the book's dedication to his daughters, Susy and Clara, to whom, along with his wife, Livy, and his longtime friend Mary Fairbanks (another ideal reader), he read his manuscript (239). See also Kaplan's account of Twain's and Warner's private readings of *The Gilded Age* (161); and Peter Stonely's *Mark Twain and the Feminine Aesthetic* (New York: Cambridge UP, 1992).

20. Letter to Howells, 17 Nov. 1889, *MTHL*, vol. 1, 279.

21. Letter to Livy, 14 Nov. 1879, *Mark Twain's Letters*, ed. Albert Bigelow Paine, vol. 1 (New York: Harper & Bros., 1917) 371. Hereafter cited as *Letters*.

22. The passage comes in a letter to Howells, quoted in chapter 1, where he proclaims his "serenity" at writing for a more dignified *Atlantic* audience, *MTHL*, vol. 1, 49.

23. *Adventures of Huckleberry Finn*, ed. Walter Blair and Victor Fischer, *The Works of Mark Twain*, ed. Robert H. Hirst, vol. 8 (Berkeley, U of California P, 1988) 196.

24. An account of Twain's use of the story can be found in *Mark Twain in Eruption: Hitherto Unpublished Pages about Men and Events*, ed. Bernard DeVoto (New York: Capricorn Books, 1968); the quotation appears on 361. See also Walter Blair's and Victor Fischer's "Explanatory Notes," *Adventures of Huckleberry Finn*, 414.

25. Letter to Livy, 14 Nov. 1879, 12 Nov. 1879, in *Letters*, vol. 1, 371, 368.

26. "The Babies. As They Comfort Us in Our Sorrows, Let Us Not Forget Them in Our Festivities," *Mark Twain Speaking*, ed. Paul Fatout (Iowa City: U of Iowa P, 1976) 133, 132.

27. The quoted phrase comes in an undelivered speech in honor of Bayard Taylor, written in 1874; *Mark Twain Speaking*, ed. Fatout, 116.

28. Letter to Mrs. Bowen, 6 June 1900 in *Mark Twain's Letters to Will Bowen, "My First, & Oldest & Dearest Friend"* (Austin: U of Texas P, 1941) 27. See also his unmailed letter of 9 Sept. 1887, where he declares, "Tom Sawyer is simply a hymn, put into prose form to give it a worldly air," *Letters*, vol. 2, 477.

29. Letter to an unidentified person, 1891, in *Letters*, vol. 2, 541. Twain added in a postscript that he subsequently deleted: "I can't get away from the boyhood period because . . . I lack . . . interest in handling the men and experiences of later times." Quoted in Walter Blair, *Mark Twain and Huck Finn*, (Berkeley: U of California P, 1960) 9.

30. On changing perceptions of childhood, see Bernard Wishy, *The Child and the Republic* (Philadelphia: U of Pennsylvania P, 1968).

31. W. A. Jones, "Children's Books," *The United States Magazine and Democratic Review* 15 (1844): 544. On boys' fiction, see Richard L. Darling, *The Rise of Children's Book Reviewing in America, 1865–1881* (New York: R. R. Bowker, 1968); Stone, *The Innocent Eye*; and Daniel T. Rodgers, *The Work Ethic in Industrial America, 1850–1920* (Chicago: U of Chicago P, 1974) 125–52.

32. Thomas Bailey Aldrich, *The Story of a Bad Boy, The Little Violinist, and Other Essays*, in *The Writings of Thomas Bailey Aldrich*, vol. 7 (Boston: Houghton Mifflin, 1911) 13.

33. Charles Dudley Warner, *Being a Boy*, in *The Complete Writings of Charles Dudley Warner*, vol. 7 (Hartford: American Publishing Co., 1904) 9.

34. Aldrich, *Story of a Bad Boy*, 3.

35. Rodgers, *Work Ethic*, 134.

36. T. J. Jackson Lears, *No Place of Grace: Antimodernism and the Transformation of American Culture, 1880–1920* (New York: Pantheon, 1981) 146.

37. The review is reprinted, in part, in *Mark Twain: The Critical Heritage*, ed. Frederick Anderson (London: Routledge & Kegan Paul, 1971) 59–61. The quotation appears on 59.

38. The phrase is from George B. Forgie, *Patricide in the House Divided: A Psychological Interpretation of Lincoln and His Age* (New York: Norton, 1979); see especially 159–200. On the middle class's "escape from history," see Douglas, *Feminization*, 197–239.

39. The phrase is taken from Christopher Lasch, *Haven in a Heartless World: The Family Besieged* (New York: Basic, 1977).

40. Mary P. Ryan, *Cradle of the Middle Class: The Family in Oneida County, New York, 1790–1865* (Cambridge: Cambridge UP, 1981) 165–78.

41. E. Anthony Rotundo, in examining a wide range of correspondence between middle- and upper-middle-class parents and sons, notes that "one of the main topics in nineteenth-century correspondence . . . was ideals of manhood." See his "Learning About Manhood: Gender Ideals and the Middle-Class Family in Nineteenth-Century America," *Manliness and Morality: Middle-Class Masculinity in Britain and America, 1800–1940*, ed. J. A. Mangan and James Walvin (New York: St. Martin's, 1987) 35–51. The quotation appears on 43.

42. Mark C. Carnes, *Secret Ritual and Manhood in Victorian America* (New Haven: Yale UP, 1989).

43. David Leverenz, *Manhood and the American Renaissance* (Ithaca: Cornell UP, 1989) 73, 74; and Charles E. Rosenberg, "Sexuality, Class and Role in 19th-Century America," *American Quarterly* 25.2 (May 1973): 141.

44. Ryan makes this point most persuasively, in *Cradle of The Middle Class*, 145–85.

45. Eli Zaretsky, *Capitalism, The Family, and Personal Life* (New York: Harper, 1976) 77. See also Stuart Blumin's cogent discussion of the paradoxes of middle-class awareness in his "The Hypothesis of Middle-Class Formation in Nineteenth-Century America: A Critique and Some Proposals," *American History Review* 90.2 (Apr. 1985): 298–338.

46. Steven Mailloux, "The Rhetorical Use and Abuse of Fiction: Eating Books in Late Nineteenth-Century America," *Boundary 2*, 17.1 (1990): 135.

47. In Twain's "Facts Concerning the Recent Carnival of Crime in Connecticut" (1876), the narrator goes on a liberating spree of mayhem and revenge after he meets and finally kills his conscience, which appears to him as a freakish and malevolent dwarf.

48. The phrase is from Ryan's *Cradle of the Middle Class*, 161.

49. Jacob Abbott, *Rollo at Work, or, The Way to be Industrious*, rev. ed. (Philadelphia: B. F. Jackson, 1853) 75. Subsequent citations will appear in the text.

50. "Children's Books of the Year," *North American Review* 102 (Jan. 1866) 246.

51. Alan Gribben, *Mark Twain's Library: A Reconstruction*, vol. 1 (Boston: G. K. Hall, 1980) 78.

52. Jacob Abbott, *Rollo at Play, or, Safe Amusements*, rev. ed. (Philadelphia: B. F. Jackson, 1853). Subsequent citations will appear in the text.

53. Maria Edgeworth, *The Parent's Assistant, or, Stories for Children* (1800; New York: Hurd & Houghton, 1869) preface.

54. Jacob Abbott, *Gentle Measures in the Management and Training of the Young* (New York: Harper & Bros., 1872) 32.

55. Abbott, *Gentle Measures*, 193.

56. On patriarchal childrearing, see Charles Strickland, "A Transcendentalist Father: The Child-Rearing Practices of Bronson Alcott," *Perspectives in American History* 3 (1969): 5–73.

57. Lydia Maria Child, *The Mother's Book* (Boston: Carter, Hendee and Babcock, 1831) preface; and Ann E. Porter, *Uncle Jerry's Letters to Young Mothers* (Boston: John P. Jewett, 1854) 55–56.

58. On mothers as the assumed audience of advice literature on children, see Nancy Cott, "Notes Toward an Interpretation of Antebellum Childrearing," *The Psychohistory Review* 6.4 (1978) 4–20.

59. See Cott, "Notes," and Wishy, *The Child and the Republic*. For a wider survey of liberalization, see N. Ray Hiner, "The Child in American Historiography: Accomplishments and Prospects," *The Psychohistory Review* 7 (Summer 1978): 13–23.

60. Abbott, *Gentle Measures*, 11, 16, 51.

61. Abbott, *Gentle Measures*, 177.

62. John S. C. Abbott, *The Mother at Home: or the Principles of Maternal Duty Familiarly Illustrated*, 2nd ed. (Boston: Crocker Brewster, 1833) 105, 159; Samuel Goodrich, *Fireside Education* (New York: Huntington, 1838) 22.

63. Goodrich, *Fireside Education*, 88; Horace Bushnell, *On Christian Nurture* (New Haven: Yale UP, 1947) 296.

64. On Twain's relationship with Bushnell, see Kenneth R. Andrews, *Nook Farm Mark Twain's Hartford Circle* (Cambridge: Harvard UP, 1950) 25–30, 103, 104.

65. Bushnell, *On Christian Nurture*, 74, 75.

66. Bushnell, *On Christian Nurture*, 74, 280.

67. Daniel Walker Howe, "Victorian Culture in America," *Victorian America*, ed. Daniel Walker Howe (Philadelphia: U of Pennsylvania P, 1976) 23. On the authority of print, see Bledstein, *Culture of Professionalism*, 65–79.

68. John Abbott, *Mother at Home*, 159.

69. H[eman] Humphrey, *Domestic Education* (Amherst: JS&C Adams, 1840) 51.

70. On advice literature for young men, see Karen Haltunnen, *Confidence Men and Painted Women: A Study of Middle-Class Culture in America, 1830–1870* (New Haven: Yale UP, 1982) 21–24, 193–94; and Allan Stanley Horlick, *Country Boys and Merchant Princes: The Social Control of Young Men in New York* (Lewisburg, Pa.: Bucknell UP, 1975) 147–78.

71. William A. Alcott, *The Young Man's Guide*, rev., 16th ed. (Boston: T. R. Marvin, 1846) 25. The importance of generational continuity lies as well behind Henry Ward Beecher's equally popular *Addresses to Young Men* (Philadelphia: Henry Altemus, n.d.). See his preface and that of S. R. Smith, *Words to Young Gentlemen and Young Ladies; or, The Path of Happiness for Young People* (Boston: James M. Usher, 1842). On the popularity of such books, see

Joseph Kett, *Rites of Passage: Adolescence in America, 1790 to the Present* (New York: Basic, 1977) 95.

72. Porter, *Uncle Jerry's Letters*, 9, 10, 11, 12.

73. While I stress what we can call their "fictionality," the extent to which the anxieties constructed in these texts reflect some element of a middle-class experience of historical rupture and feminine domestic isolation is suggested by the words of one mother who wrote privately: "There is scarcely any subject concerning which I feel more anxiety than the proper education of my children. It is a difficult and delicate subject, the more I feel how much is to be learnt by myself." Quoted in Carl N. Degler, *At Odds: Women and the Family in America from the Revolution to the Present* (New York: Oxford UP, 1980) 68.

74. Jones, "Children's Books," 537.

75. "Children's Books of the Year," 238.

76. "Pernicious Juvenile Literature," *National Quarterly Review* 39 (1879): 143, 141.

77. W[illiam] G[raham] Sumner, "What Our Boys Are Reading," *Scribner's Monthly*, 15.5 (Mar. 1878): 683.

78. Michael Denning, *Mechanic Accents: Dime Novels and Working-Class Culture in America* (London: Verso, 1987) 59.

79. Howells, "Criticism and Fiction," 51, 52.

80. Letter to Henry Rogers, Nov. 1896, *Mark Twain's Letters to His Publishers, 1867–1894*, ed. Hamlin Hill (Berkeley: U of California P, 1967) 7.

81. This is not to dismiss altogether the links Denning suggests at the end of his book between Twain and dime novelists. Certainly the "sequels" to *Tom Sawyer*—*Tom Sawyer Abroad*, *Tom Sawyer, Detective*, and "Tom Sawyer among the Indians"—solicit a market with their main characters in much the same way as do formulaic dime novels. And to the extent that Mark Twain becomes the preeminent character of his fiction, many of his other writings circulate in like manner. But even these issues must be understood in the context of Twain's aspirations to the "classic" status that Denning concedes to him; *Mechanic Accents*, 208.

82. Quoted in John Tomsich, *A Genteel Endeavor: American Culture and Politics in the Guilded Age* (Stanford: Stanford UP, 1971) 121. On the feminized home as a target for writing, see Douglas, *Feminization*.

83. Howells, "Criticism and Fiction," 75.

84. Bushnell, *On Christian Nurture*, 287.

85. Michel Foucault, *Discipline and Punish: The Birth of the Prison* (New York: Vintage, 1979) 116.

86. Bushnell, *On Christian Nurture*, 286. On authors citing prison officials, see Goodrich, *Fireside Education*, 20–21, and "Pernicious Juvenile Literature," 144. On the links between juvenile reform and domesticity, see David J. Rothman, *The Discovery of the Asylum: Social Order and Disorder in the New Republic* (Boston: Little, Brown, 1971) 206–36; and Stanley K. Schultz, *The Culture Factory: Boston Public Schools, 1789–1860* (New York: Oxford UP, 1973) 48–68.

87. See Kett, *Rites of Passage*, 111–34.

88. On the expectations for parental discipline voiced by advice writers, see Richard Brodhead, "Sparing the Rod: Discipline and Fiction in Antebellum America," *Representations* 21 (Winter 1988), especially 67–77.

89. Letter to Andrew Lang, 1889, *Letters*, vol. 2, 527–28.

90. The following discussion is based on the excellent textual commentary in *The Adventures of Tom Sawyer, Tom Sawyer Abroad, Tom Sawyer, Detective*, ed. John C. Gerber, Paul Baender, and Terry Firkins, *The Works of Mark Twain*, ed. Robert H. Hirst, vol. 6 (Berke-

ley: U of California P, 1980). See especially "Introduction," 3–30, and "Textual Apparatus," 503–619. Also of help is Hamlin Hill, "The Composition and Structure of *Tom Sawyer*," *American Literature* 32 (Jan. 1961): 379–92.

91. The two chapters between Becky's and Tom's romance and the trial–chapters 21 and 22—were inserted later.

92. The gang, according to Bernard DeVoto, was during the antebellum period "perhaps the most dangerous and certainly the most widespread criminal organization in America." *Mark Twain's America* (Boston: Little, Brown, 1932) 17.

CHAPTER FOUR. *"By the Book"*

1. Letter to Howells, 5 July 1875, *The Mark Twain–Howells Letters: The Correspondence of Samuel L. Clemens and William D. Howells, 1872–1910*, ed. Henry Nash Smith and William M. Gibson, vol. 1 (Cambridge: Harvard UP, 1960), 91. Hereafter cited as *MTHL*.

2. Mark Twain, *Adventures of Huckleberry Finn*, ed. Walter Blair and Victor Fischer, *The Works of Mark Twain*, ed. Robert H. Hirst, vol. 8 (Berkeley: U of California P, 1988) 1. Subsequent citations will appear in the text.

3. Letters to Howells, 20 July 1883, and 15 Oct. 1883, *MTHL*, vol. 1, 432, 445–46.

4. Mark Twain, *The Adventures of Tom Sawyer*, (Berkeley: U of California P, 1980) 48, 256–57.

5. The passage appears in Twain's notebooks in 1895. Quoted it Everett Emerson, *The Authentic Mark Twain: A Literary Biography of Samuel L. Clemens* (Philadelphia: U of Pennsylvania P, 1984), 138.

6. Henry Nash Smith, *Mark Twain: The Development of a Writer* (Cambridge: Harvard UP, 1962).

7. Forrest G. Robinson, *In Bad Faith: The Dynamics of Deception in Mark Twain's America* (Cambridge: Harvard UP, 1986), 126, 206.

8. St. Louis *Globe-Democrat*, 17 Mar. 1885, 1, in *The Critical Response to Mark Twain's Huckleberry Finn*, ed. Laurie Champion (New York: Greenwood Press, 1991) 13.

9. The Springfield *Daily Republican* cited that speech and Twain's latest book as evidence that "Mr. Clemens . . . has no reliable sense of propriety," 17 Mar. 1885: 4; in *Critical Response*, ed. Champion, 14.

10. Boston *Daily Globe*, 17 Mar. 1885: 2; in *Critical Response*, ed. Champion, 14. The writer then advised Twain in the future to "put a little more whenceness of the hereafter among his nowness of the here."

11. Steven Mailloux, *Rhetorical Power* (Ithaca: Cornell UP, 1989) 116.

12. Russell Reising, *The Unusable Past: Theory and the Study of American Literature* (New York: Methuen, 1986) 151–62; the quotation appears on 162. On contemporary debates over the novel's racial politics, see *Critical Response*, ed. Champion; and *Satire or Evasion? Black Perspectives on Huckleberry Finn*, ed. James S. Leonard, Thomas Tenney, and Thadious M. Davis (Durham, N.C.: Duke UP, 1992).

13. Mailloux, *Rhetorical Power*, 97, 100.

14. Victor Doyno is the latest critic to emphasize "the narrative of a minimally literate boy in conflict with a society which defines itself and exercises control *through books*." See his *Writing Huck Finn: Mark Twain's Creative Process* (Philadelphia, U of Pennsylvania P, 1991) 28. The New York *Herald* quoted one member of the Concord Library Committee as objecting to the book's "rough, ignorant dialect" and its "systematic use of bad grammar and an employment of inelegant expressions." New York *Herald*, 18 Mar. 1885: 6; in *Critical Response*, ed. Champion, 14, 15.

15. Smith, *Development of a Writer*, viii. As David Sewell has argued, despite Twain's fascination with—indeed, his seeming embrace of—the vernacular perspective, he was an author "for whom correct speech [was] still a moral norm": he counted among his favorite books Henry Breen's grammatical analysis of literature, *Modern English Literature: Its Blemishes & Defects*, and Richard Grant White's *Words and Their Uses*. See Sewell's *Mark Twain's Languages: Discourse, Dialogue, and Linguistic Variety* (Berkeley: U of California P, 1987) 89. See 15–36 for a cogent analysis of Twain's relationship to prescriptive grammar. On the larger politics of standard English, see Dennis E. Baron, *Grammar and Good Taste: Reforming the American Language* (New Haven: Yale UP, 1982) 142–50. On Breen specifically, see Alan Gribben, *Mark Twain's Library: A Reconstruction*, vol. 1 (Boston: G. K. Hall, 1980) 82.

16. On the rendering of idiomatic speech in print, see Neil Schmitz, *Of Huck and Alice: Humorous Writing in American Literature* (Minneapolis: U of Minnesota P, 1983) 65–95.

17. Schmitz, *Of Huck and Alice*, 60. Schmitz's insights into the "phonocentrism" of American humor, in general, and of the humor in *Huckleberry Finn*, in particular, have proven enormously helpful to my own conceptualization of the text.

18. See Twain's letter to Howells, 9 Aug. 1876, *MTHL*, vol. 1, 144.

19. His nephew Charles Webster, who oversaw the book's publication, thought "it would help the sale of the book and would go nicely" with the frontispiece of Huck already in place. Letter to Twain, 13 Sept. 1884, in "Textual Introduction," *Huckleberry Finn*, 478.

20. Gerhardt would later do Grant's bust. On Twain's patronage, see Walter Blair, *Mark Twain and Huck Finn*, (Berkeley: U of California P, 1960) 360. The quotation is from Justin Kaplan, *Mr. Clemens and Mark Twain* (New York: Simon & Schuster, 1966) 263.

21. William Dean Howells, "Mark Twain," *Century Magazine* (1882), reprinted in *Mark Twain: The Critical Heritage*, ed. Frederick Anderson (London: Routledge & Kegan Paul, 1971) 101. See also, in the same volume, the Harvard educator Thomas Sergeant Perry's comparison of Twain and Whitman in "An American on American Humor," *St. James Gazette* (1883), especially 106.

22. Letter to Mollie Fairbanks, 6 Aug. 1877, in *Mark Twain to Mrs. Fairbanks*, ed. Dixon Wecter (San Marino: Huntington Library, 1949) 206–7.

23. Letter to Orion Clemens, 12 May 1880; quoted in Justin Kaplan, *Mr. Clemens and Mark Twain*, 237.

24. Emerson gives a clear account of Twain's writing efforts during the period, in *Authentic Mark Twain*, 126.

25. Anonymous review, New York *Tribune*, 25 Oct. 1881, quoted in Emerson, *Authentic Mark Twain*, 111. Emerson gives a good overview of the critical reaction, both public and private, to the novel. See 108–11.

26. Letter to Annie Lucas, 31 Jan. 1881, quoted in Emerson, *Authentic Mark Twain*, 108.

27. Letter to Howells, 5 July 1875, *MTHL*, vol. 1, 91.

28. Mrs. James T. Fields, *Memories of a Hostess*, 251; quoted in Blair, *Mark Twain and Huck Finn*, 80.

29. Mark Twain, "Autobiography of a Damned Fool," *Satires & Burlesques*, ed. Franklin R. Rogers (Berkeley: U of California P, 1967) 144. The relevant episode is on 144–46.

30. For an account of Twain's uses of Franklin's *Autobiography*, see Gribben, *Mark Twain's Library*, vol. 1, 241–43.

31. For a brief overview of the publishing history of Franklin's autobiography, see "Introduction," *The Autobiography of Benjamin Franklin*, ed. Leonard W. Larabee, et. al. (New Haven, Yale UP, 1964).

32. Letter to Howells, 6 June 1877, *MTHL*, vol. 1, 180.

33. See Twain's letters to Orion Clemens, 26 Oct. 1853 and 28 Nov. 1853, *Mark Twain's Letters*, ed. Albert Bigelow Paine, vol. 1 (New York: Harper & Bros., 1917) 25–29.

34. *Roughing It* (New York: New American Library, 1980) 221. James Cox briefly but usefully analyzes the parallels between the two men's careers, suggesting that Twain's (inaccurate) account in his own *Autobiography* of leaving his brother's print shop is modeled on that of Franklin's abandonment of his apprenticeship to his brother. See Cox's *Mark Twain: The Fate of Humor* (Princeton: Princeton UP, 1966) 91–93.

35. "The Late Benjamin Franklin," *Sketches New and Old*, vol. 19, *The Writings of Mark Twain*, Hillcrest Edition (New York: Harper & Bros., 1906) 211, 212, 215; "Some Thoughts on the Science of Onanism," *Mark Twain Speaking*, ed. Paul Fatout (Iowa City: U of Iowa P, 1976) 125.

36. Sacvan Bercovitch, "The Ritual of American Autobiography: Edwards, Franklin, Thoreau," *Revue Francaise D'etudes Americaines* 7.14 (May 1982): 141, 148. The educator William Harris confessed to reading Locke's *Human Understanding* as a child, "having read somewhere that Franklin prided himself on reading that work at my age." See William T. Harris, "How I Was Educated," *Forum* 1 (Aug. 1886): 559. See also Jeannette Leonard Gilder, "Books That Have Helped Me," *Forum* 4 (Oct. 1887): 207–12, who counts the *Autobiography* as the most influential book of her childhood. She humorously recounts her efforts to follow as exactly as possible the details of Franklin's life story. For a brief survey of Franklin's place in school texts, see Ruth Miller Elson, *Guardians of Tradition: American Schoolbooks of the Nineteenth Century* (Lincoln: U of Nebraska P, 1964) 191–93.

37. Noah Porter, *Books and Reading, or What Shall I Read and How Shall I Read Them?* rev. ed. (New York: Scribner's, 1888) 211.

38. Robert Sayre makes the point that "The young man in the *Autobiography* is patently a boy's Franklin." See "Autobiography and the Making of America," *Autobiography: Essays Theoretical and Critical*, ed. James Olney (Princeton: Princeton UP, 1980) 158.

39. *A Brief Memoir of the Life of Dr. Benjamin Franklin Compiled for the Use of Young Persons* (New York: Mahlon Day, 1833) 1.

40. [William L. Mott], *The Young Franklinian, Grandfather's Story: Written for the Children of Mechanics and Farmers By their Wellwisher* (Hartford: William L. Mott, 1872) 77, and William M. Thayer, *The Printer Boy, or, How Ben Franklin Made His Mark, An Example for Youth* (Boston: J. E. Tilton, 1861) 231. Other texts consulted include *A Life of Benjamin Franklin: Embracing Anecdotes Illustrative of his Character* (Boston: Lee & Shepard, 1876); Henry Mayhew, *Young Benjamin Franklin, or, the Right Road Through Life. A Boy's Book on a Boy's Own Subject* (New York: Harper & Bros., 1862); Peter Parley, *The Lives of Franklin and Washington Illustrated By Tales, Sketches, and Anecdotes Adapted to the Use of Schools, and Young Persons* (London: Thomas Tegg, 1839); Jacob Abbot, *Franklin, the Apprentice Boy* (New York: Harper & Bros., 1855); and [Samuel Hutchins] *Benjamin Franklin: A Book for the Young and the Old: For All* (Cambridge, Mass., 1853).

41. Thayer, *Printer Boy*, 101; [Hutchins], *Benjamin Franklin*, 9. See also Abbott, *Franklin*, 24–27; Franklin, *A Brief Memoir*, 16; and *A Life of Benjamin Franklin*, 27–33.

42. *A Life of Benjamin Franklin*, 27–28; Abbott, *Franklin*, vii–viii, 27.

43. Franklin, *Autobiography*, 43. Subsequent citations will appear in the text.

44. Franklin's break with his father caused nineteenth-century pedagogues some anxiety. Some texts dealt with its implications by emphasizing the errors of Franklin's ways and pointing to the later reconciliation of father and son. Others located the source for his "rebellion" in the unjustifiably harsh ways of his brother. One went so far as to deny the problem altogether, baldly stating: "Benjamin was generally very prompt to obey his parents, even when he did not exactly see the necessity of their commands. He understood full well that

obedience was a law of the household." Thayer, *Printer Boy*, 23; see also Mayhew, *Young Benjamin Franklin*, Abbott, *Franklin*, and [Hutchins], *Benjamin Franklin*.

45. Jay Fliegelman uses the eighteenth-century term "emulation" to characterize "the apprentice/master relationship" that informs Franklin's use of *The Spectator*. As he puts it: "Emulation permitted the expression of ambition in the context of a larger reverence for the models of the past, an accommodation of authority and liberty, of ancients and moderns." *Declaring Independence: Jefferson, Natural Language, & The Culture of Performance* (Stanford, Calif.: Stanford UP, 1993) 180.

46. Christopher Looby, "'The Affairs of the Revolution Occasion'd the Interruption': Writing, Revolution, Deferral, and Conciliation in Franklin's *Autobiography*," *American Quarterly* 38. 1 (Spring 1986): 78. See also Elizabeth Davis, who describes the scene as a "paradigmatic encounter with language," in "Events in the Life and in the Text: Franklin and the Style of American Autobiography," *Revue Francaise D'etudes Americaines* 7.14 (May 1982): 190.

47. Michael Warner, *The Letters of the Republic: Publication and the Public Sphere in Eighteenth-Century America* (Cambridge: Harvard UP, 1990) 76.

48. Warner, *Letters of the Republic*, 82.

49. Insofar as his life story merges personal success and cultural continuity into a figural enactment of history, Franklin drew on the Puritan tradition of figural history in which the efforts of colonists in the New World were interpreted both individually and collectively as the fulfillment of both Christic salvation and the migration of the Jews from Egypt. The preeminent American practitioner of the art was Cotton Mather, whose major work, *Magnalia Christi Americana*, Franklin cites on 51. On figuration, see Erich Auerbach, "Figura," *Scenes from the Drama of European Literature* (Minnesota: U of Minnesota P, 1984) 11–78; and Sacvan Bercovitch, *The Puritan Origins of the American Self* (New Haven: Yale UP, 1975) 53–73.

50. As Warner argues, "Franklin's famous ambition of perfection is formed on the model of print, on the submersion of the personal in a general reproduction." Warner, *Letters of the Republic*, 89.

51. Warner, *Letters of the Republic*, 90.

52. The connection between the two books is certified all the more by Twain's inclusion of a chapter from his novel in *Life on the Mississippi* and his subsequent decision to leave that chapter out of *Huckleberry Finn* when it was printed. The whole story lies in neither book.

53. Samuel Moffett, "Mark Twain: A Biographical Sketch," in *"How to Tell a Story" and Other Essays*, vol. 22 of *The Writings of Mark Twain*, Hillcrest Edition (New York: Harper & Bros., 1906) 314–15.

54. Moffett, "Biographical Sketch," 328, 329, 332–33.

55. *A Life of Franklin*, 33–34.

56. William Torrey Harris, "How I Was Educated," *Forum* 1 (August 1886): 559.

57. William Torrey Harris, "How Far May the State Provide for the Education of Her Children at Public Cost?" *The Addresses and Journal of Proceedings of the National Education Association Session of 1871, St. Louis, Missouri* (New York and Washington: James H. Holmes, 1872), in *American Writings on Popular Education: The Nineteenth Century*, ed. Rush Welter (New York: Bobbs-Merrill, 1971) 271, 273.

58. Harris "How I Was Educated," 558.

59. Harris, "How Far May the State," 273.

60. Moffett, " A Biographical Sketch," 314–15, 316, 317.

61. Later in life, Twain tended to emphasize the educational utility of his writing. "Ours is a useful trade," he urged on receiving an honorary masters from Yale in 1888, "with all its lightness, and frivolity it has one serious purpose . . . the deriding of shams, the exposure of pretentious falsities, the laughing of stupid superstitions out of existence." Quoted in Justin

Kaplan, *Mr. Clemens and Mark Twain*, 147. In 1906, surveying the "literary graveyard" his *Library of Humor* had become in only twenty years, Twain assumed the office of teacher most explicitly: "Humor must not professedly teach and it must not professedly preach, but it must do both if it would live forever. . . . I have always preached. . . . If the humor came of its own accord and uninvited I have allowed it a place in my sermon, but I was not writing the sermon for the sake of the humor. I should have written the sermon just the same, whether any humor applied for admission or not." *The Autobiography of Mark Twain*, ed. Charles Neider (New York: HarperCollins, 1990) 15.

62. Moffett, "Biographical Sketch," 322, 319, 320–21.

63. See especially Cox, *Fate of Humor*, 105–26; Smith, *Development of a Writer*, 78–80; Schmitz, *Of Huck and Alice*, 79–94; and Leo Marx, "The Pilot and the Passenger: Landscape Conventions and the Style of *Huckleberry Finn*," in *Mark Twain: A Collection of Critical Essays*, ed. Henry Nash Smith (Englewood Cliffs, N.J.: Prentice-Hall, 1963) 49–52.

64. Mark Twain, *Life on the Mississippi* (New York: New American Library, 1961) 63. Subsequent citations will appear in the text.

65. *Life on the Mississippi*, 266.

66. *Life on the Mississippi*, 126, 131, 132.

67. Franklin, *Autobiography*, 65.

68. The literature on the confidence game in *Huckleberry Finn* is extensive. The most useful discussions can be found in William E. Lenz, "Confidence and Convention in *Huckleberry Finn*," in *One Hundred Years of Huckleberry Finn: The Boy, His Book, and American Culture*, ed. Robert Sattelmeyer and J. Donald Crowley (Columbia: U of Missouri P, 1985) 186–200; Gary Lindberg, *The Confidence Man in American Literature* (New York: Oxford UP, 1982); Warwick Wadlington, *The Confidence Game* (Princeton: Princeton UP, 1975); and Kenneth Lynn, *Mark Twain and Southwestern Humor* (Boston: Little, Brown, 1959).

69. *Life on the Mississippi*, 61.

Coda

1. *Mark Twain's Own Autobiography: The Chapters from The "North American Review,"* ed. Michael J. Kiskis (Madison: U of Wisconsin P, 1990) 190.

2. Letter to Howells, 16 Jan. 1904, *The Mark Twain–Howells Letters: The Correspondence of Samuel L. Clemens and William D. Howells, 1872–1910*, ed. Henry Nash Smith and William M. Gibson, vol. 1 (Cambridge: Harvard UP, 1960) 778. Hereafter cited as *MTHL*.

3. *Mark Twain's Autobiography*, ed. Albert Bigelow Paine, vol. 2 (New York: Harper & Bros., 1924) 246. The passage opens as a kind of argument, the first of twenty-five autobiographical excerpts published in the *North American Review* during 1906–7. For a reasoned explanation of the resemblances and divergences of the various published autobiographies, see Michael J. Kiskis's introduction and "Appendix C" in *Mark Twain's Own Autobiography*.

4. Letter to Howells, 17 June 1906, *MTHL*, vol. 2, 811.

5. "Preface," *The Autobiography of Mark Twain*, ed. Charles Neider (New York: Harper-Collins, 1990).

6. Letter to Howells, 14 Mar. 1904, *MTHL*, vol. 2, 782.

7. *Own Autobiography*, ed. Kiskis, 3.

8. *Own Autobiography*, ed. Kiskis, 234, 230.

9. *Own Autobiography*, ed. Kiskis, 242.

Index